Modern Etruscans
Close Encounters with a Distant Past

Modern Etruscans

Close Encounters with a Distant Past

Chiara Zampieri,
Martina Piperno &
Bart Van den Bossche
(eds)

Leuven University Press

Published with the financial support of KU Leuven Fund for Fair Open Access, the KU Leuven MDRN lab and Museo Nazionale Etrusco di Villa Giulia.

Published in 2023 by Leuven University Press / Presses Universitaires de Louvain / Universitaire Pers Leuven. Minderbroedersstraat 4, B-3000 Leuven (Belgium).

Selection and editorial matter © Chiara Zampieri, Martina Piperno & Bart Van den Bossche, 2023
Individual chapters © The respective authors, 2023

This book is published under a Creative Commons Attribution Non-Commercial Non-Derivative 4.0 Licence. Further details about Creative Commons licences are available at http://creativecommons.org/licenses/

Attribution should include the following information: Chiara Zampieri, Martina Piperno & Bart Van den Bossche (eds), *Modern Etruscans: Close Encounters with a Distant Past*. Leuven: Leuven University Press, 2023. (CC BY-NC-ND 4.0)

Unless otherwise indicated all images are reproduced with the permission of the rightsholders acknowledged in captions. They are expressly excluded from the CC BY-NC-ND 4.0 licence covering the rest of this publication. Permission for reuse should be sought from the rights-holders.

ISBN 978 94 6270 379 7 (Paperback)
ISBN 978 94 6166 523 2 (ePDF)
https://doi.org/10.11116/9789461665232
D/2023/1869/27

NUR: 682, 630
Layout: Crius
Cover design: Daniel Benneworth-Gray
Cover illustration: Apollo of Veii. Neg. 4632. ©Museo Nazionale Etrusco di Villa Giulia. Archivio fotografico

Table of Contents

9   Introduction
    Chiara Zampieri, Martina Piperno and Bart Van den Bossche

23 Etruscans, Victorians, and After: The Modern Sense of Beauty
    Francesca Orestano

43 The 'Walking Apollo': From Archaeological Dissemination to Literary Knowledge
    Chiara Zampieri

63 Cooking by the Book: Travel Writing and Etruscan Food Culture in the Interwar Period
    Bart Van den Bossche

81 Etruscans in Unexpected Places: Space, Temporality and Visual Agency
    Lisa C. Pieraccini

97 The Demonisation of the Etruscans: From Alfred Grünwedel to German Schoolbooks
    Martin Miller

115 Mr Lawrence and Lady Larthia: D. H. Lawrence as an Apprentice Etruscologist
    Marie-Laurence Haack

127 Etruscan Studies and the Infernal Landscape in Vincenzo Cardarelli's prose d'arte
    Gennaro Ambrosino

147 The Problem of Distance: Giorgio Bassani, The Etruscans and the Limits of Compassion
Martina Piperno

163 A Compromised Antiquity: The Post-war Italian Rejection of the Etruscan Past
Andrea Avalli

181 About the Authors

185 Index

Unless otherwise indicated, all translations are provided by the editors.

Introduction

Chiara Zampieri, Martina Piperno and Bart Van den Bossche

'L'Étrurie est à la mode', French archaeologist Salomon Reinach bluntly stated in 1927. In fact, since the 1830s, Etruria had not only been attracting the attention of archaeologists of all sorts, but it had also been a fascinating and, in some cases, captivating destination for poets, novelists, painters and sculptors from all over Europe. What charmed writers like Anatole France, Gabriele D'Annunzio, D. H. Lawrence, Aldous Huxley, Vincenzo Cardarelli, Corrado Alvaro, Curzio Malaparte or Marguerite Duras, among others, is the aura of mystery and secrecy that had been lingering over the Etruscan civilisation since the 15th century.[1] The interwar period makes for a particularly interesting moment in this regard as it corresponds to the period in which Italian and European culture were impacted by the significant archaeological discoveries in the Etruscan necropolises of Tarquinia and Cerveteri, in northern Latium. From the turn of the century onwards, new technologies and scientific methods, the rigorous cataloguing of artefacts and important institutional support for ancient history and classical studies allowed archaeologists to systematically excavate Etruscan sites as never before, thus leading to unprecedented findings and discoveries. In the first decades of the twentieth century, the results were impressive. The years between 1909 and 1936, for instance, saw the discovery and excavation of the necropolis of La Banditaccia, in the municipality of Cerveteri. Between 1913 and 1916, no less than 1200 Etruscan tombs were found during the archaeological campaign at Veii, which culminated with the stunning discovery of the Apollo of Veii in the sanctuary of Portonaccio in 1916.

The unearthing of this life-size terracotta statue by the Italian archaeologist Giulio Quirino Giglioli was a major archaeological find, but this discovery was also, and mostly, a pivotal moment in terms of cultural impact as it would also affect the institutional setting for Etruscan scholarship. As Marie-Laurence Haack has pointed out, this discovery was 'an epiphany that was as much archaeological as it was symbolic',[2] for it played a decisive role in conceiving, elaborating and defining the identity of Etruscology as a discipline as well as in the creation of what might be called an 'Etruscan myth'.[3] To begin, the exhibition of the Etruscan statue at the Museo Nazionale Etrusco di Villa Giulia in Rome in 1919 revolutionised the perception of Etruscan art and, more broadly, of Etruscan culture in the eyes of scholars but also, and for the first time, of writers and artists throughout Europe. Before the excavations at Veii, Etruscan art was still subject to the negative, if not bluntly dismissive judgements of Johann Joachim Winckelmann, Theodor Mommsen and Jules Martha. In his *Geschichte der Kunst des Altertums* (1764), Winckelmann defined Etruscan art as a clumsy copy of Greek art, which in contrast was elegant and refined, and the Etruscans as a barbaric people, a second-rate culture incapable of developing an artistic language of their own. A century later, the German historian Theodor Mommsen made a series of critical statements about the Etruscans in his *Römische Geschichte* (1861), adducing their degenerate and obscene way of life as the main cause for their inability to produce genuine works of art. In 1889, in *L'art étrusque* by the French archaeologist Jules Martha, one could still read that '[Etruria] feverishly copies from the right and from the left, it has no time to train its hand or to develop a method. In this fever of imitation, it merely develops a certain technical skill, industry predominates art and originality is smothered'.[4]

The discovery of the Apollo of Veii put an end to this long-standing critical stance by triggering an unprecedented change of perspective on Etruscan art, which was rapidly promoted 'to the rank of original and timeless art'.[5] Moreover, many modernist and avant-garde artists now turned to Etruscan art as the epitome of a primitivism that was not only pre-classical (and even anti-classical) but also, and above all, Italian and therefore quintessentially indigenous. The Apollo of Veii, with its terracotta limbs, its archaic smile, its almond-shaped eyes and its dynamic posture, is therefore promptly perceived by art historians as well as by the sculptors and artists of the time as a completely different kind of Apollo. With its malicious and cruel smile, the Etruscan statue eventually started to embody a different strand of ancient art, obscure, irrational, disturbing and diametrically opposed to smooth and balanced forms in white marble of the Greco-Latin sculpture, and its proverbial (or even stereotypical) features of proportionality, harmony and sense of measure. The interpretation of Etruscan art as primitive and indigenous, dominant in 1920s Italy, is highlighted by the words of the archaeologist Ranuccio Bianchi Bandinelli, according to whom '[a] special and widespread interest is directed today towards Etruscan art' since 'some of its characteristics coincide, singularly, with certain trends in contemporary art, and we undeniably resent Etruscan art as the least classical among the ancient arts, as the most Western'.[6] Through the lens of primitivism, several artists and intellectuals of the peninsula thus started to recognise themselves in what can be defined as one of the first truly Italian artistic manifestations. As

Carlo Pirovano has pointed out, the revaluation of Etruscan art was not only an archaeological matter, but also an aesthetic one:

> Archaeological erudition and avant-garde poetics arrived almost simultaneously at the rupture of Greco-Roman 'centrism' (the classical world par excellence) and the re-evaluation of figurative languages not related to that matrix, non-European cultures on the one hand, and archaic Mediterranean ones on the other.[7]

Such enthusiasm for the Apollo of Veii, and more generally for the kind of antiquity that it embodied, considerably affected both the arts and all areas of study on the Etruscans, especially in the Italian context. In 1925, the Comitato Permanente per l'Etruria was founded, and several national and international conferences followed suit, amongst which the Convegno Nazionale Etrusco (1926) and the Congresso Internazionale Etrusco (1928). In 1925, the first chair of Etruscan studies in Italy was awarded to Alessandro Della Seta, an archaeologist who, in 1918, had already devoted himself to the first systematic cataloguing[8] of the artefacts conserved in the warehouses of Villa Giulia. In 1927, the journal *Studi Etruschi* was founded, hosting contributions from scholars and archaeologists from all over Europe and allowing for the swift circulation of scholarly work on the Etruscans within the international scientific community. From the very first issue of the journal, the aim of the publication is clear: 'The journal will host original works as well as information and news of everything related to the progress of our knowledge concerning this ancient [...] Italian people'.[9] From its first issue, the journal is conceived as a place where all the available information could be shared easily among the members of a scientific community that was still in the process of being formally constituted. Each of these publications and academic events had the double function of promoting Etruscology as an independent scholarly discipline while guaranteeing its scientific legitimacy. Among the various sectors of Etruscan studies, the one that benefited most from the discovery of the Apollo was for sure Ancient Art History, which then experienced an unprecedented development. The publications *Etruria antica* (1925) by Pericle Ducati and *Storia dell'arte etrusca* (1927) by Giulio Quirino Giglioli are emblematic of the wish to overcome the dismissive stereotypical interpretations promoted by art historians like Winckelmann, Mommsen or Martha in the previous decades.

In this context of unprecedented archaeological fervour, archaeologists were not the only ones captivated by Etruscan antiquity. The stunning discoveries, associated with the aura of mystery lingering over the Etruscan civilisation, also attracted the attention of writers, poets, artists, and sculptors of the period. Massimo Campigli, Alberto Giacometti and Arturo Martini, among others, assiduously frequented the halls of Villa Giulia to study Etruscan sculpture to renew their own aesthetic conceptions drawing inspiration from a more primitive and, at the same time, more indigenous artistic language. Writers like D. H. Lawrence, Vincenzo Cardarelli and Corrado Alvaro visited some of the major Etruscan sites and produced sketches and short proses where present-day perspectives and the distant past are intertwined in sometimes peculiar ways. As Martina Corgnati claims, the shadow of the Etruscans is lengthy and stretches far beyond the early twentieth century. In the post-war years, for instance, Etruscan references can be found not only in a wide variety of cultural artefacts, ranging from novels, like Giorgio Bassani's *Il giardino dei Finzi-Contini* (1962), short stories, like Luciano Bianciardi's *Il campanile* (1952), and movies like *La voglia matta* (1962) or *Il sorpasso* (1962), but also in comics and photographs.

Recent research has focussed on the institutionalisation and professionalisation of Etruscology as an academic discipline in the early twentieth century within a broader cultural and institutional perspective, and with particular regard to Italy and Germany. Marie-Laurence Haack[10] paved the way with an edited volume illustrating the process which led to the recognition of Etruscology as an academic discipline; with a socio-historical approach, she also investigated how in the 1930s authoritarian regimes in Fascist Italy and Nazi Germany related to Etruscology.[11] Art historians have tackled the question from an aesthetic perspective, showing how sculptors and painters from the modernist period turned towards the Etruscan terracotta searching for unexplored and so to speak 'autochthonous' forms of primitivism.[12] Several scholars have focussed on the role of references to Etruscan culture, art and artefacts in literary and archaeological writing.[13] Compared to Martina Piperno's monograph *L'antichità "crudele". Etruschi e Italici nella letteratura italiana del Novecento*[14] – the first book-length study on the reception and adaptation of Etruscan culture from a literary perspective – the present volume aims to advance the study of the interplay between archaeological knowledge and various literary and cultural practices by launching a truly comparative and cross-disciplinary conversation on the topic. The chapters, therefore, will not limit themselves to the mere analysis of specific Etruscan and archaeological references within targeted texts, cultural practices or artefacts, but they will actively engage with a range of questions, such as: what is the relationship between literary discourse and archaeological discourse? What kind of knowledge results from such discursive interplay? What is the role of literary devices, specifically, in this knowledge production process? How do references to Etruscan culture relate to developments in academic knowledge on the Etruscans? The various contributions will also explore the symbolic value of material culture as well as of Etruscan sites dealing with questions like: what is the symbolic value of Etruscan artefacts and sites? What is the relationship between Etruscan heritage and cultural memory? By addressing these questions, the various contributors to the volume actively renegotiate the idea of 'classical reception' in favour of a more dynamic and dialogical engagement with the past. To answer these questions with a cross-disciplinary and comparative approach, the volume brings together scholars from different disciplines and traditions. The contributions, each focussing on a specific case-study yet closely linked by a common focus on Etruscan material culture and heritage, offer cross-disciplinary perspectives on the phenomenon as they take into account not only different traditions, but also various cultural artefacts and practices, including movies, art pieces, archaeological accounts, *prosa d'arte*, photographs, food culture, comic series, schoolbooks and newspaper clippings, thus opening up the field of investigation.

The contributions gathered in this book all consider a specific element of Etruscan material culture in the modernist period. Francesca Orestano delves into fascination with Etruscan artefacts in late nineteenth century Britain through the lens of John Ruskin's aesthetic and artistic theories, addressing also the multiple and wide-ranging suggestions sparked by Etruscan culture. As an Etruscan artefact *par excellence*, the statue of the Apollo of Veii discovered in 1916 is at the heart of Chiara Zampieri's reflection on the thematic and discursive interactions between archaeology and literature following the manifold reflections and suggestions sparked by the sensational discovery of the Etruscan Apollo. The materiality of archaeological artefacts is definitely a crucial factor in terms of contact with and reception of Etruscan culture, but also less tangible (or even highly immaterial) features have prompted interesting cultural and literary elaborations. In this respect, Etruscan food culture, for instance, is a striking manifestation of the fascination with Etruscan culture in the early twentieth century, as Bart Van den Bossche shows in his reading of travel writing by Corrado Alvaro, Alberto Savinio, Vincenzo Cardarelli and D. H. Lawrence. Etruscan wall-paintings in the necropolises also played a pivotal role in the construction of an 'Etruscan myth' during modernity. Frescos of demons and mysterious creatures in the painted tombs of Tarquinia, for instance, stirred the imagination of several artists and poets – even recent ones – who did not fail to recontextualise these iconographic elements in their own artistic production. As Lisa C. Pieraccini shows, however, Etruscan demons dwell not only in the tombs, on the contrary, they can also be found in the most unexpected places, ranging from American funerary monuments, to Italian postage stamps, to accessories realised by leading fashion designers and to horror movies.

Literary or aesthetic fascination for Etruscan material culture, however, was not an all-pervasive phenomenon in the European context. As Martin Miller persuasively argues, in Germany, at the turn of the century, intellectuals and archaeologists are far more interested in academic knowledge concerning the language and origin of the Etruscan civilisation rather than on the imaginations and charm of Etruscan artefacts and sites. The interplay between archaeological knowledge and literary creation is also at the core of Marie-Laurence Haack and Gennaro Ambrosino's essays. While Haack explores D. H. Lawrence's background readings before his journey through Etruscan necropolises, Ambrosino investigates how Vincenzo Cardarelli incorporates concrete archaeological data in his *prose d'arte* turning them into a personal interpretation of private and collective memory, but also in highly personal and national narratives connected to Etruria. The issue of the cultural memory of the Etruscans is further addressed in the contributions of Martina Piperno and Andrea Avalli. Martina Piperno focusses on memory through the lens of Giorgio Bassani's *Prologo* to his *Giardino dei Finzi-Contini*, where Etruscan necropolises are represented as spaces packed with symbolic values, as *lieux de mémoire* for the all too recent tragedy of the Shoah. Andrea Avalli provides yet another reading of the cultural memory linked with Etruscan culture by focussing on the relationship of postwar Italy with its ancient past. After the Second World War and the end of the Fascist regime, Avalli argues, Etruscan culture seems to be rejected and perceived with irritation, an irritation that is grounded on the perception of Etruscan civilisation (and even more so on the perception of Etruscology) – as nothing more than an erudite, boring and highly rhetorical form of memory of ancient Italy.

This book takes its cue from the research project 'Modern Etruscans' launched in 2019 by the MDRN Research Lab at the University of Leuven and focussing on the selection, mediation, and dissemination of archaeological and historical knowledge on the Etruscans and their civilisation in different literary traditions of the modernist period.[15] Some of the core concepts in the scholarly debate on the relationship between science, knowledge and literature in the modernist period have been particularly inspirational for the critical framework of this book. Three elements in particular regarding the interaction between the rapidly developing scientific knowledge of the modernist period and cultural, artistic and literary representations are closely interwoven with the topics and approaches used in this book.

First, the expanding knowledge on Etruscan culture (but this goes for the study of all ancient cultures, or even for culture in general) cannot be detached from the study of knowledge production as regards its cultural embedding and circulation and the configuration of specific knowledge cultures. Questions to be addressed in this context may focus on topics like the places of knowledge ('*les lieux de savoir*')[16], types of spatiality and temporality associated with specific forms of knowledge, the materiality of objects, tools and artefacts involved in the production of knowledge, the role of the body and embodied experience in science and knowledge production processes, factors of emotion and affect associated with different fields and types of knowledge, and, more broadly speaking, the psychological and sociological profile(s) associated with experts and other agents in the production, circulation and reception of different forms of knowledge. With regard to the study of Etruscan culture (as well as to other topics in the humanities with a broader sociocultural and political appeal) a crucial topic concerns the ways in which expert knowledge is communicated and disseminated within society, and the particular configurations in which more specialist venues (conferences, proceedings, journals, archives and collections) are combined – and not always frictionlessly – with practices of dissemination aimed at the broader public, ranging from highly institutionalised forms of dissemination (e.g. national museums, archives, major exhibitions, but also education programmes, etc.) to more loosely organised forms of popularisation which may also yield discussions and conflicts. Particularly relevant for the contributions in this volume is the interaction between expert knowledge of historians and archaeologists on the one hand, and the 'aesthetic' understanding of Etruscan culture in literary and artistic contexts. As the various chapters illustrate, this is an interaction that cannot be reduced to a plain and simple distinction between 'objective' criteria of scientific discourse and 'subjective' experience or 'aesthetic' creation on the other.

The multiple and multifaceted interactions between expert knowledge about Etruscan culture and broadly cultural engagements with Etruscan heritage are addressed, one way or another, in most of the chapters in this book. Francesca Orestano, Chiara Zampieri and Marie-Laurence Haack, in particular address the issue more comprehensively. Zampieri and Orestano highlight how the ways in which Etruscan artefacts are exhibited and displayed are informed by specific interpretations of Etruscan culture but also how, in turn, such exhibitions encourage the audience to take on a specific position vis-à-vis the Etruscans, even imposing more or less subtly a particular gaze. Orestano discusses the important role of the Campanari exhibition in London in 1837, which – in connection with the rather limited knowledge on the Etruscans at that time – encouraged fixing a (rather) exoticising and (definitely) aestheticising gaze on Etruscan artefacts, while the association between Etruscans and funerary culture also reinforced a 'metaphysical' and 'mysterious' take on Etruscan culture and world-views. The exhibition would give new impetus to images of the Etruscans in literature and the arts, as well as to scholarly interest in the Etruscans. In the same vein Chiara Zampieri details the broad impact of the so-called Apollo of Veii, discovered in 1916 and put on display from 1919 onwards; the statue proved to be of great importance for the scholarly understanding of Etruscan culture – or to be more precise, for a thorough reappraisal of the aesthetic qualities of Etruscan art – giving not only a strong impetus to the further institutionalisation of Etruscan studies but generating also a striking and lasting impact on the presence of Etruscan references in literature, in visual arts and in the broader cultural field. In the interbellum period, the Apollo of Veii became the object of a broad range of interpretations, and the statue was seen not only as a correlative of the modern condition of anxiety and unrest after the Great War, but also as an icon of an utterly different condition unspoilt by modern alienation and which could inspire modern men to change course and aspire to an alternative kind of culture.

While Zampieri's and Orestano's chapters explicitly address the interaction between the rapidly expanding scientific knowledge and cultural perceptions of the Etruscans, most of the other chapters in the book also seem to at least fully confirm Massimo Pallottino's thesis about the ongoing cross-pollination between scientific expertise on Etruscan antiquity and cultural interpretations of the Etruscans. Even in postwar Italian and Western culture, references to Etruscan culture pop up in a wide range of contexts and media, from literary texts that have become modern classics (see Piperno's chapter on *Il giardino dei Finzi-Contini*) to Italian movies and fiction of the 1950s and 1960s (as shown in Avalli's chapter) to comics, cinema, contemporary art and graveyard monuments; in particular, the various cases advanced by Lisa C. Pieraccini highlight just how surprisingly varied and astonishingly creative the engagement with Etruscan culture and heritage is in contemporary Western culture.

A second crucial point regarding the interactions between science and culture in the modernist period – one with obvious connections to the previous point – concerns the need to thematise the boundaries of what can be considered 'scientific' or 'expert' knowledge within specific historical contexts. As scientific disciplines become more institutionalised and their social and political significance increases, forms of border policing tend to become more prominent, and discussions about what can and what cannot be considered science become increasingly frequent and relevant. Consequently, the boundary between expert knowledge and its use in a broad cultural sense will also become a topic of discussion, demarcation and border policing. This in turn will trigger mechanisms of reflection and thematisation of specific discursive sectors on their own epistemic status; this may, in particular, be the case in literary and artistic uses and creative re-elaborations of expert knowledge, which are bound to thematise the specific stances of their processing of specialised knowledge. Writers, artists and intellectuals will thus begin to place the role and status of knowledge in a different light in their dealings with it. A more specific aspect for literature and the visual arts is the reflection on (and thematisation of) specific medium-related aspects of knowledge. As far as literature is concerned, it is related to the linguistic and discursive nature of knowledge and the role of specific types of language use in the articulation of knowledge, both as a specialist domain and in terms of public good and dissemination; in visual culture, this self-reflexivity and thematisation may have more to do with the role of images, illustrations and other forms of visual support in the development and dissemination of knowledge.

Especially in the second half of the nineteenth century, clear signs of increasing specialisation and forms of border policing can be observed between the increasingly institutionalised and professionalised field of expert knowledge and that of the erudite (or less erudite) enthusiast and collector. In this respect, Francesca Orestano outlines the differences between George Dennis' influential description of Etruria (still larded with many literary references and devices) and the works of John Ruskin, who clearly assumes the role of a scholar and expert, that being, as Orestano appropriately underlines, Ruskin's scholarly approach combines an art-historical and formalist view with psychological interpretations. Around the same years the Francophone world acknowledges a clear conceptual division between the '*collectioneur*' and the '*archéologue*', as is illustrated by a lemma listed in the Larousse dictionary and cited by Chiara Zampieri. Once again, it should be noted that the professionalisation of knowledge in no way seems to limit the potential of Etruscan culture to offer imaginative and creative impulses, perhaps precisely because within the professionalising and specialising field of Etruscology an important psychological-experiential and interpretive component also remains present.

The relationship between scientific knowledge on Etruscan culture and representations of the Etruscans informed by a wide range of cultural images, values and practices is thematised in several literary travelogues devoted to Etruscan heritage sites. Several chapters in the book expand upon the importance attached by writer-travellers to the experiential, emotional, existential and spiritual experience of physical contact with archaeological sites, especially, but certainly not exclusively, with the tombs. Most of the writers who have been studied would see their own approach as complementary to the more detached, objectifying and historicising perspective of specialist knowledge (as Gennaro Ambrosino in particular points out in his analysis of Cardarelli's lyrical-autobiographical prose texts on Tarquinia). As Marie-Laurence Haack demonstrates at length in her chapter, in the case of an author like D. H. Lawrence, the relationship between science and literature, between the scholar and the artist, tends to become more complex: with Lawrence, the physical experience of Etruscan culture is not only explicitly brought to the fore but also clearly opposed with what Lawrence sees as the strategies of scientific distancing, objectification and museification of the Etruscan past. At the same time, this in no way means that Lawrence does not avail himself of scholarly knowledge of the Etruscans, quite the contrary: Marie-Laurence Haack highlights the extent to which Lawrence's reflections on the Etruscans are linked to his visions of and attitudes towards history and temporality, visions he articulated through the reading of scholarly works by some of the major historians of antiquity. It is also interesting that D. H. Lawrence plans, carries out his tour in Etruria and publishes his *Sketches* while the first Etruscological congresses (the Convegno nazionale in 1926, the Congresso internazionale in 1928) are held and the first issue of *Studi Etruschi* appears (1927). In short, what emerges from Lawrence's *Etruscan Places* is the ambition to propose an alternative paradigm of knowledge of the Etruscans, one that distances itself from the scientific approach (and certainly from a one-sided empirical and objectivising approach) and advocates instead for a vital, sensory and creaturely connection with Etruscan culture (or to any form of culture, for that matter). Elaborating and communicating this kind of experience of the past is something that, according to the British writer, only literature can do. A similar perspective of literary knowledge as complementary, integrative, supplementary and corrective to scientific knowledge also speaks – albeit in less explicit terms – from texts and prose by writers like Vincenzo Cardarelli, Corrado Alvaro and Alberto Savinio; not coincidentally, these authors, as Bart Van den Bossche points out, pay great attention to food culture as an important aspect of this kind of vital, experiential, emotional and lived historical experience. In connection with this kind of complementarity, it is also interesting to note that, as Chiara Zampieri signals, in the early 20th century also a number of specialists (like Giulio Quirino Giglioli, but Pericle Ducati is also worthy of mention), disseminated historical notions and archaeological information about Etruscan art and culture through texts characterised by more literary registers and techniques able to convey the specifically experiential and aesthetic dimension of Etruscan finds.

A special situation seems to arise in Germany where the positivist-scientific tradition is so strong and long-standing that it does not seem to leave much room for speculative theories, the kind of creative-imaginary dealings with the

Etruscans present in other European cultural areas. In the interwar period, the references to the Etruscans in Alfred Rosenberg's *Der Mythus des 20. Jahrhunderts* turn this situation completely on its head: on this occasion, the Etruscans are associated with Satanism, black magic and witchcraft, and any form of historical truth about the Etruscans is sacrificed to Rosenberg's wildly speculative (to say the least) and hideous racial theories.

A third element to be taken into account when discussing science and culture in the modernist period regards what can be called the broader cultural frameworks (or 'narratives') of knowledge production and dissemination, which is of particular importance in the modernist period with its extraordinary expansion and institutionalisation of the sciences, as well as with the increasing importance of social and political valorisation of highly specialised knowledge in modern society. Again, literary, artistic and cultural elaborations of expert knowledge can be seen as an important terrain where such broader narratives are critically thematised and scrutinised. More specifically, there are interesting forms of interaction between literary elaborations of (and reflections on) knowledge and broader cultural narratives on science: not only are literary texts a reflection and a product of these kinds of broader conceptions, but they also often enter into a critical dialogue with these conceptions of knowledge and develop new visions that represent, in turn, a source of new conceptions. In the case of the Etruscans, these broader narratives combine general concepts about knowledge on ancient and silent cultures with specific local narratives about political and cultural identity, about national and local past, and they also touch on the relationship between specialised historical knowledge and subjective empathy and experience (*Erleben*). It is noticeable how literary texts devoted to the Etruscans not only parasitise scientific knowledge, but also think 'alongside' and 'in parallel with' the sciences, contributing to a language, a capacity of imagination, narrative patterns and an interpretative knowledge in the study of ancient cultures like that of the Etruscans.[17] An expression of the efficacy and interconnectedness of these narratives can also be found in the way in which cultural-identitarian, artistic and subjective interpretations and scientific habitus cross-fertilise with each other, not in the least because a number of scientists are also active in more literary-artistic and public-oriented writing about their knowledge, in which they let science and cultural representations (and cultural memory) actively enter into dialogue with each other.

The various chapters in the book explore diverse contexts and different narratives into which will be inserted references to Etruscan culture. There is, to begin with, the consistent perception of Etruscan heritage and culture as being associated with a regional scale of Etruria, or even the local scale of specific towns and landscapes. For obvious reasons, a similar take on the Etruscans is very present when authors have personal connections with the area (Tuscany and Latium), a condition that often results in the projection of a transhistorical *genius loci* aimed at establishing a connection between ancient Etruria and present-day Tuscany, often even erasing any historical distance; clear illustrations of this process can be found in the works of Curzio Malaparte (see Zampieri's chapter) and Vincenzo Cardarelli (analysed by Ambrosino and Van den Bossche). Yet writers who are not of Tuscan origin also address the regional and local embedding of Etruscan culture and tend even to see Etruscan culture as an epitome of a 'localist' interpretation of culture, emphasising the strong connections that can exist between culture and local context, as opposed to political doctrines and systems that willingly and enthusiastically ignore local differences or even actively erase them in the name of an overly homogeneous and centralist ideal of national unity, with the risk of producing a nation alienated from its own roots and identity. As Van den Bossche points out, this kind of reflection also plays out, albeit not always explicitly in reflections on the Etruscans by Italian authors like Corrado Alvaro, Alberto Savinio and Vincenzo Cardarelli. In D. H. Lawrence's *Etruscan places*, the critique becomes quite explicit, and when Lawrence repeatedly notes that Tuscan gastronomy is literally and metaphorically prepared and consumed in tasteless ways, this is to be understood as a clear symptom of local inhabitants being alienated from their own identity and having only a sterile or purely instrumental connection to the land and its produce. This alienation, in Lawrence's view, is inextricably vexed with the kind of abstract political ideology propagated by the Fascist regime.

Ambrosino's analysis of Vincenzo Cardarelli's writings indicates, however, that the status of the Etruscans in Italian culture in the 1930s was not always that clear-cut, and that it is subject to shifts, related in particular to not always frictionless incorporation of the Etruscans into the narrative of Italian national origins and identity, which revolved around Rome. With the increasing focus of Fascist ideology on racial theories in the second half of the 1930s, the relationship between Rome and Etruria (and the presumed 'oriental' origin of the Etruscans) became particularly uneasy. Either way, the association of the Etruscans with preoccupations around roots and origins, identity and memory ensured that, as Andrea Avalli demonstrates in his contribution, not only Etruscan studies as an academic pursuit but also references to all things Etruscan in postwar Italy were often ignored or even rejected as rhetorical and reactionary issues which were not only of no use but also viewed as being harmful in contemporary Italy. Yet the chapters by Pieraccini and Piperno demonstrate that this is not the whole story, as they highlight several cases in which references to the

Etruscans function in narratives that differ substantially. Pieraccini analyses a number of artworks and cultural artefacts (such as a tomb sculpture that explicitly refers to the 'Sarcofago degli sposi' but also a comic strip that combines the myth of the Far West with references to the Etruscans) from a postcolonial and decolonising perspective, showing how the subtle treatment of elements from Etruscan culture reverses the demonisation on Etruscan otherness into a critique of imperialist and patriarchal value systems of sorts: the American sculptor Patricia Cronin uses the over-familiar 'Sarcofago degli sposi' as a starting point for a funerary monument for her deceased same-sex partner (and thus also engaging the Roman critique of gender roles in Etruscan society in a subtle play of references), and when the hero from an Italian comic strip about the Far West is depicted in an Etruscan pose, this can be read as a commentary on the American myth of the frontier and the conquest of the West. Martina Piperno reads Bassani's references to the Etruscans in the *Giardino dei Finzi-Contini* within the framework of a reflection on distance and compassion, involving not only the typical connections between Etruscan culture, necropolises and death, but also the relationship with other literary treatments of funerary monuments and their cultural and political functions, linking it also to speculations about the Roman destruction of written Etruscan sources, a statement that recalls the role of poetry and narration to keep the memory of the deceased alive – as reassessed by Foscolo's *Sepolcri* and by Bassani's novel.

Notes

1. Jean-Marc Irollo, *Histoire des Étrusques. L'antique civilisation toscane VIIIe – Ier siècle avant J.-C.* (Paris: Perrin, 2004), p. 21.
2. Marie-Laurence Haack, 'L'étruscologie au XXᵉ siècle. Bilans historiographiques', in *Anabases*, 23 (2016), pp. 11-26, doi: https://doi.org/10.4000/anabases.5537. (Accessed May 2023).
3. Martina Corgnati, *L'ombra lunga degli etruschi. Echi e suggestioni nell'arte del Novecento* (Monza: Johan & Levi, 2018), p. 27.
4. '[L'Étrurie] copie à droite, elle copie à gauche, n'a pas le temps de se former la main, de se faire une méthode. Dans cette fièvre d'imitation elle ne gagne qu'une certaine habilité technique; l'industrie prime l'art et l'originalité est étouffée'. Jules Martha, *L'art étrusque* (Paris: Firmin-Didot, 1889), p. 615.
5. Marie-Laurence Haack, 'Introduction. De l'étruscomanie à l'étruscologie: L'étruscologie au début du XXᵉ siècle', in *La construction de l'étruscologie au début du XXᵉ siècle*, Marie-Laurence Haack and Martin Miller (eds) (Bordeaux: Ausonius Éditions, 2015), doi: http://books.openedition.org/ausonius/5448. (Accessed May 2023).
6. '[u]no speciale e diffuso interesse è rivolto oggi verso l'arte etrusca'; 'alcuni suoi caratteri coincidono infatti, singolarmente, con certe tendenze dell'arte contemporanea, e noi risentiamo innegabilmente l'arte etrusca come la meno classica fra quelle antiche, come la più occidentale'. Ranuccio Bianchi Bandinelli, 'Il Bruto Capitolino scultura etrusca', in *Dedalo*, vol. 1, no 8 (1927-1928), p. 275.
7. 'Erudizione archeologica e poetiche d'avanguardia approdano quasi contemporaneamente alla rottura del 'centrismo' greco-romano (il mondo classico per eccellenza) e alla rivalutazione dei linguaggi figurativi non riconducibili a quella matrice, le culture extra-europee, da una parte, e quelle mediterranee arcaiche dall'altra'.

Carlo Pirovano, 'Letture del sottosuolo', in *Fortuna degli etruschi*, Franco Borsi (ed.) (Milan: Electa, 1985), p. 443.

8. Alessandro Della Seta, *Museo di Villa Giulia* (Rome: Danesi, 1918).

9. 'La rivista accoglierà i lavori originali nonché informazioni e notizie di tutto quanto riguarda il progresso delle nostre conoscenze su questo antico [...] popolo italiano'. Quoted by Marie-Laurence Haack in 'L'étruscologie au XXe siècle. Bilans historiographiques', doi: https://doi.org/10.4000/anabases.5537. (Accessed June 2023).

10. *La construction de l'étruscologie au début du XXe siècle*, Marie-Laurence Haack and Martin Miller (eds).

11. *Les Étrusques au temps du fascisme et du nazisme*, Marie-Laurence Haack and Martin Miller (eds) (Bordeaux: Ausonius Éditions, 2016), doi: 10.4000/books.ausonius.10620. (Accessed May 2023).

12. Martina Corgnati, *L'ombra lunga degli Etruschi. Echi e suggestioni nell'arte del Novecento*; Maurizio Harari, 'Grèce ou non Grèce au Portonaccio', in *La construction de l'étruscologie au début du XXe siècle*; Maurizio Harari, 'Etruscologia e fascismo', *Athenaeum*, vol. 100 nos. 1-2 (Como: New Press, 2012), pp. 405-418; Mauro Pratesi, 'Scultura italiana verso gli anni Trenta e contemporanea rivalutazione dell'arte etrusca', *Bollettino d'arte*, vol. 28 (1984), pp. 91-106; Giuseppe Pucci, 'La sculpture étrusque dans les années vingt et trente: entre esthétique et idéologie', in *Les Etrusques au temps du fascisme et du nazisme*.

13. Giovanna Bagnasco Gianni, *Fascino etrusco nel primo Novecento, conversando di arti e storia delle arti* (Milan: Ledizioni, 2016); Giuseppe M. Della Fina, *Gli etruschi nella cultura e nell'immaginario del mondo moderno. Atti del XXIV Convegno Internazionale di Studi sulla Storia e l'Archeologia dell'Etruria* (Rome: Quasar, 2017); Maurizio Harari, 'Carducci, così pieno dell'Italia antica', *Strumenti critici, Rivista quadrimestrale di cultura e critica letteraria*, vol. 141, no. 2 (2016), pp. 213-226, doi: 10.1419/83412; Maurizio Harari, ' "À qui étrusque disait peu de chose...": Étrusques perdus et retrouvés à travers Ruskin et la Recherche', *Œuvres & Critiques*, 42 1 (2017), pp. 303-311.

14. Martina Piperno, *L'antichità "crudele". Etruschi e Italici nella letteratura italiana del Novecento* (Rome: Carocci, 2020).

15. The project is part of a large-scale interdisciplinary research programme titled *Literary Knowledge (1890-1950): Modernisms and the Sciences in Europe* which explores the multiple interactions between literature and the sciences in the modernist period in Europe.

16. *Lieux de savoir. Espaces et communautés*, Christian Jacob (ed.), vol. 1 (Paris: Albin Michel, 2007); *Lieux de savoir. Les mains et l'intellect*, Christian Jacob (ed.), vol. 2 (Paris: Albin Michel, 2011). For a synthesis see Christian Jacob, *Qu'est-ce qu'un lieu de savoir?* (Marseille: OpenEdition Press, 2014), http://books.openedition.org/oep/423. (Accessed May 2023).

17. See also Abigael Van Alst, Sascha Bru and Jan Baetens, 'Entre expérimentation poétique et savoir scientifique: sur la vérité de la littérature, 1890-1950. Entretien avec Sascha Bru et Abigael van Alst (MDRN)', *Fabula LhT*, 24 (November 2020), https://www.fabula.org/lht/24/mdrn.html. (Accessed May 2022).

Etruscans, Victorians, and After: The Modern Sense of Beauty

Francesca Orestano

Before Ruskin: Imagining Etruria

In the late eighteenth century, and during the long Victorian age, English travellers to Italy 'discovered' Etruria. Whether genuine or recreated in England by the artful crafts of the Wedgwood factory and in Victorian jewellery, or materially displayed or just fabricated by the Victorian imagination, the Etruscans would exist within a perplexing halo of mixed uncertainty as to their identity and origins. Antiquity lent them its charm as precious relics from the past: yet as they did not fit into the acknowledged cultural mould of either Rome or Greece, they would prove at once daunting, confusing, and fascinating. Michael Vickers has addressed the problem in his essay 'Imaginary Etruscans: changing perceptions of Etruria since the fifteenth century',[1] pointing out the intricacies of the reception of the Etruscans within the cultural horizon of England and Europe since the fifteenth century. Recent exhibitions in Italy, Vickers emphasises, with the display on 'The Imaginary Etruscan', show an amazing selection of items that Vickers defines as Etrusco-Kitsch. Among these, Donald Duck discovering a tomb, the famous smile of the Cerveteri couple obtained by saying 'cheese', and movies like *The Etruscan Kills Again* or *Assassination in the Etruscan Cemetery*, thriving on the thrill of the revenge of the mummy or zombie stories. Such products of the popular imagination 'neatly encapsulate the ambivalent yet pivotal role played by the Etruscans in European thought during the past few centuries. At times they have been regarded as Westerners […], at others as exotic orientals'.[2]

Going back in time, such wavering attribution is confirmed by the titles of some major works that included Etruscan antiquities within a heterogeneous list of styles, generically clustered under the umbrella of ancient art. Anne-Claude-Philippe de Tubières, Comte de Caylus, *Recueil d'antiquités égyptiennes, étrusques, grecques, romaines et gauloises* (Paris, 1752-1767), Pierre-Francois d'Hancarville, *Collection of Etruscan, Greek, and Roman Antiquities from the Cabinet of the Hon. W. Hamilton, His Britannick Majesty's Envoy Extraordi-

nary and Plenipotentiary at the Court of Naples (1766), Giovan Battista Piranesi, *Diverse maniere d'adornare i camini e ogni altra parte degli edifici desunte dall'architettura egizia, etrusca, e greca con un ragionamento apologetico in difesa dell'architettura egizia e toscana* (Roma, 1769): these were the collections that constructed an Etruscan identity, separate from the Greek and Roman heritage; and yet the collector's eye rested on the surface of the items examined and aligned without focussing in depth, as to history, chronology, origin. Thus, the gaze of the *connoisseur,* architect and decorator, dwelt on the elements of form rather than develop a discourse about the Etruscans. As I should like to suggest, formal categories of design would play a major role in the modern response to the Etruscans: possibly, but not certainly, inasmuch as the missing interpretation of their language adds cogency to the visual values embedded in their relics, but also owing to the unprecedented emphasis on form – significant form – typical of the European avant-garde movements.

Victorians and Etruscans: a Great Exhibition

The Victorian age transforms the flat categories of the above-mentioned book titles into the spectacular display of Etruscan tombs staged in London by the Campanari family. The Romantic sublime, a gothic taste for crypts, a passion for darkness, a visionary slant, all concurred in feeding such exhibition. Described as the first archaeological blockbuster of its time, it whetted the public appetite for the spectacular *mises-en-scène* that were luring Victorian spectators to dioramas, panoramas, magic lantern shows and *tableaux vivants*. A display that was no longer arranged typologically, it comprised a series of chambers with reproductions of wall-paintings, authentic stone doorways, objects hung from the walls, and genuine sarcophagi with lids left slightly open so that visitors could peep inside at skeletons and pieces of Etruscan gold jewellery.[3] The catalogue entitled *A Brief Description of the Etruscan and Greek Antiquities now Exhibited at 121 Pall Mall opposite the Opera Colonnade* complemented an article in *The Times* (January 26, 1837) that dwelt on the frightening figures of two guardian Charons placed at the entrance of the exhibition, so that visitors would feel at once like gold diggers and sacrilegious tomb-raiders, violating the tranquillity of the eternal sleep of the Etruscans.[4] The same article also called attention to the beauty of the genuine jewels on display, adding that 'The shape of these earrings perfectly matches today's fashion, as their craftsmanship is identical with what you can see today on display in the showcases of jewellery shops'.[5]

Fig. 1.1 The British Museum: the Etruscan Room, with visitors (1847). Wood engraving, 12.2 x 15.4 cm. Wellcome Library n° 38445i. Public Domain. https://wellcomecollection.org/works/hnrp8nnu

Connoisseurship, collections and museums are proof of the Victorians' fascination with Etruscan art; craftsmanship, producing cheap replicas of precious objects, would enhance the cultural contact between the two civilisations.[6] The British Museum had an Etruscan Room since 1847 (Fig. 1.1).

In the aftermath of the Great Exhibition, held in 1851 at the Crystal Palace, when the huge structure was moved to Sydenham between 1852 and 1854, experts like Matthew Digby Wyatt and Owen Jones were hired to create a series of courts that provided a narrative of the history of fine arts. There were courts illustrating Egyptian, Greek, Roman, Byzantine, Medieval and Renaissance architecture: although the Etruscans did not earn a specific court, the display was proof of the educational ambition achieved through a spectacular staging of monumental architecture and famous statues.

I should like to point out two modes of reception, one based on the formal alignment of similar items, as displayed in the engraving of the Etruscan Room at the British Museum in 1847. The other response to the Etruscans could be described by borrowing some sentences from Virginia Woolf's 1919 essay on *The Royal Academy*, where 'from first to last each canvas had rubbed in some emotion [...] the great rooms rang like a parrot-house with the intolerable vociferations of gaudy and brainless birds'.[7] As with the Royal Academy in 1919, in 1839 the lady who introduced visitors to the emotions and picturesque descriptions of the Etruscan world was Mrs Elisabeth Caroline Hamilton Grey, who, after the London exhibition, decided to travel to Italy and visit the real thing, the Campanari site at Tuscania. The result was her *Tour to the Sepulchres of Etruria in 1839*, published in London in 1843.[8] The book, although written by a non-specialist, provides vivid descriptions and insights from the '*immancabile signora Grey*' – who, according to Colonna, witnessed the discovery of a tomb containing 27 sarcophagi. The critical lexicon adopted by Mrs Grey to describe Etruscan objects and sculptures included adjectives like romantic, picturesque, rococo *ante litteram*, monstrous: the notion of grotesque was also there, inasmuch as she noted many figures bridging the borderline between human and animal, like sphynxes, mermaids, tritons and harpies. Grotesque physiognomic skill and caricature gave life to the characters lying on the sarcophagi. Mrs Grey's perception was acutely visual: in recent years such response has earned a well-deserved scholarly seal in Katherine Coty's *A Dream of Etruria: The Sacro Bosco of Bomarzo and the Alternate Antiquity of Alto Lazio*,[9] in which Coty argues that the mannerist gardens at Bomarzo, with their ugly menagerie of disproportioned baroque monsters and faux-Etruscan tombs, are intrinsically related to the rich Etruscan palimpsest of the region north of Rome explored by Mrs Grey.

Mrs Grey's enthusiasm was like that displayed by other commentators who did not belong to the disciplinary field of archaeology: travellers, poets, painters, decorators and so on. Among those who focussed on the Etruscans, George Dennis, the antiquarian, explorer then diplomat, was in Italy in 1842 and his *Cities and Cemeteries of Etruria*, published in 1848 by the British Museum, which included sketches and picturesque engravings by Samuel Ainsley, was considered a work of scholarly value. The treatise included tables in which Pelagic, early Greek and Etruscan alphabets were compared, and scholarly notes which typically suggested that Mrs Grey's was the work of a dilettante. But topography and accuracy would slide into personal impressions when Dennis summoned *The Arabian Nights* and other exotic texts to spice up his descriptions. This passage described the museum of the Campanari at Toscanella-Tuscania that included a garden full of statues. The writer responded to the magic of the place by staging a kind of Etruscan-Gothic fantasy:

> The garden is a most singular place. You seem transported to some scene of Arabian romance, where the people are all turned into stone, or lie spellbound, awaiting the touch of a magician's wand to restore them to life and activity. […]. Lucumones of aristocratic dignity – portly matrons, bedecked with jewels – stout youth, and graceful maidens – reclining on the lids of their coffins, or rather on their festive couches – meeting with fixed stony stare the astonishment of the stranger, yet with a distinct individuality of feature and expression, and so life-like withal, that 'like Pygmalion's statue waking' each seems on the point of warming into existence. Lions, sphynxes, and chimæras dire, in stone, stand among them, as guardians of the place […]. It is as strange a place as may well be conceived, and a lonely walk here by moonlight would try weak nerves and lively imaginations.[10]

John Ruskin, the Two Paths

The response of John Ruskin to the notion of Etruscan, which he embraced in its widest sense, ranging from material evidence to written accounts – Ruskin read George Dennis's treatise – typically included and oscillated between two opposing perspectives. One was the chatty, vociferous discourse attached to the visual arts, a discourse that had to do with names, dates, attributions, schools, subjects, interpretation and so on; the other perspective consisted of a sharp, exclusive focus on the elements of form. Such aporia becomes understandable when we consider Ruskin's gifted eclecticism: a skilled painter, who could handle watercolours and pencils and produce admirably finished works and sketches, he was also an art critic, a critic of society, an author of fiction and poetry, editor, collector, museum manager and teacher. His formalist statement, *The Elements of Drawing*, can be contrasted against his comments about the dubious morality of the picturesque, either noble and Turnerian, or merciless and vulgar, which can be found in *Modern Painters*, in *The Seven Lamps of Architecture* – namely, in the *Lamp of Memory* – and in many other writings about Italy and its art, monuments and landscape.[11]

The Elements of Drawing was published in 1857 for a readership of art students, amateur painters, workmen, who would need lessons and practical methods to learn to sketch and draw. Here the accent did not fall on the moral questions prompted by art: Ruskin would endorse a formalist code based on strictly visual categories, a code that, apart from the idiosyncratic language of Ruskin's preference, did bear a remarkable likeness with two other art texts of strictly aesthetic, visual, formalist vocation: William Gilpin's *Three Essays: On Picturesque Beauty; On Picturesque Travel; and On Sketching Landscape: to which is Added a Poem on Landscape Painting* (1792; 1794; 1808), and *Vision and Design* (1920) by Roger Fry.[12] Not dissimilar in substance from Reverend Gilpin's 'little rules,' Ruskin's 'laws' were meant to establish the categories that enhance visual perception and aesthetic appreciation. Starting on a similar path with 'An Essay in Aesthetics' (1909) and recalling his progress towards a modern theory of vision in 'Retrospect' (1920),[13] Roger Fry maintained that 'the eye rests willingly within the bounds of a picture', insofar as it requires 'the perception of purposeful order and variety in an object' and 'the necessity of a closely woven geometrical texture'[14] in composition. The visual horizon of modern art, according to Fry, included elements of design that determine the visual impact of an image, such as 'rhythm of the line', 'mass', 'space', 'light and shade', 'colour' and finally 'the inclination to the eye of a plane'.[15]

Ruskin's response to the Etruscans remarkably oscillated between two modes of appreciation: the aesthetic and the psychological approach; it was either a formalist vision and set of 'laws' or the spinning of verbal discourse rich in idiosyncratic story-telling and free associations. His drawings document his keen, exclusive focus on line, proportion, and geometrical correspondence, or rhythm, of curves and angles: different projections of the same object reveal his interest in the outline shape of the Etruscan vases. Ruskin would again focus on the Etruscan objects kept at the Ashmolean Museum and give ulterior relief to his first drawings with the application of colour, as in his watercolour of an Etruscan cup, made in 1875.[16]

Ruskin was even capable of extracting pure visual values from the discourse of myth. During one of his visits to the British Museum, he discovered an Etruscan bronze combining mythology and botany, described as 'Demeter sitting in the rustic car, each of the wheels in the form of an open flower, found at Amelia in Etruria'. His diary for 3rd March 1876 mentions an 'Etruscan bronze […] Chariot of Demeter with pure roses for wheels'. His drawing does not focus on the goddess or on the archaeological dating of the artefact, nonchalantly bypassed, but on the shape of the roses. The eye prompts the recognition of a similar perfect pentagon, seen elsewhere, in his own garden, at Brantwood, in the Lake District:

> if you will look into the Etruscan room of the British Museum, you will find there an Etruscan Demeter of—any time you please—B.C., riding on a car whose wheels are of wild roses: that the wild rose of *her* time is thus proved

to be precisely the wild rose of *my* time, growing behind my study on the hillside; and for my own part, I would not give a spray of it for all Australasia, South America, and Japan together.¹⁷

Ruskin, however, together with his keen vision on the elements of design, was also an art historian, a teacher, and in this role he would read the Etruscan material as an important chapter in the art history of Italy. In *The Aesthetic and Mathematic Schools of Art in Florence. Lectures Given before the University of Oxford in Michaelmas Term, 1874*, he addressed his audience on the art of Cimabue:

> I don't know if you have a distinct idea of Etruscans—who they were, or what they were. But mass them in your minds thus: — Pagan Etruscans, exactly like the Greeks, and having their chief dynasty at the same time as the Greek, contemporary with earliest Rome. [...] Christian Etruscans, converted, I don't know when, but very quietly in a group here at Florence till the thirteenth century [...]. Then the Lombard nobles intermarry with the peaceful Etruscans, quarrel with them, and there is one continual clatter of street fighting till 1250, when the peaceful Etruscans turn out the Lombards, and begin their own great Florentine life—much strengthened by their battle, taught how to hit hard with sword or chisel, and thenceforward, Etruscans re-animate, living to our own day. Then, in Cimabue you have his own Etruscan ancient and peaceful blood—the Lombardic temper mingling in its restlessness; finally, the traditional education in religious legend given him by his Greek masters. That is the way in which the grafting tells on his own nature.¹⁸

Race, blood, religion, wars... reanimation: *mutatis mutandis*, in this account the Etruscans figure like zombies from the ancient Italian civilisation, endowed with a surplus of life, stretching from antiquity to present.

Ruskin would enlarge this narrative in *The Laws of Fésole. A Familiar Treatise on the Elementary Principles and Practice of Drawing and Painting as Determined by the Tuscan Masters. Arranged for the Use of Schools* (1877-1878), where his handling of the art of Cimabue, Giotto, Brunelleschi, demonstrates the transition from a sharp focus on form towards his spirited handling of art history along a narrative that elects the Etruscans as protagonists of many important chapters in our civilisation.

> And this book is called *The Laws of Fésole* because the entire system of possible Christian Art is founded on the principles established by Giotto in Florence, he receiving them from the Attic Greeks through Cimabue, the last of

their disciples, and engrafting them on the existing art of the Etruscans, the race from which both his master and he were descended. In the centre of Florence, the last great work of native Etruscan architecture, her Baptistery, and the most perfect work of Christian architecture, her Campanile, stand within a hundred paces of each other: and from the foot of that Campanile, the last conditions of design which preceded the close of Christian art are seen in the dome of Brunelleschi [...]. [T]he methods of draughtsmanship established by the Florentines, in true fulfilment of Etruscan and Greek tradition, are insuperable in execution, and eternal in principle;[19]

In *Mornings in Florence* (1875-1877) the Etruscan evidence would acquire priority over the Greek art heritage, and even the Parthenon in Ruskin's eyes would be belittled by the Cathedral of Florence:

Giotto was a pure Etruscan-Greek of the thirteenth century; converted indeed to worship St. Francis instead of Heracles [...]. The ancient Etruscan gold and metal work and the drawing on their pottery is finer, more subtle, more wonderful as work than Athenian gold, or bronze, or pottery, but you have no Etruscan Parthenon nor Etruscan Phidias. But after Christ, these workmen became artists in the highest kind; and Michael Angelo is the Etruscan Phidias, and the Cathedral of Florence is the Etruscan Parthenon.[20]

The connexion between Greek and Etruscan art, enlarged to embrace the osmosis between myth and religion, violated the traditional boundary between paganism and Christianity, but Ruskin went on fearlessly:

[Etruscan art] remains in its own Italian valleys, of the Arno and upper Tiber, in one unbroken series of work, from the seventh century before Christ, to this hour, when the country whitewasher still scratches his plaster in Etruscan patterns. All Florentine work of the finest kind [...] is absolutely Etruscan, merely changing its subjects, and representing the Virgin instead of Athena, and Christ instead of Jupiter.[21]

According to Paul Tucker, *Mornings in Florence* is 'Ruskin's boldest historical invention, the survival in medieval and early Renaissance Tuscan Christian art of a native Etruscan tradition. This fantasy colours the whole book, as it does all of Ruskin's writings on Tuscan art after 1874.'[22] It is possible to imagine that the two paths that would be followed by the Etruscan reception in the twentieth century were already straddled by Ruskin, who either out of a moralist devotion to the purity of the line and the elements of design, or owing to flights of fantasy that allowed him to romance episodes of art history, would encapsulate and stimulate the attitudes of authors of the so-called modernist avant-garde.

Romancing the Etruscans

Nathaniel Hawthorne, John Addington Symonds, Walter Pater, Vernon Lee, Henry James, Edith Wharton, Marcel Proust: for different reasons, these and other authors introduced the Etruscan theme within their narrative discourse – whether through an Etruscan protagonist, or a strange bracelet, within a landscape description, or in a photographic reproduction – and all these performative roles activate a dissolving view into the distant past and often throw an ominous light on the narrative. Either way, the Etruscan object allows authors to move a step away from lucid realism, to open the floodgates of psychological awe, superstition, emotions, seduction. Such is the function of the bracelet donated to Hilda in *The Marble Faun: Or The Romance of Monte Beni* (1860) by Nathaniel Hawthorne; of the native from the Etruscan Luni in Walter Pater's *Marius the Epicurean* (1885); of a bracelet again in Edith Wharton's *The Age of Innocence* (1920); of the reproduction of Ruskin's copy of Botticelli's Zipporah standing on the desk of Charles Swann, as she reminds him of Odette de Crécy.[23] Marco Canani has detailed the occurrence of Etruscan landscape and objects in Vernon Lee's oeuvre;[24] Henry James, in *Italian Hours* (1909) preferred to give his readers an unashamed impressionist account of Cortona and Volterra rather that detailing a visit to the Guarnacci archaeological museum.

> I may not invite the reader to penetrate with me by so much as a step the boundless backward reach of history to which the more massive of the Etruscan gates of Volterra, the Porta all'Arco, forms the solidest of thresholds; since I perforce take no step myself, and am even exceptionally condemned to impressionism unashamed.[25]

Gabriele D'Annunzio, commenting on the relics kept at the museum Guarnacci, is the one who is supposed to have christened the long bronze statue 'L'ombra della sera' – 'The Evening Shadow' – offering his idiosyncratic comment on the elongated linear shape of the body, but also suggesting the quasi nocturnal sentiment of silence the statue inspired.

Also a very young Roger Fry, on his first seeing the Etruscan remains in Rome, seemed to proceed on the path already traced by John Ruskin – a critical position that would be deeply modified by his encounter with the art of Cézanne, by the Post-Impressionists' exhibitions of 1910 and 1912, and by the ensuing concept of significant form, then discussed in the essays collected as *Vision and Design* (1920). But in 1891, according to Frances Spalding, Roger Fry 'struggled to come to terms with Early Christian art through the study of mosaics, discovered the greatness of Raphael, admired the Pantheon, and enthused over Etruscan art.'[26] This aspect was confirmed by Virginia Woolf, in *Roger Fry. A Biography* (1940), where a letter written by Fry in 1891, from Rome, reveals a great deal about his first reaction to Etruscan things:

> I've got very keen on Etruscan things. [...] I think they will throw some light on Greek paintings because what is so interesting is the extraordinary way in which they accepted Greek art. But there is also much that is original in their art and I think I can trace all that I formerly thought the Romans had added to Greek art (namely something grotesque and picturesque) to an Etruscan origin so much so that I think what the Italians of the Renaissance selected for their model was rather what was Etruscan in Roman art than anything else. I dare say this is rather wild or else has been said before, but at present I'm rather mad on them.[27]

The discursive path, already recognisable in Ruskin's response to the Etruscans, their art and civilisation, would still mould the attitude of twentieth-century writers. D. H. Lawrence devoted a whole book, *Etruscan Places* (1932), to the Etruscan environment, art, society, after his tour of Tuscany in 1927. For Lawrence, who was witness to the Italian descent into Fascism – a regime wrapped in Roman mottoes, symbols, ideology, style – the Etruscans were the antidote against Rome, against a society based on the military order, and a belligerent morality. The Etruscans instead were coloured, light, dancing, loving, erotic as much as Lawrence desired them to be.

> However, those pure, clean-living, sweet-souled Romans, who smashed nation after nation and crushed the free soul in people after people, and were ruled by Messalina and Heliogabalus and such-like snowdrops, they said the Etruscans were vicious. *So basta! Quand le maître parle, tout le monde se tait*. The Etruscans were vicious! The only vicious people on the face of the earth presumably. You and I, dear reader, we are two unsullied snowflakes, aren't we? We have every right to judge. Myself, however, if the

Etruscans were vicious, I'm glad they were. To the Puritan all things are impure, as somebody says. And those naughty neighbours of the Romans at least escaped being Puritans.[28]

Lawrence's empathic and emphatic response adopts the rhetoric of excess and the dialogic attitude with the imaginary reader that often sounded in Ruskin's accounts of art history: but Lawrence's response easily overflows into comments about society, religion, morality, sexuality. Very much like, and yet much unlike Ruskin's, he thus comments on the tombs at Cerveteri, endowed 'with those easy natural proportions whose beauty one hardly notices, they come so naturally, physically. It is the natural beauty of proportion of the phallic consciousness, contrasted with the more studied or ecstatic proportion of the mental and spiritual Consciousness we are accustomed to.'[29] Anthony Burgess suggests that 'in the Etruscan remains he finds not just love of life but the very Lawrentian metaphysics of "phallism".'[30] Besides Lawrence's metaphysics, one may also bring into the general picture of the relationship of the literati with the Etruscans, the mirroring effect concept and theory, occurring when individuals empathise with and accept people whom they believe to hold similar interests and beliefs.[31]

'Drawing may be taught by tutors: but Design only by Heaven'[32]

Artists, especially when the demise of realism and naturalism at the beginning of the twentieth century brought to the foreground the formal elements of design, were to find in Etruscan art line, mass, composition and geometrical correspondence. Again, Ruskin's drawing of a figurine[33] seems to have started an endless reverberation of lines, proportions, curves and formal echoes. The drawing by Ruskin of an ancient statuette, and its echoes in modern figures, suggest that an art expression extremely ancient and distant could still be appropriated by the modern artist, owing to the principle of analogy and the system of the grid.[34]

Massimo Campigli (born Max Ihlenfeld, 1895-1971), whose artistic career started with the Italian Futurists, who contributed to their magazine *Lacerba*, and later consorted with the 'Paris Italians' Giorgio De Chirico, Alberto Savinio and Filippo De Pisis, was one of those artists whose work suggests that the line of design Ruskin perceived in Etruscan art was destined to enjoy a long afterlife in the following century.[35] After a first flirtation with Egyptian art, in 1928, when he debuted at the Venice Biennial, Campigli saw the Etruscan collection at the Museo Nazionale Etrusco in Rome and embraced its style.[36] In his own words, after that

Fig. 1.2 Works from the collection of the Alberto Giacometti Foundation in the rooms of the Kunsthaus Zürich (2020). By Alberto Giacometti-Stiftung, © Succession Alberto Giacometti / 2022, ProLitteris, Zürich – Own work. Licensed under CC BY-SA 3.0 via Wikimedia Commons. https://commons.wikimedia.org/wiki/File:Giacometti-Räume,_Kunsthaus_Zürich,_2020.jpg

visit, '[…] A pagan happiness entered my paintings, both in the spirit of the subjects and in the spirit of the work, which became freer and more lyrical'.[37] Today, this passage is quoted in the presentation of the exhibition *Massimo Campigli e gli Etruschi. Una pagana felicità*, held in Venice from May to September 2021.

Other Italian artists would find their personal solution to the quest for the elements of design voiced by the European avant-garde movements, by identifying the necessary formal qualities modern art was in search of in the lesson of Etruscan art. Arturo Martini (1889-1947) was one of the first artists who contributed to the identification of the major role Etruscan sculpture could play in the quest for modern art, and in the art debates of the first decades of the twentieth century. Between 1929 and 1932, Martini would forge a language based on 'plastic values' that harked back to Etruscan art as a source devoid of the sentiments of elegy and nostalgia, but still yielding the power of its formal design.[38]

Also the Italian artist Marino Marini (1901-1980) would maintain: 'I look back to the Etruscans for the same reason for which modern art has looked backwards, ignoring the recent past and drawing new strength from the expressions of

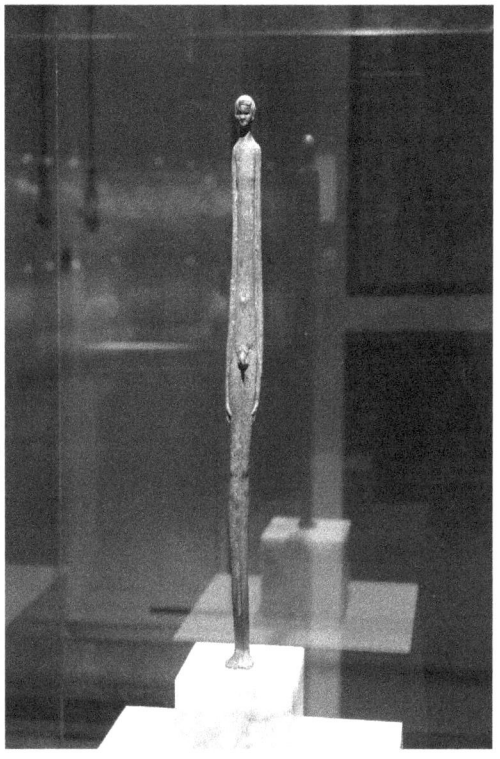

Fig. 1.3 Ombra della Sera (3rd century BC). Etruscan Bronze Figurine, 57,5 cm. Museo Etrusco Guarnacci, Volterra. By Jnn95. Licensed under CC BY-SA 4.0 <https://creativecommons.org/licenses/by-sa/4.0>, via Wikimedia Commons. https://commons.wikimedia.org/wiki/File:Ombra_della_Sera_Volterra.jpg

a virgin and remote mankind. Such coincidence is not just of a cultural kind: we all need to retrieve the elementary essence of art'.[39] Whilst born in Pistoia, that is, in Etruscan land, Marini intended to interpret on Italian soil the aspiration that moved modern European artists and critics of the 1910s and 1920s towards ancient African and Australian art. In 1921, Alessandro Della Seta wrote:

> Etruscan figures were not gods and heroes that myth made sublime; their subjects were not loaded by a deep innermost meaning; Etruscan art saw in those figures only men and human actions. As a consequence, instead of soaring towards ideal spheres it would remain on the ground, in order to fix aspects that had to do with their humanity. Those figures were caught in action, were moving in real space, and their action was made more evident by heightening the formal elements of design.[40]

The life of Marino Marini was indeed deeply entwined around his cultural roots and his early visits at the National Archaeological Museum in Florence. But the Etruscans were not only the response to a cultural background rooted in Marini's personal history. The same elements of design that had fascinated Ruskin in his Ashmolean Museum drawing were there, as in the figure of a dancer created in

Fig. 1.4 Reclining Figure by Henry Moore (1935-1936). Elm wood, 48.26 x 93.34 x 44.45 cm. Collection Buffalo AKG Art Museum, © The Henry Moore Foundation / Artists Rights Society (ARS), New York / DACS, London. Image Available Under Fair Use. https://www.albrightknox.org/artworks/rca1939121-reclining-figure

1929,[41] one of a line that belongs to Ruskin's and Campigli's dancers. And Marini's artwork also responded to the feelings described by Della Seta, in their search for a deep sense of the human life, action, ultimate destiny, as in his terracotta group entitled 'Popolo' (1929), and in his figures of mounted cavaliers.[42]

In his *Pensieri sull'arte* Marini maintained: 'My love for reality [...] is perhaps due to the Etruscans: it's a reality that appears in forms of elementary structure, but whose surfaces invite the play of light. Whilst simplification can visibly drive us away from nature, it always leads us back to it, insofar as it only tends to what is essential.'[43] To conclude, in 1961 Marini was interviewed by the Swedish sculptor Staffan Nilhén, who inquired about his Etruscan inspiration. Marini's answer was concise and full of intransigent pride: 'I am not inspired! I am Etruscan! The same blood fills my veins. As you know a culture can remain dormant for generations and suddenly wake up to a new life. In Martini as well as in myself the Etruscan art is reborn, we take on from the point at which they stopped.'[44]

But it was not only in Italy that Etruscan art exerted its deep fascination through its elements of design, its freedom from realism, its plastic values. Swiss-born artist Alberto Giacometti (1901-1966), for example, after visiting

Fig. 1.5 Sarcophagus of Velthur Vipinana, case with Niobids, Centauromachia, Achilles and Hector (late 4th century BC). By Fabrizio Garrisi. Licensed under CC BY-SA 4.0 <https://creativecommons.org/licenses/by-sa/4.0>, via Wikimedia Commons. https://commons.wikimedia.org/wiki/File:Sarcofago_di_Velthur_Vipinana,_fine_del_IV_sec._a.C._Coperchio_calco_in_gesso_-FG2.jpg

the Guarnacci Museum in Volterra in the early 1960s created the sculpture of the 'Standing Woman' (1956) inspired by the Etruscan bronze 'The Shadow of the Evening' that Gabriele D'Annunzio had christened (Fig. 1.2 and Fig. 1.3). Also 'L'homme qui marche' by Giacometti was inspired by the Apollo of Veii. Drawing inspiration from the Etruscan deity, Giacometti would start to produce many thin elongated figures that soon became the mark of his art style.

To conclude this brief survey of sculptors who took after the elements of design in Etruscan art, British-born artist Henry Moore (1898-1986) should be mentioned. His first 'Reclining Figure' (1929) (Fig. 1.4) was compared to the factuality of Etruscan funerary monuments (Fig. 1.5). In 1921, after having fought in World War One, Moore studied in London, and the British Museum archaic art rooms proved inspiring.[45] The so-called primitive style artwork from Egypt, Pre-Columbian America, Africa, and indeed the Etruscan sculptures, offered lasting inspiration to his work. In 1924, Moore won a six-month travelling scholarship which he spent in Northern Italy studying the great works of artists like Michelangelo, Giotto, Giovanni Pisano and so on. Michelangelo would prove an early inspiration to Moore dating back to his Yorkshire schooldays, but the triangulation with the Etruscan-Florentine Renaissance of Ruskin's art history is there as well. Another strong link would be Moore's passion for D. H. Lawrence's works, and here again Tuscany would be the common ground where the two artists met, namely in *Etruscan Places*, as detailed by Jane Costin.[46] Moore's reclining figures, his archetypes of womanly figures, are connected to Lawrence's vision and the concept of 'a sense of touch':

> While Moore was inspired by his visits to the Etruscan exhibitions at the British Museum, as he freely acknowledged, Lawrence's work was a 'considerable' influence on his thought. We know that Moore avidly read all of Lawrence's novels and that he had a 1933 edition of *Sketches of Etruscan Places* on his bookshelf together with a book about the trial of *Lady Chatterley's Lover*. Indeed, as we will see, looking at some of Moore's sculptures suggests that it was Lawrence's emphasis on the importance of touch that had a particular influence on Moore's later works.[47]

Coda: Alberto Savinio, 'Non conviene svelare il segreto degli Etruschi'

My last paragraph returns to the two paths, insofar as the artist Alberto Savinio (1891-1952) seems to open up notions that, simultaneously, take both directions. Greek by birth, brother of Giorgio De Chirico, Alberto Savinio did stride the artistic horizon of post-war avant-garde, the *rappel-à-l'ordre*, literature and painting, but also music, opera and stage production. His article 'Non conviene svelare il mistero degli Etruschi' (1950) confirms that to love the Etruscans means to not love Rome: 'Between the Romans and the Etruscans, my sympathy goes to the Etruscans'.[48] We find more than one echo of Lawrence's response to the Etruscans, an acerbic comment on Mussolini's dictatorial *romanitas* included.

> In comparison with Roman classicism, the Etruscans […] represent the romantic element; the sentiment for the object that beyond the limit classicism imposes on it, produces its continuation, *ad infinitum*. The aversion Rome felt for Christianity was really for romanticism. Etruscans had reduced the romantic sentiment of life to its simplest form, to its most practical and egoistic form […]: it was to be the continuation of life beyond life;[49]

The passage repeats what in this essay has been expressed by many voices, dating back to John Ruskin; but Savinio also underlines that Etruscan language, with its mystery, must not be unveiled: much to his dismay, near Cosa he meets a group of American archaeologists who intend to dispel the mystery. As a coda, he remarks that most men cannot tolerate whatever is mysterious, deep, or sublime, to use a romantic word and concept that basically points to a wordless sentiment of awe. Actually he remarks that the Italians seem hostile to whatever ignores, breaks and transgresses the boundary of realism. Savinio's metaphysical art, instead, while expressing his careful attention for lines, masses, composition, and the elements of design, abounds with dreams, and oneiric visions that chime in with the eerie past that is one with the notion of 'Etruscan' and with the modern artist's strong response to their powerful material presence.

Notes

1. Michael Vickers, 'Imaginary Etruscans: Changing Perceptions of Etruria Since the Fifteenth Century', in Michael Vickers, *Parerga: Selected Essays on Literature, Art and Archaeology*, Alexander Rubel (ed.) (Bucharest: Editura Academiei Române, 2019), pp. 293-318. Once again, I am grateful to Professor Michael Vickers for his invaluable comments, guidance, and for his many essays about the history of antiquity that have highlighted our changing perceptions of beauty, taste and value of the arts and relics of antiquity.
2. *Ibid.*, p. 294.
3. Francesca Orestano, 'Gli Etruschi nella memoria culturale britannica tra Otto e Novecento: ovvero il fascino sublime di un braccialetto', in *Fascino Etrusco nel primo Novecento, conversando di arti e storia delle arti*, Giovanna Bagnasco Gianni (ed.), *Aristonothos. Scritti per il Mediterraneo antico*, vol. 11 (Milan: Ledizioni, 2016), pp. 145-170.
4. Documents related to the Campanari exhibition in London in *Tuscania*, Giovanni Colonna (ed.) (Siena: Nuova Immagine, 1986).
5. *The Times*, 26 January 1837, in *Tuscania*, pp. 21-22.
6. I have dealt with the Victorians' ability to reproduce marble, silver, rugs and other items in Francesca Orestano, 'The Chemistry of Taste. Aesthetics, Literature, and the Rise of the Impure', in *English Literature. Theories, Interpretations, Contexts*, Maria Concetta Costantini (ed.), 2 (2015), pp. 177-202.
7. Virginia Woolf, 'The Royal Academy' [1919] in *The Crowded Dance of Modern Life*, Rachel Bowlby (ed.) (London: Penguin, 1993), pp. 13-18 (p. 17).
8. Mrs Hamilton Grey also authored *The History of Etruria. Tarchun and his items from the foundation of Tarquinia to the foundation of Rome*, vol. 1 (London: John Hatchard, 1843).
9. Katherine Coty, *A Dream of Etruria: The Sacro Bosco of Bomarzo and the Alternate Antiquity of Alto Lazio*, master dissertation, University of Washington, 2013.
10. George Dennis, *The Cities and Cemeteries of Etruria*, 2 vols. (London: John Murray, 1848), vol. 1, pp. 442-443. https://books.google.it/books?id=kLc_AAAAcAAJ&pg=PR21&hl=it&source=gbs_toc_r&cad=3#v=onepage&q&f=false (Accessed July 2021). In the same volume, Dennis describes Tarquinia by referring to 'Ariosto's pictures in Etruscan tombs', fancying the Etruscan priest in a procession as a 'wise Merlin', *ibid.*, p. 309.
11. I have tried to represent this aporia in Francesca Orestano, 'Across the Picturesque: Ruskin's Argument with the Strange Sisters', in *Strange Sisters: Literature and Aesthetics in the Nineteenth Century*, Francesca Orestano and Francesca Frigerio (eds) (New York, London: Peter Lang, 2009), pp. 99-122.
12. Francesca Orestano, 'Pictures of Modernity, the Modernity of the Picturesque: A Chiasmus', in *Pictures of Modernity: The Visual and the Literary in England, 1850-1930*, Loretta Innocenti, Franco Marucci and Enrica Villari (eds) (Venezia: Cafoscarina, 2008), pp. 103-118. Gilpin's attention to claro-obscuro and 'intricacy' was rephrased by Ruskin as the 'Law of Mystery'; the 'Law of Principality' was expressed by Gilpin as the strategy of 'grouping'; the 'Law of Repetition' echoes the succession of coulisses or screens that frame the

principal object of the scene; the 'Law of Continuity' expressed the rhythm of simplified, receding perspective plans; the 'Law of Curvature' is, namely, the line of beauty; the 'Law of Radiation' is the increasingly complicated pattern of a simple form; the 'Law of Contrast' is, literally, 'Contrast'; the 'Law of Interchange' heightens the effect of the Law of Contrast by enforcing the unity of opposite things; the 'Law of Consistency' is the effect of colour and line which Gilpin indicated as 'Keeping', conferring a homogeneous 'tone' to a composition of contrasting parts; the 'Law of Harmony' recommends that colours be kept in the 'middle range'. One may conclude that since Gilpin, Ruskin, Fry, unanimously identify and define the categories which determine the formal value of design, one may also decide whether Gilpin and his picturesque theory are modern, and so Ruskin and Fry are as well, or whether Fry and Ruskin are outdated. The definition of modernity is at stake, rather than the modernity of the picturesque. John Ruskin, 'The Elements of Drawing', in *Works*, Edward Tyas Cook and Alexander Wedderburn (eds), 39 vols. (London: George Allen, 1903-1912), vol. 15, pp. 120-200.

13. Roger Fry, 'An Essay in Aesthetics' and 'Retrospect', in *Vision and Design* [1920] (London: Penguin, 1961), pp. 22-39 and pp. 222-237.
14. *Ibid.*
15. *Ibid.*, p. 39. Fry had jettisoned the classic categories drawn from the field of verbal discourse, in his attempt 'to divide works of visual art [without] adopting the classification already existing in poetry into Epic, Dramatic, Lyric, and Comedic.' Roger Fry, 'Retrospect', pp. 222-237.
16. John Ruskin, 'Study of an Etruscan Cup', in *Works*, vol. 21, p. 254. Illustrations available online, URL: http://ruskin.ashmolean.org/collection/8990/9168/9286/14553;http://ruskin.ashmolean.org/collection/8990/9169/9324/14554. (Accessed May 2023).
17. Letter 66 of *Fors Claviger*a, for June 1876, in *Works*, vol. 28, p. 621, Ruskin's emphasis, with the note: 'Etruscan bronze statue with iron centre splitting, and lambent drapery. Chariot of Demeter with pure roses for wheels. Roses and stars in early Greek vases confused. Etruscan and Camirus gold quite undistinguishable in dotted-dew workmanship.' Most of the objects thus noted may be seen in 'The Room of Gold Ornaments' and 'The Etruscan Saloon' at the British Museum.
18. John Ruskin, *Works*, vol. 33, pp. 202-203.
19. *Ibid.*, vol. 15, pp. 345-346.
20. *Ibid.*, vol. 33, p. 472.
21. *Ibid.*, vol. 23, p. 342.
22. Paul Tucker, 'Adrian Stokes and the "Anti-Ruskin Lesson" of British Formalism', in *Ruskin and the Twentieth Century: The Modernity of Ruskinism*, Toni Cerutti (ed.) (Vercelli: Mercurio, 2000), pp. 129-144 (p. 137).
23. In 1874 in Rome, Ruskin was intrigued by the Etruscan-like lettering on the hem of Botticelli's Zipporah; he copied the image and when he was teaching in Oxford, when he gave a lesson on the Schools of Florence, he defined Zipporah the Etruscan Athena: his copy from Botticelli would become the frontispiece for volume 23 of Ruskin's *Works*. This is the reproduction mentioned in Marcel Proust, *Du côté de chez Swann* (1913).
24. Marco Canani, 'Vernon Lee e la modernità etrusca, tra eredità artistica e memoria culturale', in *Fascino Etrusco nel primo Novecento. Conversando di arti e storia delle arti*, Giovanna Bagnasco Gianni (ed.), pp. 177-192.
25. Henry James, *Italian Hours* (New York: The Ecco Press, 1987), p. 327.
26. Frances Spalding, *Roger Fry. Art and Life* (Berkley and Los Angeles: University of California Press, 1980), p. 35.
27. Virginia Woolf, *Roger Fry. A Biography* (London: The Hogarth Press, 1940), p. 68.
28. D. H. Lawrence, *Etruscan Places* in *D. H. Lawrence and Italy*, with Introduction by Anthony Burgess (London: Penguin, 1972), pp. 1-214, p. 2
29. *Ibid.*, p. 10.
30. *Ibid.*, 'Introduction', p. XI.
31. Philippe Rochat, Claudia Passos-Ferreira, 'From Imitation to Reciprocation and Mutual Recognition', in *Mirror Neuron Systems*, Jaime Pineda (ed.) (New York: Springer Nature, 2008), pp. 191–212, doi: https://doi.org/10.1007/978-1-59745-479-7. (Accessed June 2021).
32. John Ruskin, 'The Laws of Fésole', in *Works*, vol. 15, p. 344.
33. John Ruskin, 'Studies of Greek Terra-cotta on Two Sides. Girl Dancing'. Illustration available online, URL: http://ruskin.ashmolean.org/collection/8990/9286. (Accessed May 2023).
34. Francesca Orestano, 'Victorian Arts and the Challenge of Modernity: Analogy, the Grid, and Chemical Transformations', *Cahiers Victoriens et Edouardiens*, 89 (spring 2019), doi: https://doi.org/10.4000/cve.5059. (Accessed June 2021).
35. See, among others, Massimo Campigli's 'Figura in blu', oil on canvas, 1960.
36. Biographical notes from https://www.settemuse.it/pittori_scultori_italiani/massimo_campigli.htm. (Accessed June 2021).
37. '[…] Nei miei quadri entrò una pagana felicità tanto nello spirito dei soggetti che nel-

lo spirito del lavoro che si fece più libero e lirico'. Quoted in the presentation of the exhibition 'Massimo Campigli e gli Etruschi. Una pagana felicità', Venice 2021. URL: http://www.arte.it/calendario-arte/venezia/mostra-massimo-campigli-e-gli-etruschi-una-pagana-felicit%C3%A0-75521. (Accessed July 2021). All translations are by Francesca Orestano.

38. See the article by Federica Grossi, 'Gli Etruschi di Arturo Martini. Rielaborazioni d'Avanguardia', in *Fascino Etrusco nel primo Novecento, conversando di arti e storia delle arti*, Giovanna Bagnasco Gianni (ed.), pp. 111-144.

39. 'Io guardo agli etruschi per la stessa ragione per cui tutta l'arte moderna si è voltata indietro saltando l'immediato passato ed è andata a rinvigorirsi nell'espressione più genuina di un'umanità vergine e remota. La coincidenza non è soltanto culturale; ma noi aspiriamo a una elementarità dell'arte'. Marino Marini quoted in Finestre sull'Arte. Rivista online d'arte antica e contemporanea, URL: https://www.finestresullarte.info/opere-e-artisti/io-sono-un-etrusco-marino-marini-e-l-arte-etrusca. (Accessed June 2021).

40. Alessandro Della Seta (1879-1944), Jewish archaeologist, museum director, writer, academic, member of the Accademia dei Lincei until the racial laws of 1938 decreed his expulsion, wrote in *Dedalo*, 1921: 'le figure non erano per gli Etruschi dèi ed eroi resi sublimi dal mito; il soggetto non si presentava grave di un profondo significato interiore; l'arte etrusca finiva per scorgervi solo uomini ed azioni umane. Quindi anziché ascendere verso le sfere dell'ideale si fermava a terra per cogliere questo lato di umanità. Le faceva figure realmente operanti, le voleva veder muoversi nello spazio, ne accresceva con modificazioni della forma il carattere dell'azione.' Quoted in Finestre sull'Arte. Rivista online d'arte antica e contemporanea, URL: https://www.finestresullarte.info/opere-e-artisti/io-sono-un-etrusco-marino-marini-e-l-arte-etrusca. (Accessed June 2021).

41. See Marino Marini's 'Danzatrice', painted terracotta, 1929.

42. See Marino Marini's 'Piccolo cavaliere', terracotta, 1943.

43. 'Il mio amore della realtà [...] lo devo forse agli Etruschi: una realtà che appare in forme che hanno lo spessore dell'elementare e sulle cui superfici gioca la luce. La semplificazione può, visibilmente, scostarsi dalla natura – ma ad essa riconduce perché tende all'essenziale'. Marino Marini, *Pensieri sull'arte. Scritti e interviste* (Milan: Scheiwiller, All'insegna del pesce d'oro, 1998), URL: https://www.finestresullarte.info/opere-e-artisti/io-sono-un-etrusco-marino-marini-e-l-arte-etrusca. (Accessed June 2021).

44. 'Io non sono ispirato! Io sono etrusco! Lo stesso sangue riempie le mie vene. Come sai, una cultura può rimanere in letargo, dormire per generazioni e all'improvviso risvegliarsi a nuova vita. In Martini e in me rinasce l'arte etrusca, noi continuiamo da dove loro si sono fermati', URL: https://www.finestresullarte.info/opere-e-artisti/io-sono-un-etrusco-marino-marini-e-l-arte-etrusca. (Accessed June 2021).

45. Roger Berthoud, *The Life of Henry Moore* (London: Faber and Faber, 1987).

46. Jane Costin, 'A Sense of Touch: Henry Moore and D. H. Lawrence', *Etudes Lawrenciennes*, 46 (2015), doi: https://doi.org/10.4000/lawrence.243. (Accessed June 2021); also see Joyce Dallaportas, *D. H. Lawrence and Henry Moore: the positive and negative manifestations of the archetypical feminine* (Ann Arbor: UMI, 1990).

47. Jane Costin, 'A Sense of Touch: Henry Moore and D. H. Lawrence'.

48. 'Tra Romani ed Etruschi, la mia simpatia va agli Etruschi'. Alberto Savinio, 'Non conviene svelare il segreto degli Etruschi', *Corriere della sera*, 9 July 1950, now in *Opere. Scritti dispersi. Tra guerra e dopoguerra (1943-1952)*, Leonardo Sciascia and Franco De Maria (eds) (Milan: Bompiani, 1989), pp. 1194-1197.

49. 'Gli Etruschi [...], di fronte al classicismo romano, rappresentano l'elemento romantico; il sentimento della cosa che, di là dal limite imposto alla cosa dal classicismo, continua la cosa: all'infinito. L'avversione di Roma al cristianesimo era in fondo avversione al romanticismo. Il senso romantico della vita [...] gli Etruschi lo avevano ristretto alla sua forma più semplice, più pratica, più egoista: al continuarsi tale quale della vita di là dalla vita'. *Ibid.*, p. 1195.

The 'Walking Apollo': From Archaeological Dissemination to Literary Knowledge

Chiara Zampieri

From Collection to Archaeology

From the Renaissance to the nineteenth century, the study of the past and its ancient civilisations and languages were the preoccupation of a small elite, including groups of amateurs, philosophers, intellectuals, and aficionados who established and developed their knowledge and fascination for the past around the practice of collection. It is only in the second half of the 19th century that the experience of excavation and the recovery of ancient objects started to be conceived differently. Around the turn of the century, the practice of unearthing ancient objects underwent a process of unprecedented institutionalisation and specialisation which gradually led to the recognition of archaeology as a scientific and independent field of studies. As for many other scholarly disciplines in the period, this process was only possible through the increasing institutional power of academia, the establishment of professional associations of experts and the circulation of scientific publications in specialised journals.

The epistemic shift represented by the transition from collection to archaeology in the praxis, is also exemplified by the invention of the terms 'collector' and 'archaeologist', both coined in the late nineteenth century precisely to distinguish two practices that were originally inseparable.[1] The 1870-edition of *Le Grand Dictionnaire Universel* by Pierre Larousse clearly illustrates this process: 'The roles are now clear: on the one hand, we have the archaeologist, a scholar who engages in the study of antiquity and, on the other, the antiquarian or collector, who indiscriminately accumulates objects from the past'.[2] The various definitions of the word 'archaeology' are also eloquent, in the sense that in several late nineteenth century dictionaries the practice of archaeology is defined by its negative, that is, as an anti-collection.[3] Nevertheless, archaeology cannot exist without collections: if in the late nineteenth century the practice of collection is gradually depreciated vis-à-vis the more specialised and professionalised discipline of archaeology, collections as sets of objects still represent an important part of archaeology as a field of studies. With the institutionalisation of archaeology, collections are no longer a matter of disordered accumulation but rather of careful selection and exposition with a specific narrative aim. Ancient artefacts are therefore gradually organised and catalogued by professional archaeologists; they are systematically exposed in the first examples of archaeological museums where ancient civilisations, with their customs and traditions, resurrect before the visitors' eyes telling stories of a lost everyday life.

In other words, with the institutionalisation of archaeology, the relationship to ancient objects is also redefined. It is the archeo-*logos*, the rationale on ancient times and origins which prevails over the random accumulation and collection of artefacts. As a consequence, archaeological remains are no longer perceived as dead and dusty objects to be collected and exposed in a bourgeois living room, but rather as artefacts imbued with meaning, as a matrix of new narratives able to expand the boundaries of reality and foster new understandings of the past.[4] Therefore, while developing as an independent domain, archaeology also fostered a new imaginative arena, full of dramatic potential and ghostly scenarios that became the subject of several archaeological fantasies, thus offering a compelling space for both imaginative resurrection and reconstruction.[5]

In the early twentieth century, several artists and writers started to question the very materiality of ancient objects and the possible relations that one can establish with the past (and the present) through these objects. Particularly compelling is the case of the Apollo of Veii, a life-size Etruscan statue dating from the sixth century BC, which was discovered and unearthed in Portonaccio in 1916, but not displayed in full until 1919.

Material Culture and the Poetics of Discovery

The early twentieth century saw a growing interest for the Etruscans and their silent and mysterious civilisation whose legacy only survived through several artefacts and funerary frescos discovered in their necropolises in Tuscany and Northern Latium. Such ferment, both archaeological and artistic,[6] was sparked by a number of excavations[7] that occurred in the early twentieth century in central Italy: the years between 1909 and 1936 saw the discovery and excavation of the necropolis of La Banditaccia, near Cerveteri (Northern Latium); from 1913 until 1916, 1200 Etruscan tombs were unearthed during the archaeological campaign of Veii, that culminated in the stunning discovery of the Apollo of Veii by the Italian archaeologist Giulio Quirino Gigliolio. It was only in 1919, after the war, that the statue was restored and displayed in the Museo Nazionale Etrusco di Villa Giulia (Rome).

The discovery of the Apollo of Veii corresponds to a decisive moment in the history of archaeology, as it marks the emergence of Etruscology as an independent and professionalised discipline.[8] This has something to do with the fact that the exhibition of the Etruscan deity completely revolutionised the perception of Etruscan art and, more broadly, of Etruscan culture. In the early twentieth century, the ideas on Etruscan art were still heavily indebted to the criticisms of Winckelmann and Mommsen's: in his *Geschichte der Kunst des Altertums* (1764) Winckelmann had defined Etruscan art as nothing but a poor copy of the elegant and refined Greek art, and the Etruscans as barbarous people, a second-rate civilisation unable to develop an individual artistic language.[9] A century later, the German historian Theodor Mommsen, for his part, had made a series of critical assertions about the Etruscans and their degenerated and obscene way of life in his *Römische Geschichte* (1861). In 1889, the French archaeologist Jules Martha wrote in his *L'art étrusque*: '[Etruria] feverishly copies from the right and from the left, it has no time to train its hand or to develop a method. In this fever of imitation, it merely develops a certain technical skill, industry predominates art and originality is smothered'[10]. The discovery and exhibition of the Apollo of Veii showcased what could now be considered a specific, autonomous, and hitherto unknown Etruscan artistic language.

Furthermore, this archaeological discovery happened in a crucial phase in the development of European art,[11] marked by the turmoil of avant-gardes of all sorts, who were restlessly on the lookout for new forms of primitivism. Several sculptors and painters of the period turned towards the Etruscan terra cotta – an earthly and domestic material – while searching for unexplored, anti-classical and, so to speak, more 'autochthone' forms of primitivism. Massimo Campigli, Mario Sironi, Arturo Martini, Marino Marini and Alberto Giacometti are just a few of the artists who studied Etruscan artefacts at the Museo Etrusco di Villa Giulia and selected them as primitive, chthonian and anti-classical models for their own sculptures.[12]

After the first display of the restored Apollo of Veii, in 1919, pictures and photographs of the statue could be found in periodicals and specialised journals across Europe.[13] The descriptions and graphic representations of the Etruscan statue sparked the imagination of several artists and writers, who, through their works, started to select, mediate, and transform into literary *topoi* a set of very specific iconographic and material features of the statue. The English writer, translator and poet Edward Storer, author of an essay entitled 'The Apollo of Veii' published in the literary magazine *Broom: An International Magazine of the Arts* (June 1922), summarises this process of fascination and growing interest for the Etruscan statue well:

> On the 19th May 1916, in the middle of the great war, a new Apollo was brought to light by the excavators of the Italian government at Veio, the ancient Veii of the Etruscans. Although the professor superintending the work knew that his discovery was of prime importance, not only archaeologically but also artistically, the discovery remained the secret of a few persons until 1920. Then the director of the Etruscan Museum in Rome gave photographs and particulars to the Italian press, and the new Apollo caused a momentary flutter of excitement among those interested in antique art.[14]

This passage is eloquent not only because Storer identifies the discovery of the Apollo as a crucial moment in art history, but also because the author mentions that pictures and descriptions of the Apollo of Veii started to circulate through the press and illustrated periodicals.

The archaeologist who unearthed the statue, Giulio Quirino Giglioli, initiated this process of dissemination. In 1919, after his demobilisation as a soldier, Giglioli restored the Apollo and published the official account of its finding during the Portonaccio campaign in the scientific journal *Notizie degli scavi di antichità*[15] under the title 'Statue fittili di età arcaica'. As the title anticipates, the article is highly detailed and includes several pictures of the Apollo taken by Giglioli himself on 19 May 1916, that is, on the very same day the statue was unearthed. Right from its incipit, the publication explicitly addresses 'the scientific world'[16], and its scientific nature is confirmed by the predominant technicity of the language, the presence of a rich bibliography, the schematic structure through bullet points, and the presence of precise data like the measurements of the statue. The passage relating the discovery of the Apollo reads like an impersonal account, as it is predominantly written in the passive form, thus conveying a feeling of scientific objectivity and reinforcing the idea of an analytical approach: 'in a large trench parallel to the course of the hill [...] the sculptures that are the subject of this report were discovered'[17] or 'The statues [...] removed [...] with all due care from the ground, were shortly afterwards taken to the Museo Nazionale di Villa Giulia and then purchased by the State together with all the remaining excavated material.'[18]

In February 1920, the monthly periodical of graphic arts *Emporium* printed another account[19] by Giglioli, with different pictures and a graphic reconstruction of the whole statuary group found at Veii. As it is evident from the title, 'Veio, la città morta', the article adopts a completely different perspective, and the discursive register radically changes as well. More literary and less scientific in the vocabulary, 'Veio, la città morta' is clearly not addressed to a readership of experts or archaeologists. Giglioli employs a more informal style that involves and engages the reader through direct addresses ('It would take too long to elaborate on the various locations explored.'[20] or 'Let us look at these two antefixes'[21]) and a first-person narrative, especially to describe the discovery of the statues ('They were in pieces […] This is how I photographed them on 19th May 1916 a few hours after the discovery'[22]). Moreover, in 'Veio, la città morta' Giglioli omits the schematic structure with bullet points, the bibliographical references and the precise measurements and descriptions of the statues he included in his previous article.

The article, whose title is a clear reference to Gabriele D'Annunzio's archaeological tragedy *La città morta*[23] (1896), opens with a romantic and decadent vision of Veii as a city in ruins awakening in the visitor a strong sense of the transience and fragility of the human condition and civilisation: 'Few places give such a sense of the transience of human affairs as that where Veii once stood'.[24] Despite the apparent emptiness and desolation of the site, Giglioli informs the reader that 'important ruins sleep in that desert, buried under the bush or the green meadow'.[25] The metaphor of sleep to describe the statue's location in the underground and that of deliverance to relate the process of upheaval – the statues are in fact 'freed from the ground'[26] – clearly hint at archaeology's power of upheaval and resurrection to increase the *pathos* of Giglioli's discovery. While recontextualising in a more literary discourse some dynamics of excavation – most notably the process of unearthing – Giglioli's choice of terms and images clearly ties in with the archaeological metaphors that will affect a whole generation of poets and writers in the modernist period.

The description of the Apollo is also affected by the different discursive register adopted in 'Veio, la città morta'. In *Notizie,* the description of the deity is precise and neutral, almost clinical in its short sentences: 'nine long black curls fall to his shoulders. He wears a rather short chiton that ends above the knees […] Apollo looks forward, downwards, his mouth set in a serene impassivity';[27] in 'Veio, la città morta', instead, the language is almost poetical: the nine curls merge into 'long […] hair', Apollo is 'clothed in a chiton and a cloak that envelops him completely', its gaze is an 'intense […] a pensive gaze' and the body is 'full of youthful robustness and boldness'.[28] Giglioli clearly drops the precision and the technical vocabulary of his official account in favour of a more evocative and figurative language that allows him to convey a more holistic and dynamic picture of the Etruscan Apollo. The precise details are no longer analysed individually, on the contrary, just like in the case of the nine curls, they merge into a homogeneous and full-scale vision.

The statue is no longer perceived as an archaeological artefact made up of different parts, but as a harmonious whole. Changing the discursive register, Giglioli thus infuses new life into the statue, which seems to come alive and actually walk out of the page: 'Above all, the movement is admirable: the statue truly walks: looking at it from behind, we see it moving swiftly with great strides, while the robe flutters backwards, with extraordinary boldness […]'.[29] These examples clearly illustrate how, switching from 'une scène d'énonciation liée à la science' [a scientific enunciative scene] to 'une scène d'énonciation esthético-littériare' [an aesthetico-literary enunciative scene],[30] Giglioli transforms the archaeological artefact into a living and dynamic creature. The resurrection is no longer an archaeological operation associated with a set of scientific and discursive procedures but it is a symbolical event packed with a wide range of meanings and performed through the specific discursive strategies applied in Giglioli's text.

It did not take long before other periodicals reproduced not only Giglioli's pictures but also his descriptions of the Apollo of Veii. The most striking cases can be found in France. In 1920 the January issue of *La Revue de l'art ancien et moderne*, founded in 1897 by Jules Comte, a six-page dossier is dedicated to 'L'Apollon archaïque de Véies'. The author, the Belgian philologist, historian, archaeologist and epigraphist Franz Cumont,[31] emphasises the importance of the discovery claiming that:

> […] no discovery of the past equals in importance the one made in 1916, during the excavations assiduously pursued by the Directorate of Fine Arts despite the difficulties of the war: these excavations brought to light the fragments of a life-size terracotta group, which is a masterpiece of Etruscan art.[32]

Cumont's words hint at how the discoveries in Portonaccio affected the perception of Etruscan art, in fact the word 'chef-d'oeuvre' had hardly ever been used before to describe an Etruscan artefact. As far as the description of the statue is concerned, Cumont almost literally translates into French the official Italian description provided by Giglioli in his *Notizie degli scavi di antichità*. Interestingly, both texts emphasise a specific aspect of the Apollo, that is the idea of movement that the statue embodies. In *Notizie*, Giglioli describes the god's posture:

> The god, […] bending his person forward, leans strongly on his right foot, brought forward, and raises his left foot slightly to take the step, while his muscles are tensed in the effort. In the swift move the wind compresses the dress, which is clinging to the figure, making its sex appear as well, while the lower flap flutters noticeably backwards.[33]

In *La Revue*, Cumont describes how 'The reproduction shows the powerful vigour of his modelling and the movement that animates him'; 'The young god strides towards his opponent with both feet planted flat on the ground'; 'The quick step presses the garment against the body to the extent that the sex protrudes' and 'The vigour of the execution, the nervous and powerful musculature – look at the feet and the legs – distinguish our Apollo'.[34]

Giglioli's and Cumont's texts clearly illustrate how different discursive registers and intertextual references affected the representation and, above all, the understanding of the Apollo of Veii. Despite the different discourses implemented in the three articles, it is already possible to single out one connotation that will soon become a recurrent *topos* associated with the Apollo: that of movement and dynamism.

One Step Forward

In the wake of Giglioli, it is worth noticing that in 1920 the archaeologist Carlo Anti published in *Bollettino d'arte* an illustrated piece entitled 'L'Apollo che cammina' – with a clear reference to Rodin's 'L'homme qui marche'[35] – in which the Italian scholar claims that 'The characteristic that makes Apollo a masterpiece, full of mighty vigour and everlasting youthfulness, so that its vision subjugates us and almost inspires awe, is in the construction of the figure, which truly moves, walks, advances, superhuman'.[36] The emphasis on the idea of movement bestowed upon the Etruscan Apollo by leading archaeologists of the period did not pass unnoticed, especially among poets and artists of the period who started to look at the walking Apollo as the embodiment of modernity, especially in terms of movement and dynamism.

In the aforementioned essay 'The Apollo of Veii', Edward Storer highlights all the iconographic features of the Apollo that Giglioli and Cumont had already stressed. The first element is the idea of movement embodied by the statue: 'The pose of the advancing figure, the tremendous force of the head and face', but, above all, the mysterious expression of the god, with its cruel and inaccessible smile: 'the curious malignity in the mask-like countenance', and the general 'expression of the face', where there is 'something sinister and cruel, dark and hermetic'.[37] According to Storer, these specifically Etruscan features are evidence of an individual and mature artistic language which adds something fresh and mysterious to the traditional conception of Apollo. Storer's essay 'The Apollo of Veii' stresses yet another crucial point in terms of dissemination and appropriation of archaeological knowledge: 'the archaeological details do not concern us here so much as the artistic interest of the life-size god'.[38] Through this declaration of poetics, Storer explicitly outlines the perspective he intends to adopt towards Etruscan material culture. Storer is not looking at the Apollo of Veii as an archaeologist or as a philologist, he is not interested in the statue as such but rather in what the statue evokes, in what it may represent.

Storer's text is crucial as not only does it represent the archaeological object through an accurate, panoramic, and encyclopedic description, on the contrary, it also participates in a process of selection and singularisation of a set of iconographic elements of the Apollo. Thus, the statue is pointed out not only as the quintessential Etruscan artefact, but also as the carrier of new meanings and unedited tales linked with its mysterious smile and cruel expression. Borrowing Krzysztof Pomian's notion, under Storer's pen, the Apollo of Veii becomes a 'semiophore',[39] that is, a material object which has been torn from any circuit of practical use, but which is enriched with new meanings and understandings precisely through its public exhibition. Through the process of discursive selection and singularisation accomplished by Storer's aesthetic gaze, the archaeological object undergoes a transformation that challenges its historical identity as an object of religious worship and turns it into an uncanny and mysterious correlative of the modern condition.

Storer's ideas are taken to the ultimate consequences in the poem 'The Apollo of Veii'[40] by the American poet Carleton Beals. The poem appeared in *Broom: An International Magazine of the Art* in March 1923, that is, nine months after Storer's essay. The poem is a full-scale vision of the statue, whose resurrection before the reader's eyes is marked by the obsessive repetition of the adverb 'forward' associated with the various body parts of the statue. Beals' vision of the Apollo of Veii – half statue and half machine – goes from the bottom to the top, starting from the advancing foot, and its steel muscles, moving up to the cruel facial expression. Although the poem focusses on the idea of movement conveyed by the statue – an idea reinforced by the poem's own rhythm – Beals follows in Storer's footsteps while describing the malignity of the smile: 'Lewd malignancy of cheek-drawn lips' and the reddish colour of the terracotta: 'Hips holding that tawny torso'. Under Beals' pen we can clearly see how the Apollo of Veii starts to be perceived not only as the deity fighting against Hercules – as in the original statuary group – but also, and mainly, as a symbol of speed, action, and movement. Apollo's step is perceived as a further step towards a new modern world.[41]

Fresh meanings and new understandings thus start to deposit onto the statue. Not only does the Apollo embody the quintessential modern features of movement, dynamism, and speed, but with his cruel and hermetic facial expression, it also comes to express the widespread uncertainties and existential anxieties of post-war Europe. As convincingly argued by Mauro Pratesi, with its earthly colour and the humble use of terracotta, 'Etruscan art implicitly represents, compared to ideal Greek beauty, a more uncertain attitude towards life'.[42]

Within the Walls of Villa Giulia

This is particularly evident in the fifth chapter of Aldous Huxley's short story *After the Fireworks*,[43] first published in 1930 as part of *Brief Candles*, Huxley's fifth collection of short stories. The scene takes place at the Museo Etrusco di Villa Giulia, right in front of the Apollo (Fig. 2.1), where the famous novelist Miles Fanning presents and describes the statue to a beautiful young American, Pamela Tarn, who is a fervent admirer of Miles' work but who knows nothing about the Etruscans and their culture.

The Apollo of Veii is introduced through a descriptive sequence, provided by the third-person narrator: 'The God stood there on his pedestal' – hence

Fig. 2.1 Apollo of Veii in the 'Sala di Veio' at the Museo Nazionale Etrusco di Villa Giulia in Rome (1930s). Neg. 3427. ©Museo Nazionale Etrusco di Villa Giulia. Archivio fotografico.

accessible to the visitors' gazes – 'one foot advanced, erect in his draperies. He had lost his arms, but the head was intact and the strange Etruscan face was smiling, enigmatically smiling'. Just like Storer and Beals, Huxley emphasises the posture, the advancing foot and the mysterious smile as the most striking elements of the statue. Huxley, however, goes beyond the mere description of the parts. Archaeological notions are in fact grafted in the text through a dialogical sequence where the knowledgeable Miles provides – not without irony – a panoramic and encyclopedic description of the statue to both the naïve Pamela and the reader. Miles explains that the statue was created in the late sixth century BC, most likely by the artist Vulca, and that it is made of terracotta in its original colour.

It is however after this first exchange between the two characters that a new understanding of the Etruscan Apollo emerges from the text, adopting the statue as a key to understand the war and the postwar condition. This is quite evident when Miles evokes the moment when he first saw the Apollo of Veii: 'I shall never forget when I came back to Rome for the first time after the War and found this marvellous creature standing here. They only dug him up in 'sixteen, you see. So there it was, a brand new experience, a new and apocalyptic voice out of the past'. Almost ironically, the silent Etruscans, 'the voiceless Others',[44] are the ones capable, through the 'apocalyptic voice' of their material culture, to give expression to the unspeakable: the absurdity of the Great War and the traumatic postwar condition. As Miles points out, the statue draws its meaning precisely from the historical moment in which the discovery occurred:

> And then the circumstances gave him a special point. It was just after the War that I first saw him—just after the apotheosis and the logical conclusion of all the things Apollo *didn't* stand for. You can imagine how marvellously new he seemed by contrast. After that horrible enormity, he was a lovely symbol of the small, the local, the kindly. After all that extravagance of beastliness – yes, and all that extravagance of heroism and self-sacrifice – he seemed so beautifully sane.

Huxley's choice of the Etruscans as a counterpoint to the absurdity of the war is no coincidence. For Miles the Apollo of Veii becomes the metonymy of the pre-war condition, of that feeling of wholeness, stability and security which precedes the sense of fragmentation and confusion brought about by the war. In the wake of Nietzsche, Miles is claiming the fragmentation of reality, and the fragmentation of the subject, who is no longer perceived as capable of making sense of the world around him. This is evident when Miles claims the impossibility of putting into written words – an operation that requires a certain degree of synthesis – the effect that the Apollo had on him after the war: '"Some day I shall try to get it on to paper, all that this God has taught me." […] "Some day," he repeated. "But it's not ripe yet. You can't write a thing before it's ripe, before it wants to be written. But you can talk about it, you can take your mind for walks all round it and through it"'. Finally, in a final effort to voice out how he feels, 'stretching out a hand, [Miles] touched a fold of the God's sculptured garment, as though he were trying to establish a more intimate, more real connection with the beauty before him'.

Miles's use of the ancient Etruscan statue to talk about the post-war condition is even clearer in the passage where Miles affirms that the Etruscans are better suited than the Greeks to describe the absurdity of the world for the simple reason that they could actually see it: 'The Greeks didn't see that divine absurdity as clearly as the Etruscans'. While the Greeks found themselves inside that absurdity, the Etruscans were outside of it. According to Miles, the Etruscans lived in fact before the 'the great split – the great split that broke life into spirit and matter, heroics and diabolics, virtue and sin and all the other accursed antitheses'. They lived in an enchanted world, where men looked like god and gods were in all things human, and it is precisely this *pre*-historical condition that made them 'whole' and 'complete', a wholeness and completeness that cannot be recovered after the tragedy of the war. The Apollo of Veii stands there, in front of Miles, as a witness of a different and bygone way of being in the world. Diametrically opposed to modern life, dominated by 'the tragic sense', the Etruscan way of life embodied by the Apollo was one of full 'acceptance'.[45] In describing the Apollo, Miles seems to revitalise the sacred function of the smiling deity, declaring himself not only a worshipper but also a 'self-appointed priest' of this 'other' Apollo, dramatically different from the Apollo of Delphi:

> How poetical and appropriate, […] that the God should have risen from the grave exactly when he did, in 1916! Rising up in the midst of the insanity, like a beautiful, smiling reproach from another world. It was dramatic. At least I felt it so, when I saw him for the first time just after the War. The resurrection of Apollo, the Etruscan Apollo. I've been his worshipper and self-appointed priest ever since.

Willing to reach the all-encompassing acceptance of the Apollo – hence the worship attitude – Miles is however forced to come to terms with the frustrating fact that he simply cannot: 'You can't. Not nowadays. Acceptance is impossible in a split world like ours. You've got to recoil. In the circumstances it's right and proper. But absolutely it's wrong. If only one could accept as this God accepts, smiling like that…'.

In this chapter, Huxley realises not only a selection of the Apollo of Veii as the perfect metonymy for Etruscan antiquity, but he also includes the archaeological object in a new discourse – a literary one – that allows him to express in words something that is far from being digested and ready to be represented: the trauma of the Great War. The Apollo of Veii, in its wretched, mysterious and silent nature, thus becomes the perfect correlate of the difficulties to understand, reflect on and talk about the postwar condition and the memory of the absurd catastrophe of the war.

Modern Etruscans

In the 1930s, while Huxley turns to the Apollo of Veii searching for the ideal correlate of the modern condition, the Italian writer and journalist Curzio Malaparte articulates in his prose writings a vision of rural Tuscany in which modern Tuscans are depicted as the direct heirs of the ancient Etruscans, and the Apollo of Veii as their own Tuscan god:

> Those who, travelling through Tuscany, and I mean classical Tuscany, let their eyes wander over the valleys, the hills, the fields, the trees, the serene gulfs of the horizon, naturally wonder if the Tuscans ever had a god of their own, a god that was all Tuscan from head to toe, and what was his name, his face, his nature, what were the personal attributes of his divinity.[46]

This is the question Malaparte puts forward in an *elzeviro* published in the Milanese paper *Corriere della sera* under the title 'Apollo Toscano'. In this article Malaparte identifies the Etruscan deity, 'the so-called Apollo of Veii, which for twenty years has walked ironically and menacingly through the halls of the Villa Giulia Museum[47]' as the mythical ancestor of the modern Tuscans: 'If it is true that the Tuscans are sons of the Etruscans, the father of the Tuscans is this Apollo of Veii'.[48]

In his *prosa d'arte*, as well as in other writings on the Tuscans and their character (later collected in the volume *Maledetti toscani*, 1956) – Malaparte uses archaeological data (most notably the statue of the Apollo) to retrace a genealogy that, beginning from the ancient Etruscans, passes through the Renaissance and stretches all the way to post-war Tuscany in the 1950s. The genealogical operation undertaken by Malaparte results in the identification of Etruscan culture as the source of a trans-historical *genius loci* whose final offspring can be recognised in Malaparte's own writing.[49] It is through the principle of analogy that the writer tailors such lineage, thus succeeding in neutralising the temporal distance that exists between the Etruscans and himself.[50] The analogy established by Malaparte relies on Etruscan material culture and, in particular, on the Apollo of Veii and its most salient iconographic features, which Malaparte recognises as the quintessential Tuscan traits. To establish this trans-historical analogy based on material culture, Malaparte refers to those iconographic elements that had already sparked the imagination of Storer, Beals and Huxley, namely, the advancing foot and, above all, the 'uncanny look', the 'secretive smile', which is an 'untrustworthy smile', imbued with 'irony', 'sarcasm' and 'invective'.[51] A smile that, *inter alia*, is the most distinctive trait of the modern inhabitants of ancient Etruria: 'And they all have that strange smile, that kind of cruel grin that the Apollo of Veii has, the Etruscan Apollo'.[52] The Apollo of Veii becomes for Malaparte a benchmark, a standard by which the Tuscan spirit can possibly be not only recognised but also measured.

In describing the Apollo of Veii's mysterious smile as a quintessential symbol of irony, Malaparte refers to a widespread cultural tradition according to which irony is the most distinctive trait of true Tuscans. In his *Maledetti toscani*, for example, he asserts that '[t]here was something inside the eyes of the [Tuscan] people that was not in the eyes of other Italians: an irony, a contempt, a mocking cruelty'.[53] The Apollo, according to Malaparte, is therefore not only the ancestor of the Tuscans, but also the primeval emblem of their ironic attitude, as is evident from his definition of Apollo as 'The father of irony, of measure, of the concrete and subtle intelligence of the Tuscans'.[54] Through the characterisation of the archaic smile as an ironic smile, Malaparte bestows yet another symbolic meaning on the Etruscan statue, which thus becomes the embodiment of the Tuscan character. Just like in Huxley's text, the Apollo of Veii, through its materiality, becomes the tangible representation of an abstract concept, that is, the Tuscan spirit and all the weight of its trans-historical nature.

The idea of a trans-historical Tuscan spirit passing through material culture is also developed by Malaparte in another article[55] initially released in the *Corriere della sera* (12th October 1937) and thereafter further developed and published in *Prospettive*,[56] the periodical created and edited by Malaparte himself, under the title 'Il surrealismo e l'Italia'. The whole article revolves around the opposition between French surrealism and what Malaparte identifies as Italian surrealism.[57] While French surrealism is described as a 'trend', an 'attitude', 'a new tag on an old thing'[58] – hence as something artificial – Italian surrealism, for its part, is depicted as something instinctive, intuitive and imaginative: 'a living, natural element of our artistic genius'.⁵⁹ In this article, Malaparte indicates that Etruscan art is the very first example of surrealist art, thus claiming that the French movement – criticised for its style, techniques and intellectualistic attitude – has much older roots, and that these roots are to be found in Tuscany, where surrealism 'is connatural with the climate, with the character of the inhabitants, with the landscape itself '.⁶⁰ Malaparte goes so far as to claim that 'the whole of Italian civilisation, from the Etruscans onwards is surrealist', that 'even the Italian landscape is typically surrealist' and that '[s]ince the Apollo of Veii, nothing has been created, truly great and authentic in Italy, that was not surrealist'.⁶¹

In this issue of *Prospettive*, Malaparte explicitly responds to Breton's *Manifeste du Surréalisme* (1924) when he claims that the French origin of the word 'surréalisme', coined by Gérard de Nerval and first used by Apollinaire, is misleading as it does not account for the Greek and Italian roots of the surrealist aesthetic. While the French word is simply 'a new tag', Surrealism is 'an ancient thing', even 'extremely ancient'.⁶² After all, Breton himself had called Dante one of the first surrealists. Referring to Alberto Savinio's geometry of the classical and romantic souls in ancient times,⁶³ Malaparte claims that Italian surrealism is characterised by 'a romantic soul' allowing for the creation of an art 'not intended to marvel, but to create reality anew, to invent it, to interpret it magically, as opposed to logic and its objective realism'.⁶⁴ While French surrealism seeks shelter 'in the oneiric freedoms and irresponsibilities' and 'in the Freudian mechanics of the subconscious',⁶⁵ Italian surrealism has always turned toward imagination and a magic interpretation of reality – also known as 'magical realism', to adopt Massimo Bontempelli's definition.⁶⁶

In his article in the *Corriere*, Malaparte divides history into moments of vast surrealist production and moments of decadence, when human beings forget or misplace their intimate, natural and spontaneous relationship with reality. The sequence of surrealist periods as flourishing moments is evident in this passage, starting precisely from a reference to Etruscan material culture:

> Emilio Cecchi, one of the few among us who know the subject well, could give us a very intelligent essay on Italian surrealism, showing us how, from the terracottas of Vulci of Veii to the poems of Burchiello, from the novellas of Lasca, Sacchetti, and Boccaccio himself to the poems of Campana and Palazzeschi, the best periods of our literature, painting, sculpture and architecture […] are surrealist periods.⁶⁷

When Malaparte affirms that the Apollo of Veii is the very first example of surrealist art, he is drawing yet another bridge between Etruscan antiquity and modern times to enhance the idea of a *genius loci* that resurfaces regularly over the centuries through the Tuscan soil: Giotto, Masaccio, Piero della Francesca are just some representatives of this trans-historical Tuscan spirit, whose final manifestation coincides with Malaparte's own writing. The association of Etruscan material culture and surrealist art allows Malaparte to root both his work and himself in the Tuscan soil, where surrealism as a form of 'fantasy' or 'magical realism' is inherently tied to the landscape, and more specifically to the soil. Almost fertilised by the Etruscan remains buried in the numerous tombs, the Tuscan soil, according to Malaparte, seems to have absorbed a certain number of features that allow for the perpetuation of some physical, artistic and cultural characteristics, all embodied by the Etruscan Apollo, the progenitor of modern Tuscans.

Towards a Cultural Biography of the Apollo of Veii

In 1927, the French archaeologist Salomon Reinach stated that 'Etruria is in fashion and Etruscan art is again attracting attention for its intrinsic qualities, its rugged originality, instead of being seen as a somewhat barbaric echo of Greek art'.[68] Giglioli, Cumont, Storer, Beals, Huxley and Malaparte's texts, however, showed that Etruria was not just a fashionable topic, it was a great deal more.

As this overview of texts engaging with Etruscan material culture has shown, the Apollo of Veii travelled across different languages, traditions, societies, and cultures which reshaped and redefined not only its understanding but also its meaning and social function in a given context. The case-study offered by the Apollo of Veii, among other Etruscan artefacts, allowed retracing how writers and poets of the modernist period achieved a careful selection and appropriation of certain iconographic elements of the statue – the walking posture, the ironic smile, the almond-shaped eyes, the reddish colour, and the use of terracotta – to integrate the archaeological object not only in a different context, but also in different discourses, connected to the literary, artistic and broadly cultural domain. These operations show to what extent knowledge surrounding Etruscan culture is malleable and suited to transaltion, transposition and import into new discourses. Were we to retrace the 'cultural biography of the object', to use Marta Caraion's terminology, the archaeological object would turn out to be the repository, the support and the trigger of new narratives precisely by virtue of its multiple and ever-changing identities. The selection of texts engaging with the Apollo of Veii shows how the statue's identity evolves through time and responds to different values and understandings – in this process following the writers' needs and awareness. While preserving its heraldic function, the Etruscan Apollo is no longer the prophet of the gods will, but rather the announcer of the complexities, anxieties and ambiguities of the modern world in the aftermath of the Great War. In the 1930s, another world conflict was just around the corner, and with his cruel and eerie smile, the Apollo of Veii seemed to know what was in the air. Hence, during the interwar period, the Etruscan Apollo, so dramatically different from the Homeric or Aeschylean one, becomes a herald not just of an ever more dynamic world, but also of a more unstable and fragmented reality.

Notes

1. Dominique Pety, 'Archéologie et collection', in *La plume et la pierre. L'écrivain et le modèle archéologique au XIXe siècle*, Martine Lavaud (ed.) (Nîmes: Lucie éditions, 2007), p. 205.
2. '[L]es rôles sont donc maintenant bien clairs: d'un côté, on a l'archéologue, un savant qui se livre à l'étude de l'antiquité, de l'autre l'antiquaire ou le collectionneur, qui accumule sans discernement les objets du passé'.
3. *Ibid.*, p. 207.
4. Marta Caraion, *Comment la littérature pense les objets* (Paris: Champ Vallon, 2020), p. 42.
5. Sasha Colby, *Stratified Modernism. The Poetics of Excavation from Gautier to Olson* (New York: Peter Lang, 2009), pp. 1-7.
6. See *Fascino etrusco nel primo Novecento, conversando di arti e storia delle arti*, Giovanna Bagnasco Gianni (ed.) (Milan: Ledizioni, 2016); Martina Corgnati, *L'ombra lunga degli Etruschi. Echi e suggestioni nell'arte del Novecento* (Monza: Johan & Levi, 2018); *Gli etruschi nella cultura e nell'immaginario del mondo moderno. Atti del XXIV Convegno Internazionale di Studi sulla Storia e l'Archeologia dell'Etruria*, Giuseppe M. Della Fina (ed.) (Rome: Quasar, 2017).
7. See *La construction de l'étruscologie au début du XXe siècle*, Marie-Laurence Haack and Martin Miller (eds) (Bordeaux: Ausonius Éditions, 2015), doi: 10.4000/books.ausonius.5448; *Les Étrusques au temps du fascisme et du nazisme*, Marie-Laurence Haack and Martin Miller (eds) (Bordeaux: Ausonius Éditions, 2016), doi: 10.4000/books.ausonius.10620. (Both accessed May 2023).
8. Massimo Pallottino, *Etruscologia* (Milan: Hoepli, 1963), p. 12; Maurizio Harari, 'Grèce ou non Grèce au Portonaccio', in *La construction de l'étruscologie au début du XXe siècle*, Marie-Laurence Haack and Martin Miller (eds), p. 29.
9. Lucy Shipley, *The Etruscans: Lost Civilizations* (London: Reaktion Books, 2017), pp. 69-70.
10. '[L'Étrurie] copie à droite, elle copie à gauche, n'a pas le temps de se former la main, de se faire une méthode. Dans cette fièvre d'imitation elle ne gagne qu'une certaine habilité technique; l'industrie prime l'art et l'originalité est étouffée'. Jules Martha, *L'art étrusque* (Paris: Firmin-Didot, 1889), p. 615.
11. See Maurizio Harari, 'Grèce ou non Grèce au Portonaccio', in *La construction de l'étruscologie au début du XXe siècle*, Marie-Laurence Haack and Martin Miller (eds); Mauro Pratesi, 'Scultura italiana verso gli anni Trenta e contemporanea rivalutazione dell'arte etrusca', in *Bollettino d'arte*, 28 (1984), pp. 91-106; Giuseppe Pucci, 'La sculpture étrusque dans les années vingt et trente: entre esthétique et idéologie', in *Les Etrusques au temps du fascisme et du nazisme*, Marie-Laurence Haack and Martin Miller (eds), pp. 241-250.
12. Andrea Avalli, 'La questione etrusca nell'Italia fascista' (PhD dissertation, Università degli Studi di Genova, Université de Picardie Jules Vernes, 2020), pp. 49-58.
13. Giovanna Bagnasco Gianni convincingly argues that the Apollo of Veii might have also inspired one of Helen Nutting's xylographies in the Etruscan issue of the illustrated periodical *Atys. Foglio d'arte e di letteratura internazionale*, managing editor Edward Storer and published in December 1918. In 1918, the Apollo of Veii had not yet been restored, the upper part of the Apollo's bust, however, was intact and the statue's various fragments had already been exposed at Villa Giulia. It is therefore possible that the very first reproduction of the Apollo of Veii is the one included in *Atys*. See Giovanna Bagnasco Gianni, 'Atys, l'etrusco', in *L' uomo nero. Materiali per una storia*

delle arti della modernità, vol. 6: 'L'etrusco' (Milan: CUEM, 2019), pp. 27-29.
14. Edward Storer, 'The Apollo of Veii', *Broom: An International Magazine of the Arts*, 3 (1922), p. 238.
15. Giulio Quirino Giglioli, 'Statue fittili di età arcaica', *Notizie degli scavi di antichità*, vol. 16 (Rome: Tipografia della Reale Accademia dei Lincei, 1919).
16. '[I]l mondo scientifico'. *Ibid.*, p. 16.
17. '[I]n una grande trincea parallela all'andamento della collina […] furono scoperte le sculture oggetto di questa relazione'. *Ibid.*, p. 15.
18. 'Le statue […] levate […] con ogni riguardo dalla terra, furono poco dopo portate al Museo Nazionale di Villa Giulia e poi acquistate dallo Stato insieme con tutto il rimanete materiale scavato'. *Ibid.*
19. Giulio Quirino Giglioli, 'Veio, la città morta', *Emporium*, vol. 302. (Bergamo: Istituto Italiano di Arti Grafiche, February 1920).
20. 'Sarebbe troppo lungo intrattenerci sulle varie localitè esplorate'. *Ibid.*, p. 62.
21. 'Osserviamo queste due antefisse'. *Ibid.*, p. 63.
22. 'Erano a pezzi […] Così le fotografai il 19 maggio 1916 poche ore dopo la scoperta'. *Ibid.*, p. 64.
23. Gabriele D'Annunzio's tragedy *La città morta* (1989) is one of the few tragedies of the *fin-de-siècle* period where archaeology and the practice of excavation are not only thematised but also selected as structural elements of the play. See Maurizio Harari, 'La favola risorge dal suolo: Gabriele D'Annunzio e l'archeologia immaginata', in *Rêver l'archéologie au XIXe siècle: de la science à l'imaginaire*, Éric Perrin-Saminadayar (ed.) (Saint-Etienne: Publications de l'Université de Saint-Etienne, 2001), pp. 177-199.
24. 'Poche località danno tanta sensazione della caducità delle cose umane quanto quella dove un giorno sorgeva Veio'. Giulio Quirino Giglioli, 'Veio, la città morta', p. 59.
25. '[I]mportanti rovine dormono in quel deserto, sepolte sotto la boscaglia o il verde prato'. *Ibid.*, p. 60.
26. '[L]iberate dalla terra'. *Ibid.*, p. 64.
27. '[N]ove lunghi boccoli neri gli scendono sulle spalle. Veste un chitone piuttosto corto che termina sopra il ginocchia […] Apollo guarda in avanti, in basso, atteggiando la bocca a una serena impassibilità'. Giulio Quirino Giglioli, 'Statue fittili di età arcaica', p. 16.
28. '[L]unghe […] chiome'; 'vestito d'un chitone e d'un mantello che tutto l'avvolge'; 'intento […] sguardo pensoso'; 'pieno di giovane robustezza e di baldanza'. Giulio Quirino Giglioli, 'Veio, la città morta', p. 64.
29. '[S]oprattutto ammirevole è il moto: la statua veramente cammina: nella veduta posteriore noi lo vediamo procedere veloce a grandi passi, mentre la veste svolazza indietro, con ardimento straordinario […]'. *Ibid.*, p. 64.
30. Dominique Maingueneau, 'La scène d'énonciation', in *Analyser les textes de communication*, Dominique Maingueneau (ed.) (Paris: Armand Colin, 2016), pp. 83-90.
31. Franz Cumont and Giulio Quirino Giglioli had an epistolary relationship and exchanged articles on and photographs of the Apollo of Veii. In a letter from March 1920, Giglioli sent 'new photographs' to Cumont, different from those included in *Notizie* and that would soon be published in *Emporium*. I thank Danny Praet (Ghent University) for bringing this letter to my attention. The letter is preserved at the Academia Belgica in Rome.
32. '[…] aucune découverte du passé n'égale en importance celle qui fut faite en 1916, au cours de fouilles poursuivies assidûment par la Direction des Beaux-Arts malgré les difficultés de la guerre: ces recherches ont mis au jour les fragments d'un groupe de terre cuite, grandeur nature, qui est un chef-d'œuvre de l'art étrusque.' Franz Cumont, 'L'Apollon archaïque de Véies', *La Revue de l'art ancien et moderne*, vol. 37 (January 1920), p. 257.
33. 'Il dio […] chinata la persona in avanti, pianta fortemente sul piede destro, portato innanzi e solleva un poco il sinistro per compiere il passo, mentre i muscoli sono tesi nello sforzo. Nella mossa veloce il vento comprime il vestito, che è aderente alla figura, facendone apparire anche il sesso, mentre il lembo inferiore svolazza sensibilmente indietro'. Giulio Quirino Giglioli, 'Statue fittili di età arcaica', p. 16.
34. 'La reproduction fait apparaître la vigueur puissante de son modelé et le mouvement qui l'anime'; 'Le dieu, juvénile, s'avance d'un pas assuré vers son adversaire, les deux pieds nus posés à plat sur le sol'; 'La marche rapide plaque le vêtement contre le corps au point de faire saillir le sexe'; 'La vigueur de l'exécution, la musculature nerveuse et puissante, – qu'on observe les pieds et les jambes – distinguent notre Apollon'. Franz Cumont, 'L'Apollon archaïque de Véies', pp. 259-260.
35. Andrea Avalli, 'La questione etrusca nell'Italia fascista', p. 33.
36. 'La caratteristica che fa dell'Apollo un capolavoro, pieno di possente gagliardia e di perenne

giovinezza, per cui la sua visione ci soggioga e quasi incute timore, è nella costruzione della figura, che veramente si muove, cammina, avanza, sovrumana'. Carlo Anti, 'L'Apollo che cammina', *Bollettino d'Arte*, 5-8 (1920), p. 74.
37. *Ibid.*, p. 239.
38. *Ibid.*
39. See Marta Caraion, *Comment la littérature pense les objets*, p. 102.
40. Carleton Beals, 'The Apollo of Veii', in *Broom: An International Magazine of the Art*, 4 (March 1923), p. 265.
41. Among other examples, this is also evident in the manifestos for the 'V Triennale di Milan' (1933), where the Apollo of Veii is elected as a symbol of modern architecture and technical advancement. On the usage of the Apollo of Veii in various manifestos see Andrea Avalli, 'La questione etrusca nell'Italia fascista', pp. 36-37.
42. '[L]'arte etrusca implicitamente rappresenta, rispetto alla bellezza ideale greca, un atteggiamento più incerto di fronte alla vita'. Mauro Pratesi, 'Scultura italiana verso gli anni Trenta e contemporanea rivalutazione dell'arte etrusca', p. 103.
43. Aldous Huxley, *After the Fireworks: Three Novellas* (London: Harper Collins Publishers, 2016). All the following quotes are taken from the e-book edition.
44. Rachel Blau DuPlessis, *The Pink Guitar: Writing as Feminist Practice*, Charles Bernstein and Hank Lazer (eds) (Tuscaloosa, AL: University of Alabama Press, 2006), p. 3.
45. In the wake of D. H. Lawrence's theories about the Etruscan civilisation, Huxley had already used the reference to the Etruscans to criticise the modern condition in his novel *Point Counter Point* (1928). In the novel, the character Rampion claims in fact that 'those naked sunburnt Etruscans in the sepulchral wall-paintings […] they knew how to live harmoniously and completely, with their whole being', while this is no longer possible for him and the other characters. Aldous Huxley, *Point Counter Point*, vol. 1, (Leipzig: Albatross, 1937), p. 136.
46. 'A chi, viaggiando per la Toscana, e intendo la Toscana classica, lascia scorrere l'occhio sulle valli, sui poggi, i campi, gli alberi, i golfi sereni dell'orizzonte, vien naturale di domandarsi se i Toscani abbiano mai avuto un dio proprio, un dio tutto toscano dalla testa ai piedi, e quale fosse il suo nome, il suo viso, la sua natura, quali gli attributi personali della sua divinità'. Curzio Malaparte, 'Apollo Toscano', in *Corriere della sera*, 31 March 1936. All the quotes that follow refer to this article.
47. '[I]l così detto Apollo di Veio, che da venti anni cammina ironico e minaccioso nell'uggia del Museo di Villa Giulia'. *Ibid.*
48. 'Se è vero che i Toscani son figliuoli degli Etruschi, il padre dei Toscani è questo Apollo di Veio'. *Ibid.*
49. This process has been thoroughly explored in Martina Piperno, *L'antichità "crudele". Etruschi e Italici nella letteratura italiana del Novecento* (Rome: Carocci, 2020), p. 69.
50. Through the process described by David Martens, 'L'hier et l'aujourd'hui dans le portrait de pays. Neutralisations de l'historicité', in *Portraits de pays illustré: un genre photolittéraire*, Anne Reverseau (ed.) (Paris: Minard, 2017).
51. '[S]guardo inquietante', 'sorriso segreto', 'sorriso da non fidarsene', 'ironia', 'sarcasmo', 'invettiva'. Curzio Malaparte, 'Apollo Toscano'.
52. 'E tutti hanno quel sorriso strano, quella specie di ghigno crudele che ha l'Apollo di Veio, l'Apollo etrusco'. Curzio Malaparte, *Benedetti Italiani*, (Florence: Vallecchi, 1961), p. 138.
53. 'Dentro gli occhi della gente [toscana] c'era qualcosa che non c'era negli occhi degli altri italiani: un'ironia, un disprezzo, una crudeltà beffarda'. Curzio Malaparte, *Maledetti toscani*, (Milan: Adelphi, 2017), p. 117.
54. 'Il padre dell'ironia, della misura, della concreta e sottile intelligenza dei Toscani'. Curzio Malaparte, 'Apollo Toscano'.
55. Curzio Malaparte, 'Il Surrealismo e l'Italia', in *Corriere della sera*, 12 October 1937.
56. Curzio Malaparte, 'Il Surrealismo e l'Italia', in *Prospettive*, 15 January 1940.
57. On Malaparte and Surrealism see Maria Pia De Paulis, 'Malaparte et la littérature: de la théorie à la praxis', in *Cahier de l'Herne Malaparte*, Maria Pia De Paulis (ed.) (Paris: Éditions des Cahiers de l'Herne, 2018), pp. 235-240.
58. '[M]oda', 'atteggiamento', 'un'etichetta nuova a cosa antica'. Curzio Malaparte, 'Il Surrealismo e l'Italia', p. 3.
59. 'È un elemento vivo, naturale, proprio del nostro genio artistico'. Curzio Malaparte, 'Il Surrealismo e l'Italia'.
60. '[È] connaturato col clima, col carattere degli abitanti, con lo stesso paesaggio'. *Ibid.*
61. 'Tutta la civiltà italiana, dagli Etruschi in poi è surrealista'; 'Perfino il paesaggio italiano è tipicamente surrealista'; 'Dall'Apollo di Veio in poi, nulla è stato creato, di veramente grande e autentico in Italia, che non fosse surrealista'. *Ibid.*
62. '[C]osa antica', 'antichissima'. *Ibid.*
63. See Alberto Savinio, *Dico a te, Clio* (Milan: Adelphi, 2011), p. 94.

64. '[U]n'anima romantica'; 'non intesa a meravigliare, ma intesa a creare nuovamente la realtà, a inventarla, a interpretarla magicamente, in opposizione alla logica e al suo realismo obbiettivo'. Curzio Malaparte, 'Il surrealismo e l'Italia'.
65. '[N]elle libertà e irresponsabilità oniriche'; 'nella meccanica freudiana del subcosciente'. *Ibid.*
66. 'Realismo magico'. See Massimo Bontempelli, L'avventura novecentista, in *Opere scelte*, Luigi Baldacci (ed.) (Milan: Mondadori, 1978).
67. 'Emilio Cecchi, uno dei pochi fra noi a conoscer bene l'argomento, potrebbe darci un intelligentissimo saggio sul surrealismo italiano, mostrandoci come, dalle terrecotte di Vulci di Veio alle poesie del Burchiello, dalle novelle del Lasca, del Sacchetti, dello stesso Boccaccio alle poesie di Campana e di Palazzeschi, i periodi migliori della nostra letteratura, della nostra pittura, scultura, architettura [...] siano periodi surrealisti'. Curzio Malaparte, 'Il Surrealismo e l'Italia'.
68. 'L'Étrurie est à la mode et l'art étrusque attire de nouveau l'attention par ses qualités intrinsèques, son originalité rude, au lieu d'être considéré comme un écho un peu barbare de l'art grec'. Salomon Reinach, *Revue archéologique*, July-December 1927, p. 314.

Cooking by the Book: Travel Writing and Etruscan Food Culture in the Interwar Period

Bart Van den Bossche

Eating & Etruscans in the Interwar Period

In the first half of the twentieth century, the available knowledge on Etruscan culture undergoes several major transformations. Archaeological excavations (with the unearthing of the Apollo of Veii in 1916 as the most spectacular discovery) provide new insights in Etruscan civilisation, ensuring an increasing public interest in and appreciation for Etruscan culture. These developments in turn lay the foundations for a stronger institutional visibility of research on the Etruscans, leading also to the emergence of Etruscan studies or Etruscology as a specific field within ancient history, a branch that interacts in obvious and less obvious ways with the cultural and scientific policies of the Fascist regime. Writers and artists visiting Etruria in the interwar period therefore engage in a multilayered dialogue with what they observe, hear and read (and are quite aware of doing so). It is the case that their fascination with Etruscan culture sometimes echoes earlier and long-standing representations associated with the 'silent people' of ancient Tuscany, their interpretations of Etruscan civilisation create a fruitful dialogue between the cultural anxieties of their time and the shifting understandings of Etruscan culture in the first decades of the twentieth century.

Writers visiting Etruscan places and heritage sites during the modernist period quite often seem to attach a distinctive and strikingly important meaning to all things connected to food, from frescoes representing banquets and commensality over kitchenware to clues about staple foods, drinks, ingredients and actual dishes. The attention for food culture is connected to the archaeological material that has been preserved and immediately catches the eye: visitors to the tombs cannot but remain impressed by the images of banquets, feasts, hunting and fishing, and the large amount of preserved artefacts directly connected to everyday life (and in particular to cooking and eating) are contrasted with the very different nature of Greek and Roman heritage, dominated as it is by impressive and highly canonised monuments and documents. But apart from the archaeological record, already in Greek and Roman culture the Etruscans are frequently (and almost topically) characterised as a people hooked on the pleasures of life, including food and wine, to the extent that they became seen as obese, idle and weak.[1]

For writers visiting Etruria during the interwar period,[2] the perceived centrality of eating and drinking in Etruscan culture is not just a matter of the archaeological record at hands, but turns out to be instrumental, if not pivotal, in the literary articulation of the anxieties, obsessions and fantasies stirred by their visits of archaeological sites. Given the manifold and multimodal cultural, social, political, psychological and ecological meanings associated to food, this is hardly a surprise. Still, it remains striking how in the writings on Etruria by D. H. Lawrence, Alberto Savinio, Vincenzo Cardarelli or Corrado Alvaro, references to the production and consumption of food, to commensality and cooking spark some remarkable and at times surprising connections between their fascination for Etruscan culture and anxieties about modern Italy and the modern world in general.

Etruscan Banquets and the 'Science of Life'

The idea of Etruscan culture being strongly attached to the concrete and material dimension of earthly life was triggered mainly by the specific features of the archaeological finds, and in particular by the impressive frescoes of banquets and the large quantities of everyday utensils in Etruscan tombs. At the same time, the Etruscan care for the concrete materiality of the everyday life is also embedded in a broader overarching vision of life and death. In an Etruscan tomb, every artefact seems to be displayed in its 'right' place and in balance with the rest of the chamber. To the visitors, the archaeological finds are fascinating not so much for what they reveal on the pleasures of Etruscan wining and dining as such (matters on which archaeologists of the interwar period still did not have that much to say), but because they suggest a culture that highly values joyful rituals of commensality and even more broadly an all-encompassing art of living in which the everyday is fused with the sacred in a smooth and natural way. Hence D. H. Lawrence's constant emphasis on 'naturalness', 'spontaneity' and 'simplicity' as the core elements of a typically Etruscan 'science of life' that can easily be appreciated in the skilful and careful arrangement of the tombs, and in the manifold scenes of actual life (and in particular of banquets and conviviality) depicted in the frescoes.[3]

Quite telling is also the scene in which D. H. Lawrence, while observing a group of peasants heading back home to Tarquinia after a long day of work in the fields, imagines a similar scene in the Etruscan age, emphasising the sharp contrast between the miserable state of modern-day Tarquinians and the radiant appearance of naked Etruscans – peasants on foot, noblemen on horseback – welcomed back home by musicians and priests, with the whole party later on passing a splendid evening with music and dinner.[4] And the proof of the pudding is once again in the eating, for the splendours of the Etruscan's imaginary conviviality contrast sharply with the poor makeshift and chaotically served meal D. H. Lawrence and his travel companion are offered the same evening in a small hotel in Tarquinia.[5]

This is actually a recurrent scene in *Etruscan Places*: already at the onset of their journey, near Cerveteri, D. H. Lawrence and his travel companion, the young American artist Earl Brewster, are served an unkempt meal made up of ill-prepared and ill-combined ingredients that lack any connection whatsoever with local traditions.[6] Throughout their trip in Etruria, both visitors cannot help but notice how little care the present-day inhabitants of the area devote to the quality and ingredients of the food they cook, in an unsettling contrast to the joyful art of living and celebrating they associate with the ancient Etruscans. In short, modern Tuscans definitely seem to be out of touch with their ancestors' culture, and have lost the typically Etruscan ability to value the beauty and fullness of life in a gracious and spontaneous way and to experience even the most humble moments of everyday life in its connections with the concrete environment as well as with the all-encompassing sacred meanings of life and death.

Just as for D. H. Lawrence, for Italian writers like Corrado Alvaro and Alberto Savinio, the manifold artefacts often connected to daily life that can be found in Etruscan tombs convey the idea of a culture that values the down-to-earth moments and events of everyday life in its seamless connections to humanity's place in the cosmos. Together with the recurrent banquet scenes in the tombs, the Etruscan care for the simple pleasures of life epitomises a deeper understanding of the continuity between life and death, and of the ability to see death as intimately connected to life. Corrado Alvaro, for instance, is struck by the abundant presence of everyday objects in the tombs, from jars over lamps and clocks to what Alvaro calls 'the perennial memory of indispensable water, wine and oil'.[7] The nature of the archaeological finds of Etruscan civilisation convincingly shows to what extent Etruscans valued life in its most straightforward and plain aspects, and how they apparently, much in contrast with Greeks and Egyptians, did not want to leave any other traces of their presence on earth than those of a people bestowed with eminently human aspirations.[8]

Alberto Savinio, too, reads the arrangement of the tombs as an attempt to create a cosy homelike atmosphere, with all the comfort of a richly furnished house, well stocked with food and drinks. The 'Tomba degli stucchi', for instance, is described almost in the manner of a real estate ad: 'there is no lack of comfort. There is room for forty-eight people. The beds for the head of the family and "his lady" are alcove beds, you go up three steps and in the middle is the small bedside table. […] And here is the cane for me and the fan for you. Here is the game bag for me to go hunting, and the mountaineer's equipment […]. And here's the cruet for the cognac, the shredder, the saucepan, the rolling pin to open the dough'.[9]

Art of Living and Living Art

Visitors almost invariably pitch the Etruscan care for the down-to-earth objects and necessities of everyday life and their allegedly laid-back rituals of commensality against other civilisations. Alvaro contrasts the Etruscan tombs packed with utensils of all sorts with the overwhelming *grandeur* of Roman and Greek civilisations (an opposition that, as we will see later on, is also important from a political point of view).[10] Savinio opposes the 'horizontal' and 'centrifugal' inclinations of the inherently romantic Etruscan soul to the vertical, centripetal and antiromantic disposition of Roman civilisation. Lawrence values Etruscan art for its ability to strike the right balance between earthly mass and uplift, as opposed to the exclusive and ill-tempered Roman privilege for 'mass' and the Greek inclination towards uplift.[11]

Interestingly, in his attempts to contrast the qualities of Etruscan art with those of Greek art as codified and idealised in the traditional Western aesthetic canon, D. H. Lawrence turns to several culinary metaphors. According to D. H. Lawrence, the attempts to achieve the pure and sublime forms of ancient Greek sculpture produces art that is 'well-cooked – like a plate of spaghetti':[12] what canonised art values as the 'aesthetic quality' of an artefact actually 'takes the edge off everything, and makes it seem "boiled down". A great deal of pure Greek beauty has this boiled-down effect. It is too much cooked in the artistic consciousness'. Etruscan art, instead – even when the subjects and techniques are Greek – will strike the visitor because 'The Greek and Roman "boiled" sort of form gives way to a raggedness of edge and a certain wildness of light and shade which promises the later Gothic, but which is still held down by the heavy mysticism from the East'. The attention to events and experiences directly connected to a sense of life and death seems the obvious outcome of this way of conceiving art. Etruscan art, like its cuisine, values genuine ingredients and steers away from processes that alter the nature of these ingredients. In terms of Lévi-Strauss's food triangle, Etruscan food is clearly associated to the *roasted* rather than to the *boiled*, signaling its attachment to a cuisine valuing a direct connection between culture and nature (in this case the element of fire) rather than the more elaborate cultural mediation associated with boiled food.[13]

Further on in the same chapter of the book, Lawrence turns to another culinary metaphor, to criticise the way in which Etruscan findings (objects and artefacts, but also entire tombs) are collected and put on display in museums. The rearranging and recombining of artefacts of all sorts and taken from various locations provokes a complete distortion of their meaning. In a museum context, what prevails is the 'object-lesson', and behind it a 'theory' or 'thesis', much to the detriment of what should be an 'experience'.[14] The museification of Etruscan archaeological materials (or, for that matter, any other heritage) is compared to the baking of an omelette in which the single ingredients lose their shape, identity and meaning ('You break all the eggs, and produce an omelette which is neither Etruscan nor Roman not Italic nor Hittite, nor anything else, but just a systematised mess').[15] – and given the importance of the egg in Etruscan commensality rituals,[16] the omelette metaphor and the image of the 'breaking' of the eggs are definitely not randomly chosen. In the same wake, even the idea of trying to synthesise 'Etruscan' culture in a museum comes under fire, as it threatens to produce an indigestible mishmash: 'If you try to make a grand amalgam of Cerveteri and Tarquinia, Vulci, Vetulonia, Volterra, Chiusi, Veii, then you won't get the essential *Etruscan* as a result, but a cooked-up mess which has no life-meaning at all.'[17] The conclusion seems quite clear: Etruscan culture, just like its cuisine, is about pure and simple ingredients that remain close to their natural origin, and that should be kept intact or at least genuinely recognisable, each with its distinctive flavour and the connection to a local context. Experiencing the Etruscans is a menu of roasted meat and fish, fruit and vegetables, wine and oil. Omelettes and macaroni are definitely off the table.

Down to Earth

Considering the above, it will not come as a surprise that visitors to Etruria closely associate Etruscan food culture with the ancient Etruscans' connection with the natural environment of the area. In fact, if it holds true that the Etruscan art of enjoying the good life manages to seamlessly merge a care for the concrete and the everyday with a profound sense of the sacred, then the same kind of relationship may also determine their connection with the environment in which they live, the land that sustains their art of living, the landscapes in which they built their cities and necropolises. Cardarelli and Alvaro (but the topic is also present in Savinio and Lawrence) characterise Etruscan culture in quite outspoken terms as imbued with a strong sense of the local dimension. It is a culture that, although invariably focussed on the role of cities, has highly valued its attachment to the rural areas and regional landscapes surrounding the cities. In its preference for the scale of the small regional space, Etruscan culture sharply contrasts with cultures – such as that of ancient Rome – that looks at space primarily from a supra-local, strategic and even imperial perspective of conquest and expansion. And once again, Etruscan food culture epitomises this distinctive Etruscan sense of space and place: for the Etruscans, the connection with the *terroir* is central, while for Rome, food becomes a matter of strategic supplies and planning, of granaries and colonies, trade and exploitation. That this contemporary interpretation of Etruscan culture has important, broad and potentially far-reaching cultural and political implications is quite obvious. In 'Gli Etruschi e la civiltà popolare' (a chapter in his *Itinerario italiano*), Corrado Alvaro interprets the difference between Etruria and Rome in terms of an opposition, and even a conflict, between a culture characterised as an 'all-out provincial and country civilisation' ('civiltà tutta provinciale e paesana')[18] and a culture that values territorial and urbanistic expansion, at the risk of losing the connection with (or even totally doing away with) the 'country life' of the previous stages of its history, which are – even in a very literal sense – the foundations for the greatness of Rome. Similar remarks resonate strongly with ongoing debates in 1930s Italy, not just with regard to the Fascist cult of ancient Rome but even more so with broader social and cultural anxieties about how ambitions to become an efficient, unified (and, one could add, highly centralised and Rome-centered) modern nation can be reconciled with the image of Italy as a patchwork of local and regional identities. For Alvaro, to focus on the relations between Etruscans and Romans eventually comes down to acknowledging the undeniable regional and rural core of Italian culture. Ancient Rome may have tried to incorporate, assimilate or destroy this core element, but the lesson that modern Rome should not forget or deny is that modern nation-building should be respectful of these 'rural and land-based origins' ('origini rustiche e terriere'), just as writers should bear in mind that the *anima paesana* of Italy survives in a literature that maintains a playful 'popular flavour'.[19]

In 'Il mio paese', a prose text by Cardarelli dedicated to his hometown Tarquinia, the writer evokes a modern-day Etruria whose inhabitants share with their ancestors a natural and intuitive connection with the land and the earth.

The modern-day visitor to Tarquinia may initially see a largely desolate, dusty, windy and half-wild landscape,[20] but at a closer look one will still spot the signs of the rural communities that live on the land in a peaceful and harmonious way, on which the passing of ages does not seem to have any impact whatsoever.

> Then, however, coming up from the station, as one approaches the town again, one begins to see, on the slope of the hill, enclosed land, cultivated with vines and orchards, dark and sparse olive groves on the rock, and the countryside suddenly takes on a pleasant and noble aspect. (…) Down below one hears the gardener talking, placidly attending to his work. High, bewildered voices, voices calling, rise from time to time from the fields and mingle with the clamour of the waterfall. The women flap their laundry at the fountain and sing, in a voice that carries far, their usual chant, while the sun boils in their ears and the air is full of rumbles and rustles. The chariot, thrown at breakneck speed for the descent, rolls and bounces with a thunder-like roar. And to all this sometimes is added, from the slaughterhouse below, the bellowing of the recalcitrant ox, the furious barking of the dog that tries to drag it down by the tongue, and the grim thud of the thrashing.[21]

This (blatantly idealised) connection with the land also spills over in the natural skilfulness with which local craftsman work the red-colored *argilla* to make sculptures of all sorts, with the harmonious and spontaneous gestures of a local *panettiere* or baker preparing his bread.[22] Whereas Roman and Greek art was made of the finest marble, to be found in far-off places, Etruscan artists turned, once again, and in a very literal way, to the soil of the land they lived on.[23]

This natural way of living of and with the land seemingly contrasts with another, darker representation of the earth, which the Etruscans, like other ancient peoples, saw as a dark underworld. It is an aspect that Cardarelli explores in 'Elegia etrusca', a prose text touching upon Etruria's strong cultural connections with the *argilla*, the characteristic red clay of the area, stating that Etruscan culture 'baked the myth of hell and perhaps created the most fiery and red version of its gigantic deities'.[24] The red-baked underworld of the Etruscans seems to condemn or deny the 'georgic' vision of nature as *alma nutrix*, but it is also an underworld steeped in a strong nostalgia for life, as the ubiquitous banquet scenes in Etruscan painting seem to recall. Perhaps both visions of the earth, the saturnine and the georgic, belong strongly together, just as the Etruscans combine life and death, the profane and the sacred, the earthly and the afterlife.

The broader cultural, social and political implications of this emphasis on the *anima paesana* of Etruscan culture and the connection to the local landscape certainly were not lost on an Italian reader of the 1930s. While Italian writers hint at the topic in rather general terms, D. H. Lawrence's *Etruscan Places* addresses the subject in an explicit fashion, seeing the *dodecapoli* or league of twelve Etruscan cities as the political translation of what he calls 'the Italian instinct', inclined 'to have single, independent cities, with a certain surrounding territory, each district speaking its own dialect and feeling at home in its own little capital, yet the whole confederacy of city-states loosely linked together by a common religion and a more-or-less common interest'.[25] Etruria must have been by no means a uniform and centralised state, but on the contrary a patchwork of locally embedded comunities, 'an endless confusion of differences'.

As already pointed out, several writers address what they see as a complicated and somewhat twisted relationship between ancient Etruria and modern-day Tuscany. In the eye of many a visitor, contemporary Etruria is not just a region scattered with ruins, it is also to some extent a country in ruins. The remnants of a long forlorn culture tell a story of loss that is also reflected in the landscape of Etruria, the villages and towns, the way of life of the current inhabitants. During his visits to various necropolises, Corrado Alvaro notes how the characteristic red earth of Etruria is crumbling and cracking everywhere, covering the entire area with soft and fine dust ('incredibly soft, tiny dust')[26]; yet it is not just the necropolises who create this impression of silence and dusty desolation; also other parts of the landscape, like the *Montagna spaccata* near Ortebello, strike the writer for their desert-like desolation and abandonment ('Not a blade of grass grows there and there is no trace of life').[27] As has been pointed out earlier, Vincenzo Cardarelli manages to spot some idyllic 'georgic' corners of farmland and pastures, yet he cannot help to note how vast stretches of his native Etruria are occupied by abandoned wildlands, home to mysterious animals like the tarantula. To D. H. Lawrence the sleepy towns and villages of Etruria seem in the grip of poverty and disarray, governed by a bureaucratic apparatus totally out of touch with the true nature of the region. Especially for Lawrence, the disappearance of ancient Etrurian culture is reflected in the poor quality of the food and the disconcerting lack of food culture and commensality. Good food is hard to find, and the meals they are served are prepared with limited skill and served without any particular care. The devastating conquest of Etruria by the Romans has profoundly marked the area well into the modern era, as everything speaks of an all-encompassing loss and disarray: from the vanished cities to the desolate countryside, from the destitute and silent peasants to the empty tables in the local hotels, the *joie de vivre* of ancient banquets and natural ingredients prepared and served with care has given way to meager and unappetising meals. To Lawrence, this is not an exclusively Tuscan disease, but a phenomenon of decay that can be observed in modern civilisation as a whole, as shown in the passage already quoted where he contrasts his vision of ancient Tarquinia with the desolate character of the new Tarquinia:

> It is different now. The drab peasants, muffled in ugly clothing, straggle in across the waste bit of space, and trail home, songless and meaningless. We have lost the art of living; and in the most important science of all, the science of daily life, the science of behaviour, we are complete ignoramuses. We have psychology instead. Today in Italy, in the hot Italian summer, if a navvy working in the street takes off his shirt to work with free, naked torso, a policeman rushes to him and commands him insultingly into his shirt again. One would think a human being was such a foul indecency altogether that life was feasible only when the indecent thing was as far as possible blotted out. The very exposure of female arms and legs in the street is only done as an insult to the whole human body. 'Look at that! It doesn't matter!'.[28]

Yet this is not the whole story. The Etruscan culture may have been wiped off the map by Rome, it has not been wiped out entirely. You can still discern the traces of it in present-day Etruria; an attentive observer may note some physical resemblance between Etruscan statues and frescoes and modern-day Tuscans, and in some of the traditions of the area one may still catch some genuinely surprising glimpses of the ancient way of living. Once again, references to food culture play a crucial role in this entanglement between distant past and present. In fact, some of the traditional *feste paesane*, as well as an occasional delicious meal, make the ancient banquets come alive. Upon his arrival in the small town of Cerveteri, Corrado Alvaro has the sensation of being thrown back in time by the sight of the fountain, the scent of must and wine, and the conversation between a couple of patrons in the local *osteria* on the 'old Etruscan pastime' ('vecchio svago etrusco') of hunting.[29] While this first Etruscan echo may have the somewhat superficial charm of a picturesque snapshot, Alvaro's description of the banquet at the *Fiera dell'Impruneta* is of a different nature.[30] Observing the local village festival as it unfolds, Alvaro cannot help but notice the absence of the kind of drunken exuberance that is so typical of this kind of country fairs. There is not a trace of 'thrill, collective exaltation, jubilation, delirium'[31] at the *Fiera dell'Impruneta*: the villagers eat in silence, caught in an eery and almost palpable unrest as if a catastrophe is about to strike the party. Alvaro is tempted to see this tense silence as the sign of the villager's deeper understanding of what is at stake in a *fiera paesana* such as the one they are celebrating: rather than just enjoying good food and local wines, the village feast is about experiencing a vital energy that transcends individual lives and reinstates the deeper natural bond between human beings in the community. To be sure, any traditional feast may be seen as an encounter between a concrete human element and what Alvaro calls 'occult forces',[32] but in Tuscany, so it seems, still reigns the typically *civilissimo* Etruscan sense of the ritual and spiritual dimension of similar feasts.[33] The calm and measured demeanor of the locals during the *Fiera dell'Impruneta* evokes the atmosphere surrounding Etruscan banquets (or at least, the atmosphere a visitor of the 1930s apparently associated with Etruscan banquets).[34] And just as their ancient ancestors, local Tuscans apparently still know how to combine a carefully crafted banquet with a deeper sense of belonging. The food, from the wine and bread to the succulent *arrosto* are 'a haven for simple tastebuds, a return to the manipulations of yesteryear, a true museum of the regional art of cooking'[35] and 'an ancient popular fantasy'.[36] Towards the end of the evening, in a kind of apotheosis, the final scenes of the feast seem to merge completely with the Etruscan frescoes: the women collecting the entrails in baskets look like *auguri* or prophets, and two female figures dressed in green and red seem to come straight from a fresco ('capitate là da un affresco').[37] The *anima paesana* of Etruria definitely is still alive, and there could be no greater contrast than that between its spontaneous respect for the true necessities of life and modern civilisation's spurious, tasteless and frenzy dealings with goods and people.[38]

Obviously, the sensation of vanishing time and the presentification of the Etruscan past is not exclusively connected to food. The sensations stirred by direct physical contact with archaeological sites (the tombs in the first place) and with the Etrurian landscape are also very powerful means that seem to dissolve and erase temporal differences and give the visitor the feeling of being in close connection with eras long past. However, food culture seems to play a special role in this respect, due to the fact that food is pre-eminently located at the intersection of two forms of experiencing time, which are respectively linked to land and landscape on the one hand and to the Etruscan necropolises on the other hand: creaturely time and ritualised time.

In terms of creaturely time, food is clearly linked to a number of natural cycles of life and death, with on the one hand the annual cycles of flowering and fruit-bearing vegetation and the activities of agriculture and harvesting related to it, and on the other hand the creaturely-existential rhythms that dominate animal life, ranging from bodily processes of continual generation and degradation to the life stages of birth, growth, maturity and death and the alternation of generations. In the preparation of food, these different rhythms become entangled and merge with each other: every meal that is prepared and every dish that is consumed is the result of a combination of all sorts of cyclically repeated processes of germination, growth, harvesting, killing, preparation, fermentation, digestion. And all these cycles are in turn linked to the land that sustain these processes and the uses that human beings make of it. To the twentieth-century visitors to Etruria discussed in this article, the vital and natural Etruscan relationship with food as they see it is the result of the healthy balance that Etruscan civilisation established with the creaturely cycle of life and death. The depictions of banquets in tombs express the way in which, for the Etruscans, life was intimately and naturally linked to death, their rituals of commensality being a strong symbol of how human beings are part of the same natural cycles that also produce the very food they are served – *you are what you eat*.[39] And conversely, for someone like D. H. Lawrence, the messy meals of contemporary Etruria are a figment of the disturbed relationship with the landscape and the state of alienation from natural life forces that is so characteristic of modern society.

The Etruscan banquets also illustrate how the connection between food and creaturely time is further associated with a cultural ritualisation of time, as meals are prepared, served and consumed according to certain rules and habits that are repeated over time according to certain syntagmatic relations.[40] In this way, food culture transforms the natural cycles of flora and fauna (dictating the availability of resources) in symbolic codes. This culinary code, often enshrined in dietary rules, menus and combinations of all sorts, in a sense codify the availability and combinability of natural resources into the ritualised patterns of a culinary calendar. This syntagmatic dimension of food culture not only has to do with patterns that are repeated over time but is also connected to what could be called the regenerative temporality of food. Through the symbolic patterns in which food is cast, the contact with certain ingredients, techniques, types of meals, codes of commensality may be seen as an efficient means to connect with cultures and communities from a distant past; through food, such a distant culture may be seen not as a fixed and remote origin that should be unearthed, unpacked or unraveled, but rather as something that can be experienced through participation and performance. Preparing, serving and consuming food can therefore establish or reactivate living, dynamic connections with communities past.

D. H. Lawrence is an author who (not coincidentally) comments in rather explicit ways on the politics of memory and time contained in his experiences of Etruscan culture. To look at the frescoes representing Etruscan banquets, to imagine a particularly Etruscan way of experiencing life and death as inextricably intertwined, allows to immerse oneself in an experience of time and space which at its core can also become accessible to modern visitors, because it is founded on a vitalistic-existential anthropology whose most forceful and most easily accessible expression can be a particular food culture. This kind of vital, natural and even bodily connection with the past is definitely at odds with the 'imperial' temporality of Rome, based on linearity, conquest, homogenisation and erasure of the past. For D. H. Lawrence, this kind of imperial temporality resonates with the modern Fascist state apparatus and its tendencies to centralise and homogenise time and space, which in turn epitomise in a radical and even caricatural way the flaws of modern civilisation.[41]

On the whole, Italian authors visiting Etruria in the interwar period express themselves in less straightforward terms than Lawrence when it comes to the politics of memory that underpins their reflections on Etruscan culture, but the topic is still addressed in one way or another. Apart from the various authors' respective positions vis à vis the Fascist regime (or, to be more precise, the different and shifting trajectories of their literary authorship and public persona in the interwar period), their comments on the relations between Etruria and Rome are loaded with broader (and at times also contradictory) implications and meanings.[42] But beyond Cardarelli's melancholic aloofness, Savinio's tongue-in-cheek banter, Alvaro's engagement with localism, their reflections on ancient Etruria and its connections with modern-day Tuscany invariably convey some kind of cultural critique of the homogenising and destructive logics of modernisation in contemporary societies. Yet it is a critique that can definitely be taken in different directions. Focussing on the destruction of Etruscan culture by Roman expansion can become a veiled (or, in the case of Savinio, more explicit) warning against tendencies to centralising and eventually repressive homogenisation of the wide diversity of traditions within Italian culture. In this respect, the Fascist regime's policies of modernisation and industrialisation as well as its identity politics of national greatness in past and present (epitomised in the cult of ancient Rome) could be seen as a threat to the cultural make-up of the country. At the same time, reflections on Etruscan culture can also trigger a critique of modern civilisation quite in tune with the localist, traditionalist and autochthonous tendencies that are also present in Fascist culture and its identity politics. Just like Rome did not just wipe Etruscan culture off the map but absorbed some of its core elements into Roman civilisation, the Fascist regime's policies could value the manifold local traditions of Italy and turn them into an asset and maybe a factor of national cohesion.

The various writings taken into consideration in this contribution show how important reflections on food culture are in the interpretation of Etruscan culture and in the ways it is made to be meaningful for modern-day visitors. In fact, it can be argued that interpretations of food culture play a crucial role in the manifold meanings, fantasies and obsessions associated with the culture, art and history of ancient Etruria and with its adoption in a cultural critique of present-day societies. Through its role as an interface between nature and culture, food allows for multiple symbolical connections, both with natural environments and the different temporalities associated with it, but also with traditions, identities and conventions of local communities and their specific connections with history and geography. Reflections on food culture can be a powerful tool for establishing connections between a distant past and contemporary visitors' sensorial and physical immersive experience of landscape, vegetation, agricultural and culinary traditions, and in allowing these forms of identification, food culture can even epitomise a specific cultural paradigm of naturalness and embodiment, as opposed to cultural paradigms based on abstract categories that may turn into symbolical violence against the natural and the body (as is the case in Lawrence and Savinio). Yet precisely this interpretation of food as concrete lived experience means that food culture can also be strongly anchored within specific settings, temporalities and geographies, that in their turn can undergo shifts, transformations, ruptures, such as the combination of conquest and assimilation that has characteriesd the relation between Rome and Etruria. The dynamics of immersion and that of transformation may also coexist, but the nature of that coexistence can also be thematised in different ways (as is illustrated by the writings of Alvaro and Cardarelli).

Notes

1. Among the most famous images figure the *obesus etruscus* in Catullus's *Carmina* 39, v. 11, Vergil's description of the Etruscans as being more interested in honouring Venus and Bacchus than in the battlefield (*Aeneid*, 11, vv. 736-738), and Vergil's image of the 'pinguis [...] Tyrrhenus' blowing the ivory flute to honour Bacchus (in *Georgica*, II, v. 194). See on this topic Maria Beatrice Bittarello, 'The Construction of Etruscan "Otherness" in Latin Literature', in *Greece & Rome*, second series, 2, 56 (2009), pp. 211-233; Jean MacIntush Turfa, 'The Obesus Etruscus. Can the trope be true?', in *A Companion to the Etruscans*, Sinclair Bell and Alexandra A. Capino (eds) (Oxford-Chichester-Malden: Wiley, 2016), pp. 321-335.
2. Quotes are from the following texts and editions: Corrado Alvaro, *Itinerario italiano* (1933) (Milan: Bompiani, 1995); Vincenzo Cardarelli, *Il sole a picco* (1929), *Il cielo sulle città* (1939), *Il viaggiatore insocievole* (1943), in Vincenzo Cardarelli, *Opere*, Clelia Martignoni (ed.) (Milan: Mondadori, 1981), resp. pp. 371-511, pp. 513-642 and pp. 643-739; D. H. Lawrence, *Etruscan Places* (1932) foreword by Massimo Pallottino (Siena: Nuova Immagine, 1986); Alberto Savinio, *Dico a te, Clio* (1939) (Milan: Adelphi, 1992). On Cardarelli, Savinio and Alvaro, see Martina Piperno, *L'antichità "crudele". Etruschi e italici nella letteratura del Novecento* (Rome: Carocci, 2020), pp. 57-91. On D. H. Lawrence's *Sketches of Etruscan Places*, see Stefania Michelucci, 'D. H. Lawrence's Etruscan Seduction', *Etruscan Studies*, 22 (2019), pp. 1-2, as well as Marie-Laurence Haack's chapter in this book.
3. 'The tombs seem so easy and friendly, cut out of rock underground. One does not feel oppressed, descending into them. It must be partly owing to the peculiar charm of natural proportion which is in all Etruscan things of the unspoilt, unro-

manised centuries. There is a simplicity, combined with a most peculiar, free-breasted naturalness and spontaneity, in the shapes and movements of the underworld walls and spaces, that at once reassures the spirit. The Greeks sought to make an impression, and Gothic still more seeks to impress the mind. The Etruscans, no. The things they did, in their easy centuries, are as natural and as easy as breathing. They leave the breast breathing freely and pleasantly, with a certain fullness of life. Even the tombs. And that is the true Etruscan quality: ease, naturalness, and an abundance of life, no need to force the mind or the soul in any direction.' 'Cerveteri', in *Etruscan Places*, pp. 42-43.

4. 'But in those days, on a fine evening like this, the men would come in naked, darkly ruddy-coloured from the sun and wind, with strong, insouciant bodies; and the women would drift in, wearing the loose, becoming smock of white or blue linen; and somebody, surely, would be playing on the pipes; and somebody, surely, would be singing, because the Etruscans had a passion for music, and an inner carelessness the modern Italians have lost. The peasants would enter the clear, clean, sacred space inside the gates, and salute the gay-coloured little temple as they passed along the street that rose uphill towards the arx, between rows of low houses with gay-coloured fronts painted or hung with bright terra-cottas. [...] Then a few words [*by the Lucumo*] – and the chariot of gilt bronze swirls off up the hill to the house of the chief, the citizens drift on to their houses, the music sounds in the dark streets, torches flicker, the whole place is eating, feasting, and as far as possible having a gay time.' 'The Painted Tombs of Tarquinia, 2', in *Etruscan Places*, p. 93.

5. See the conversation with Alberto, the young waiter serving the guests (or trying to do so) in the small hotel: '[he] says exactly what we knew he'd say, in a bright voice, as if announcing the New Jerusalem: "There are eggs and beefsteak and there are some little potatoes." We know the eggs and beefsteak well! However, I decide to have beefsteak once more, with the little potatoes left over by good fortune from lunch fried. Off darts Albertino, only to dart back and announce that the potatoes and beefsteak are finished ("by the Chinese," he whispers), "but there are frogs." "There are what?" "*Le rane*, the frogs!" "What sort of frogs?" "I'll show you!" Off he darts again, returns with a plate containing eight or nine pairs of frogs' naked hind-legs. B. looks the other way and I accept frogs-they look quite good. In the joy of getting the frogs safely to port, Albertino skips, and darts off: to return in a moment with a bottle of beer, and whisper to us all the information about the Chinese, as he calls them. [...] And so the boy continues, till I ask what about *le rane*? Ah! Er! *Le rane!* Off he darts, and swirls back with a plate of fried frogs' legs, in pairs.' 'The Painted Tombs of Tarquinia 2', in *Etruscan Places*, pp. 95-96.

6. 'Everybody is perfectly friendly. But the food is as usual, meat broth, very weak, with thin macaroni in it: the boiled meat that made the broth: and tripe: also spinach. The broth tastes of nothing, the meat tastes almost of less, the spinach, alas: has been cooked over-in the fat skimmed from the boiled beef. It is a meal – with a piece of so-called sheep's cheese, that is pure salt and rancidity, and probably comes from Sardinia; and wine that tastes like, and probably is, the black wine of Calabria wetted with a good proportion of water. But it is a meal.' 'Cerveteri', in *Etruscan Places*, p. 34.

7. '[...] these Etruscans [...] have brought to our fantasy the colour of a people, the shape of the house in their tombs, and all these goods for daily use: cups, jars, pitchers, lamps, clasps, instruments for measuring time, situlae, cysts; the everlasting memory of indispensable water, wine, oil; the vision of a market of small ordinary things, the emotion of simple people with the little spots in their house, their habits, their needs' ('[...] questi Etruschi [...] hanno portato nella nostra fantasia il colore d'un popolo, la forma della casa nelle loro tombe, e tutta questa merce d'uso quotidiano: coppe, orci, brocche, lampade, fibbie, strumenti per misurare il tempo, situle, ciste; il ricordo perenne dell'acqua necessaria, del vino, dell'olio; la visione d'un mercato di piccole cose comuni, il sentimento della gente piccola coi suoi angoli di casa, le sue abitudini, i suoi bisogni'), *Itinerario italiano*, p. 35.

8. See, apart from the quote in the previous note, the characterisation of Etruscan civilisation as a 'provincial civilisation, good to live in as long as one is alive, and which is not to leave any evidence in history other than of an industriousness linked to human aspirations' ('civiltà di provincia, buona per vivere fino a che si è in vita, e per non lasciare nella storia altro attestato che di un'operosità legata ad aspirazioni umane'). *Itinerario italiano*, p. 33.

9. '[...] le comodità non mancano. C'è posto per quarantotto persone. I letti per il capofamiglia e per la "sua signora" sono ad alcova, ci si sale per tre gradini e in mezzo sta il comodino. [...] Ed ecco il bastone per me e il ventaglio per te. Ecco il carniere per me cacciatore e gli attrezzi d'al-

pinista [...]. Ed ecco l'ampollina per il cognac, il trincetto, il tegame, lo stendarello per aprire la pasta.' *Dico a te, Clio*, p. 108.

10. In fact, for Alvaro one of the main reasons for the impact of Etruscan culture on present-day visitors has to do with the Etruscan archaeological record, dominated by 'goods for daily use' ('merci della vita d'ogni giorno') being so staggeringly different from the 'great attestations, signs of a life that is eternally public, solemn, elevated' ('grandi attestati, segni di una vita eternamente pubblica, solenne, alta') dominating the heritage of Roman and Greek civilisations. *Itinerario italiano*, p. 35.

11. 'It is useless to look in Etruscan things for 'uplift'. If you want uplift, go to the Greek and the Gothic. If you want mass, go to the Roman. But if you love the odd spontaneous forms that are never to be standardised, go to the Etruscans.' 'Tarquinia', in *Etruscan Places*, p. 66.

12. 'Art is still to us something which has been well cooked like a plate of spaghetti. An ear of wheat is not yet "art". Wait, wait till it has been turned into pure, into perfect macaroni.' 'Volterra', in *Etruscan Places*, p. 146.

13. 'A un double titre, par conséquent, on peut dire que le rôti est du côté de la nature, le bouilli du côté de la culture. Réellement, puisque le bouilli requiert l'usage d'un récipient, objet culturel; symboliquement, pour autant que la culture est une médiation des rapports de l'homme et du monde, et que la cuisson par ébullition exige une médiation (par l'eau) du rapport entre la nourriture et le feu, absente dans le cas de rôtissage.' Claude Lévi-Strauss, 'Le triangle culinaire' (reprint of the original article in *L'Arc*, 26 (1965), pp. 19-29), in *Food and History*, vol. 1 no. 2 (2004), p. 11. In the article, Lévi-Strauss subsequently incorporates 'smoking' (*fumage*) in the culinary triangle, but he will elaborate and apply the various categories throughout the four volumes of *Mythologiques*. As regards D. H. Lawrence's depreciation of the 'boiled', Lévi-Strauss' remarks on the 'aristocratic' and 'prodigal' nature of roasting as compared to the 'democratic' and 'common' technique of boiling are also relevant. *Ibid.*, p. 13.

14. 'Volterra', in *Etruscan places*, p. 153.
15. *Ibid.*, p. 154.
16. See Lisa C. Pieracini, 'The Ever Elusive Etruscan Egg', *Etruscan Studies*, vol. 2 no. 17 (2014), pp. 267-292.
17. *Ibid.*, p. 154.
18. *Itinerario italiano*, p. 31.
19. *Itinerario italiano*, p. 32. For a broader perspective on the scepticism towards Rome since Italian unification, see Joshua Arthurs, 'The Eternal Parasite: Anti-Romanism in Italian politics and culture since 1860', *Annali d'Italianistica*, vol. 28 (2010), pp. 117-136, and Antonino de Francesco, *The Antiquity of the Italian Nation: The Cultural Origins of a Political Myth in Modern Italy 1796-1943* (Oxford: Oxford University Press, 2013).

20. 'Paese eminentemente malinconico: la polvere e il vento sono d'ogni mese' ('Eminently melancholic country: the dust and wind are of every month'). *Il sole a picco*, p. 374.

21. 'Ecco, però, che venendo su dalla stazione, via via che ci si riaccosta all'abitato, si cominciano a vedere, sul declivio del colle, terreni chiusi, coltivati a vigna e frutteto, uliveti scuri e magri sulla roccia, e la campagna prende di botto un aspetto ridente e nobile. (...) Si ode giù sotto l'ortolano che parlotta. placidamente attendendo alla sua opera. Voci alte e smarrite, voci che chiamano, sorgono di tanto in tanto dai campi e si confondono col clamore della cascata. Le donne sbattono i panni alla fontana e cantano con voce che va lontano, la loro cantilena consueta, mentre il sole bolle negli orecchi e l'aria è piena di rombi e di fruscii. Il carro, lanciato a rotta di collo per la discesa rotola e rimbalza con un fragore simile a quello del tuono. E qualche volta ci si aggiunge, dal sottostante mattatoio, il mugghio del bove recalcitrante, l'abbaiare furioso del cane che cerca di strascinarlo azzannandolo per la lingua e il tonfo cupo della mazzata.' *Il sole a picco*, pp. 375-376. In 'Vita delle tombe etrusche' (published in *Il cielo sulle città*), Cardarelli sees a celebration of this kind of harmonious and euphoric connection with nature in the 'Tomba della caccia e della pesca': '[...] it is interesting to note that in all the tomb's paintings there is not a single captured or dead beast to be seen, except in one frame detail, in which a hunter is depicted returning with a hare, killed and hanging from a stick poised over his shoulder, while his trusty hound follows him sniffing and wagging its tail. Rather than episodes of hunting and fishing, the large paintings depict the joy, the exultation of men and animals for the beautiful season that has returned'('[...] è interessante notare come in tutte le sue pitture non s'incontri una sola bestia catturata o morta, fuorché in un particolare di cornice, nel quale è raffigurato un cacciatore che torna con una lepre, uccisa e appesa a un bastone in bilico sulla spalla, mentre il fido bracco lo segue annusando e scodinzolando. I grandi quadri vogliono descrivere, più che episodi di caccia e di pesca, la gioia, l'esultanza degli uomini e degli animali per la bella stagione che è ritornata'). *Il cielo sulle città*, pp. 523-524.

22. 'I saw the Etruscans again, who manipulated clay with refined roughness and deft skill; and they made homemade sculpture, not unlike the way a baker makes bread and a patissier makes cakes.' ('Ho rivisto gli Etruschi, che manipolarono la creta con ricercata grossolanità e lesta bravura; e fecero della scultura casereccia, non altrimenti di come fa il panettiere il pane e il pasticciere i dolci.'). *Il sole a picco*, p. 382. Interestingly, the sculptor Arturo Martini also uses a culinary metaphor to describe the Etruscan techniques of sculpturing: 'The Etruscans made statues the way our women make ravioli: they even used a pasta wheel to cut' ('Gli Etruschi facevano le statue come le nostre donne fanno i ravioli: usavano persino la rotellina per tagliare'). Gino Scarpa, *Colloqui con Arturo Martini* (Milan: Rizzoli, 1968), p. 118; on Arturo Martini, see also Martina Corgnati, *L'ombra lunga degli Etruschi. Echi e suggestioni nell'arte del Novecento* (Monza: Johan & Levi, 2018), pp. 50-59, and Federica Grossi, 'Gli Etruschi di Arturo Martini: rielaborazioni d'avanguardia', in *Aristonothos. Scritti sul mediterraneo antico*, vol. 11 (2016), pp. 111-142. (the passage from the *Colloqui* is also quoted in Grossi's essay, resp. on p. 51 and p. 118).
23. In 'Gli Etruschi' (published in *Il cielo sulle città*), Cardarelli sees the sculpture in terracotta as an illustration of the Etruscan's obsession with the earth they live on, turning them into a kind of profoundly ctonic culture: '[…] they seem to have invented terracotta sculpture and worked preferably the most caducous and perhaps vile stones, provided they were local, they did not live on the surface, but almost inside the earth. The most impressive reminders that the Etruscans have left us, apart from their necropolises, are pits, tunnels, gashes in the rock, mining waste, semi-natural bridges, falls' ('pare abbiano inventato la scultura in terracotta e lavorarono di preferenza le pietre più caduche e magari ignobili, purché locali, non vivevano alla superficie, ma quasi dentro la terra. I ricordi più impressionanti che ci abbiano lasciati gli Etruschi, oltre alle loro necropoli, sono cave, cunicoli, squarci nella roccia, rifiuti minerari, ponti seminaturali, cascate'). *Il cielo sulle città*, p. 531.
24. '[…] portò a cottura il mito dell'inferno e creò forse, dei suoi giganteschi numi, i più infuocati e rossi'. *Il sole a picco*, p. 392.
25. *Etruscan Places*, p. 71.
26. '[…] incredibilmente molle, minuta polvere'. *Itinerario italiano*, p. 34 (on the necropolis of Cerveteri); see also the description of the necropolis of Veii: 'nothing else but dust, and the colour of that dust' ('niente altro che polvere, e il colore di quella polvere', p. 33) and Orbetello (p. 38).
27. '[…] Non vi cresce un filo d'erba e non v'è traccia di vita'. *Ibid.*, p. 38.
28. *Etruscan Places*, pp. 94-95.
29. *Itinerario italiano*, p. 34.
30. *Ibid.*, p. 43.
31. '[…] ebbrezza, esaltazione collettiva, tripudio, deliquio'. *Ibid.*, p. 44.
32. *Ibid.*
33. 'Here, among a highly civilised people, this huge feast, this easy joy of eating and drinking, seemed the ultimate celebration of a rite lost, but alive in the deep memory of instincts' ('Qui, tra un popolo civilissimo, quell'enorme festino, quella facile gioa del mangiare e del bere, parevano la celebrazione estrema di un rito perduto, ma vivo nella memoria profonda degli istinti'). *Ibid.*, pp. 44-45. See also Vincenzo Cardarelli in 'Vita delle tombe etrusche': 'I will simply say that in my hometown every excuse is good to have a lunch, a dinner, a snack. The convivial ritual consecrates every work done in common, consecrates the fruits of the season, sanctifies anniversaries, gains, joys, whatever satisfaction one may have from life' ('Mi limiterò a dire che al mio paese tutto è buono a giustificare un pranzo, una cena, una merenda. Il rito conviviale suggella ogni lavoro fatto in comune, consacra i frutti della stagione, santifica le ricorrenze, i guadagni, le gioie, qualunque soddisfazione si possa avere dalla vita.'). *Il cielo sulle città*, p. 535. And all these moments of conviviality, Cardarelli adds, are celebrated in an atmosphere of modesty, silence and mutual respect, with a great sense of the sacred nature of the event. *Ibid.*, p. 537.
34. 'It was easy to recall the supreme Etruscan indifference amidst the earth's goods, the sense of blissful peace and fullness, that of the full belly that stretched them out on their cots and brought them closer to contemplation' ('Era facile ricordare la suprema indifferenza etrusca fra I beni della terra, il senso di pace beata e di pienezza, quella del ventre pieno che li stende sui loro lettucci e li avvicina alla contemplazione'). *Itinerario italiano*, p. 45.
35. 'un paradiso di gole semplici, un ritorno alle manipolazioni di una volta, un vero museo dell'arte regionale nella cucina'. *Ibid.*, p. 45.
36. '[…] un'antica fantasia popolare'. *Ibid.*, p. 46.
37. *Ibid.*, p. 47.
38. It is interesting to contrast Alvaro's impressions of the *fiera dell'Impruneta* with D. H. Lawrence's dismissive and even disdainful remarks on the official banquet in honour of the newly appointed *podestà di Volterra*, which for Lawrence is just a

feast of vanity ('stacks of glittering glass'), existential *ennui* ('out-of-work young men' coming from some kind of 'nowhere') and grotesque devotion (the banquet does not produce sounds of music or partying, just 'roaring noises'): 'They [= the waiters preparing the banquet] were so thrilled getting all the glasses and goblets and decanters, hundreds of them, it seemed, out of the big chiffonnier-cupboard that occupied the back of the dining-room, and whirling them away, stacks of glittering glass, to the banquet-room: while out-of-work young men would poke their heads in through the doorway, black hats on, overcoats hung all over one shoulder, and gaze with bright inquiry through the room, as though they expected to see Lazarus risen, and not seeing him, would depart again to the nowhere whence they came. A banquet is a banquet, even if it is given to the devil himself; and the *podestà* may be an angel of light. [...] And we, not bidden to the feast, went to bed. To be awakened occasionally by sudden and roaring noises – perhaps applause – and the loud and unmistakable howling of a child, well after midnight'. *Etruscan Places*, p. 143.

39. A satirical wink at the glorification of ancient Etruscan civilisation and its connection with the natural and creaturely dimension of food can be found in a passage in Aldous Huxley's novel *Those Barren Leaves*, set in the anglophone expat community in Tuscany in the early twentieth century. At some point, two of the main characters, Miss Thriplow and Mr. Cardan, visit a grocery, and are overwhelmed by the powerful smells of the produce. 'It [= the shop] was dark within and filled with a violent smell of goat's milk cheese, pickled tunny, tomato preserve and highly flavoured sausage.

"'Whee-ew!" said Miss Thriplow, and pulling out a small handkerchief, she took refuge with the ghost of Parma violets. It was a pity that these simple lives in white aprons had to be passed amid such surroundings.

"'Rather deafening, eh?" said Mr. Cardan, twinkling. "Puzza," he added, turning to the shopkeeper. "It stinks."

The man looked at Miss Thriplow, who stood there, her nose in the oasis of her handkerchief, and smiled indulgently. "I forestieri sono troppo delicati. Troppo delicati," he repeated.

"'He's quite right," said Mr. Cardan. "We are. In the end, I believe, we shall come to sacrifice everything to comfort and cleanliness. Personally, I always have the greatest suspicion of your perfectly hygienic and well-padded Utopias. As for this particular stink," he sniffed the air, positively with relish, "I don't really know what you have to object to it. It's wholesome, it's natural, it's tremendously historical. The shops of the Etruscan grocers, you may be sure, smelt just as this does. No, on the whole, I entirely agree with our friend here."' *Those Barren Leaves. A Novel*, 1925 (London: Chatto & Windus, 1960), p. 212.

40. On the syntagmatic relations connecting meals, ingredients and food habits, see the classical essay by Mary Douglas, 'Deciphering a Meal', *Daedalus*, vol. 1 no. 101 (1972), pp. 61-81, later included in *Implicit meanings. Essays in anthropology* (London: Routledge, 1975).

41. Lawrence's pitching of Etruscan culture against Rome and his critical remarks on Italian Fascism in *Etruscan Places* should obviously be read within the context of his complex, ambiguous and contradictory ideas on authoritarian leaders, crowd psychology and modern politics; see, in this respect the important analysis in Nidesh Lawtoo, 'Lawrence Contra (New) Fascism', *College Literature*, vol. 2 no. 47 (2020), pp. 287-317.

42. On the ambiguous and contradictory elements in many representations of Etruscan culture, see Martina Piperno, *L'antichità "crudele"*, pp. 70-71 and 80-82.

Etruscans in Unexpected Places: Space, Temporality and Visual Agency

Lisa C. Pieraccini

The subject of this chapter, *Etruscans in Unexpected Places*, highlights the assumption that there is a proper place and space for Etruscan objects, art, things and even discourse.[1] Broadly speaking, both the expected and unexpected norms of society's collective imagination govern the ways in which we see and experience the world – and the past is no exception. In the case of an ancient culture like the Etruscans, their *place* is still very much an ongoing conversation in the general field of history, art history and archaeology.[2] This is due, in part, to the tightly structured classical curriculum which traditionally focuses on the exceptionalism of Greece and Rome; to the great loss of all the many cultures that existed beyond and within that boundary. The Etruscans are a prime example of surviving in a state of 'otherness' within a curriculum that has just started to decolonise itself.[3] Subsequently, the concept of otherness enlarges the spaces where these cultures materialise in unexpected ways. This chapter hopes to shed light on those very *spaces* by looking at examples of how the visual agency of Etruscan art emerges in surprising and unforeseen ways. It seeks to explore new and innovative modes for understanding Etruscan art and its reception – all the while revealing how their material culture has been negotiated, received and experienced through various time periods and geopolitical dynamics from the last few centuries. In addition, it calls for the dismantling of the old classical canon where the Etruscans were frequently marginalised and it seeks to look at them through a fresh new lens – broadening the view of their past, present and future.

It may not seem odd, when examining the Etruscans, that I begin this inquiry by focusing on a funerary monument. However, what may be surprising is that the monument is not in Italy, but rather in the United States. The tomb of American Civil War officer, Egbert Ludovicus Viele was built at the turn of the twentieth century by Viele himself who set out to construct a tomb to honor his wife, his own life and house their sarcophagi.[4] The tomb is known today not simply

Fig. 3.1 Tomb monument of Egbert Ludovicus Viele, West Point Cemetery, New York. Photo by Colleen McArdelle, Office of Memorial Affairs, West Point.

because it is one of the largest funerary monuments at the West Point Cemetery in New York, but rather because it reflects a form of hybrid that is rather unusual for the late nineteenth and early twentieth centuries (Fig. 3.1).[5] Its Egyptian style pyramid may seem a fitting tribute to an afterlife monument of the Egyptian revival period in late nineteenth century America, but its Etruscan inscription which boldly faces the viewer was not. Upon facing the tomb, one reads: EBGERT LUDOVICUS VIELE-KIZI ZILACHNKEI MEANI-MUNIKLETH-JULIETTE-NUPPHZIKANTHKE. In fact, the inscription was ignored for most of the twentieth century and tour-guides to the cemetery took great liberties with loose translations in an attempt to make sense of the epitaph. Something to the effect of 'Egbert Ludovicus Viele his body occupies this sepulchre with Juliette his wife and beloved companion' was commonly stated when groups toured the cemetery.[6] A simple visit to the inner chamber of the tomb might reveal the subtle Etruscan ethos Viele achieved in the design; choosing finely carved stone sarcophagi where he and his wife are each carved laying on their backs, life-size, on their sarcophagus lids (Fig. 3.2). A remarkable aspect of this tomb

Fig. 3.2 The inner chamber of the Viele tomb with two sarcophagi depicted Egbert and Juliette Viele, West Point Cemetery, New York. Photo by Colleen McArdelle, Office of Memorial Affairs, West Point.

(and there are many fascinating aspects to mention),[7] is the Etruscan inscription on the exterior which must have mystified and confused viewers since the time of its completion. Evidently, Viele was not concerned with viewers understanding the Etruscan words, but rather with the words themselves (Fig. 3.3). In fact, he most likely was inspired by an inscription published in Alexander William Crawford's 1872 book, *Etruscan Inscriptions*, which mentioned an epitaph found just outside the 'Ceisinie' Tomb discovered in Tarquinia in 1735.[8] The inscription reads: LARTH KEISINIS VELUS KLAN KIZI ZILACHNKE MEANI MUNIKLETH METHUM NUPPHZI KANTHKE KALUS LUPU.[9] Viele, as argued elsewhere, must have been motivated by the Etruscan name, 'Velus' which appeared on the 'Ceisinie' tomb inscription – seeing a direct link to his own name, Viele.[10] By cherry-picking some words and combining them with his name and that of his wife, Viele created a tomb 'message board' that he must have realised no one could read. Apparently, he made no effort to offer visitors any clues as to the meaning of the words; as this was not the scope of the inscription.[11] As to the reason why Viele decided to inscribe this Etruscan

Fig. 3.3 Etruscan inscription on the exterior of the Viele tomb, West Point Cemetery, New York. Photo by Colleen McArdelle, Office of Memorial Affairs, West Point.

message on the entrance of his tomb, one could point to his inclination towards superstition and beliefs of life after death, in particular, towards the religious traditions from two ancient cultures known for their dedication to the afterlife. The combination of Egyptian and Etruscan, which is a unique blending unseen in any other funerary monument of the time in the United States, represents an eclectic form of hybridity which must have appealed to Viele. Perhaps because it eased *his* deeper anxieties about death and secured a symbolic ancient portal for his final resting place.[12] Interestingly, the tomb also features a number of Christian elements, as Viele and his wife Juliette are shown fully clothed as they lay atop of their sarcophagi – Juliette even holds a cross. No doubt, Viele must have felt measured by how far he could go with ancient pagan architecture, design and inscriptions. The Christian elements may also speak to priorities that were far more in keeping with Juliette's religious beliefs than with her husband's. Thus, Viele's tomb, with its amalgamation of pagan and Christian components, exercised its own agency as a hub for relieving angst and assuring a safe journey to the afterlife. That this was accomplished through artistic expressions in archi-

Fig. 3.4 Patricia Cronin, Memorial To A Marriage, Carrara marble, 2002, 27" x 84" x 47", © 2023 Patricia Cronin / Artists Rights Society (ARS) New York.

tecture, sculpture and inscription, was nothing less than a funerary triumph for Viele. But apart from these considerations on the form and *décor* of the tomb, Viele's decision to use the Etruscan language on his Egyptian tomb *façade* speaks to the place the Etruscans occupied in Viele's own imagination. For Viele, the Etruscan inscription and the life-size 'Etruscan' sarcophagi were enough to grant access to an afterlife. Although Viele's memorial monument, located at the West Point Cemetery in New York, may seem a highly unusual and unexpected site for an Etruscan funerary inscription, it speaks quite clearly to the appeal of the Etruscans outside of their own space and time.

Cemeteries and funerary art, in fact, could be considered as a place in which Etruscan references should easily and naturally fit, as Etruscan culture is renowned for its monumental tombs and funerary art in ancient Italy. However, a modern funerary sculpture in Woodlawn Cemetery in the Bronx, New York, entitled 'Memorial to a Marriage' (2002), by Patricia Cronin is a recent example of the timeless impact of Etruscan art and values (Fig. 3.4).[13] Patricia Cronin's personal commemoration carved in three tons of Carrara marble pays tribute to her wife, artist Deborah Kass. It is nothing short of a love set in stone and remains one of the only equity marriage monuments in the world.[14] The embracing bodies, shown reclining in the nude with a thin blanket softly covering them from the waist down (except for their feet protruding from the fabric), exists as both a memorial and an insurance policy against oblivion. The exposed feet with toes gently touching pay homage, not only visually but sentimentally, specifically to the fourth century BC Etruscan sarcophagus lid housed in the

Fig. 3.5 Stone sarcophagus of *Ramtha Visnai* and *Arnth Tetneis* from the Ponte Rotto necropolis in Vulci, 4th BCE, Boston Museum of Fine Art.

Boston Fine Arts Museum of 'Ramtha Visnai and Arnth Tetneis' from the Ponte Rotto necropolis in Vulci (Fig. 3.5). Cronin was inspired by the funerary embrace seen on so many iconic Etruscan works of art. Growing up in Boston, she visited the famous Etruscan sarcophagi from Vulci housed in the Boston Museum of Fine Arts (both sarcophagi feature couples embracing into the afterlife). Moreover, she also lived in Rome, the city with the largest Etruscan museum in the world (the Museo Nazionale Etrusco di Villa Giulia).

Etruscans are one of those rare cultures in the ancient Mediterranean who celebrated the married couple in their art. Embracing couples into eternity became a fundamental artistic convention; much to the chagrin of the Greeks and Romans who were not only unsympathetic to Etruscan women dining or drinking with their husbands, but often hostile to the very notion of the couple in joyous occasions.[15] What is of special interest in Cronin's sculpture is that she flips the ancient Greco-Roman patriarchal and patrilinear world upside down – two women celebrating their intimate union for eternity. The same can be said for the well-known examples of heterosexual couples in Etruscan art. Etruscan literature, which has not survived (save for funerary inscriptions and a few long fragments), would have certainly provided us with ideas on love, couples and same sex unions. But if the funerary markers in

Fig. 3.6 Movie poster for, *The Etruscan Kills Again*, 1972.

tomb chambers at cemeteries like the Banditaccia at Caere are any indication of same sex relationships, then Cronin's work is an even more fitting tribute, not just to her wife, but to Etruscan women from long ago. The stone-carved pediment finials on funerary beds at Caere, which have been understood as denoting females (right side in the tomb) with the half circle relief lines denoting males (left side in the tomb), often represent same sex couples. Not only, more and more funerary evidence suggests that same sex burials require new and careful interpretations.[16]

This commemorative work holds a distinct space at the Woodlawn Cemetery. One of the oldest cemeteries in the United States, Woodlawn Cemetery features hundreds of funerary monuments inspired by neoclassical rubrics, but until Cronin's work not a single monument exudes Etruscan inspiration. Therefore, Cronin's 'Memorial to a Marriage' not only breaks gender barriers, but it also breaks away from the neoclassical canon and its Greco-Roman models which have dominated the arts for centuries.

Demonising the Etruscans is a common aspect of modern perceptions of the Etruscans. From the early discoveries of their painted tombs with alleged 'demons' colourfully displayed on the walls to the 1972 Italian *giallo* (horror) film entitled *The Etruscan Kills Again* ('L'Etrusco uccide ancora'), demonology has had a tight grip on the popular imagination of the Etruscans and their underworld dynamics (Fig. 3.6). And yet, these so-called demons actually reveal fascinating aspects of the Etruscan conception and practicalities of the underworld. In fact, these funerary figures, I would argue, most likely functioned as guardians, guides and assistants protecting the deceased as she/he made the journey down to the underworld. These 'guides' are frequently depicted with blue/grey skin tones and/or wings and on occasion, animal features like donkey ears or a beak nose (one need only think of Tuchulcha from the Orcus Tomb in

Tarquinia). Such images led to the modern creation of the main protagonist in the mystery novel written by Brian Edgar Wallace on which the 1972 film, *The Etruscan Kills Again*, was based. Tulchulcha (as referenced in the film) embodies an underworld demon who goes about murdering young couples visiting Etruscan tombs. For the Etruscans, he may have been the keeper of the cosmic underworld order – and not a heavy breathing monster as portrayed in the 1972 movie. The film, directed by Armando Crispino, one of Dario Argento's contemporaries,[17] brings the vilifying of Etruscan underworld figures to the big screen. In the film, the necropolis becomes a crime scene, not a cultural heritage site. Viewers learn that Etruscan archaeological parks are dangerous places. Jason Porter, played by Alex Cord, is an archaeologist surveying the Banditaccia cemetery at modern Cerveteri. Porter opens up the film with an ominous statement, 'An entire civilisation buried for over 2,000 years...we hardly know anything about them. The Etruscans, they came, they stayed for a while, and then they disappeared'. The cliché of disappearing mysteriously along with the statement 'they came,' typify deep stereotypes which ignore the indigenous nature of the Etruscans, not to mention, the damaging 'vanishing race' trope. Of course, settler colonisation erases cultures, language and identity – in this case, Roman manifest destiny extinguished Etruscan voices. From the seventeenth century onwards, the Etruscans have often been packaged as a spectral people whose cultural imprint was ambiguous at best. In the film, Porter discovers Tuchulcha's image painted on a tomb wall and viewers are led to believe that he accidentally awakens an Etruscan 'demon'. The resurrected Tuchulcha preys on young couples making love in tombs (while breathing heavily to Verdi's *Requiem*). The murders continue outside the tomb until the real demon is discovered to be the son of a wealthy movie director whose fetish for high heels and Verdi's *Requiem* was disguised as an Etruscan underworld figure. Porter embodies a typecast archaeologist – an unstable alcoholic and a loner who opens up the tomb of doom (a theme used many times over in 20th century films).[18] Not only, the demonifization of the Etruscans, through Tuchulcha's on screen persona, type-cast them as terrifying and brutal at a time in Italy when the Etruscans were considered 'mysterious' by many. Tuchulcha, whose name is inscribed on a single tomb in Tarquinia dating to the fourth century BC (the Orcus Tomb), remains an anomaly (Fig. 3.7).[19] Animal ears, snakes in his hair and a beak for a nose, Tuchulcha brandishes bearded serpents whose reptilian pattern matches the very colourful wings he so proudly displays. And yet, we see no gruesome acts by Tuchulcha or any other such winged figures in Etruscan tomb painting.

Since Crispino's film, more so-called 'demons' have been discovered on tomb walls, the most iconic being the 1985 discovery of the Tomb of the Blue Demons

Fig. 3.7 Detail of Tulchulcha from the Orcus Tomb (back right wall), Tarquinia, end of 4th BCE. Photograph by Marvin Morris, Minstero dei Beni e delle Attivita' Culturali e del Turismo-Soprintenza Archeologia, Belle Arti e Paesaggio per l'Area Metropolitana di Roma, la provincial di Viterbo e l'Etruria Meridionale.

at Tarquinia.[20] The sole combination of the words 'demon' and 'tomb' in the title of this burial chamber undoubtedly triggers fear and mystery. But the more we read the visual narratives of these funerary paintings, the clearer it becomes that the demonising reception of these underworld figures are indicative of post-modern Christian anxieties rather than of Etruscan underworld 'demons' who, when carefully examined, can often be seen escorting the deceased to the afterlife.

The Etruscans are still heavily typecast in modern media – take for example the recent 2018 American film[21] *The Etruscan Smile*, in which an Etruscan funerary sarcophagus becomes a catalyst for an elderly Scottish man's will to live after a terminal diagnosis (Fig. 3.8). Etruscan demons have no place here, it is rather the Etruscan *joie de vivre* that is type-cast in the movie. The Etruscan zest for life and their smiles which prevent or ease impending death flex their agency on the modern screen. The movie has nothing to do with antiquity or the Etruscans and was not even filmed on Italian soil. Instead, most of the film takes place in San Francisco where the main character Rory (an elderly Scottish man played by Brian Cox) visits a museum (presumably the Legion of Honor in San Francisco) where he stumbles upon an Etruscan sarcophagus on display. A larger-than-life clay Etruscan couple smiles as they recline on a funerary couch/bed. The sarcophagus in the film is a fake and a far cry from the iconic Etruscan sarcophagus of the married couple (Sarcofago degli sposi) from ancient Caere housed in the Museo Nazionale Etrusco di Villa Giulia in Rome (clearly the source of inspiration for this modern piece). With his Scottish accent, Rory exclaims, 'They look like they are having a right ball those two!' His soon-to-be

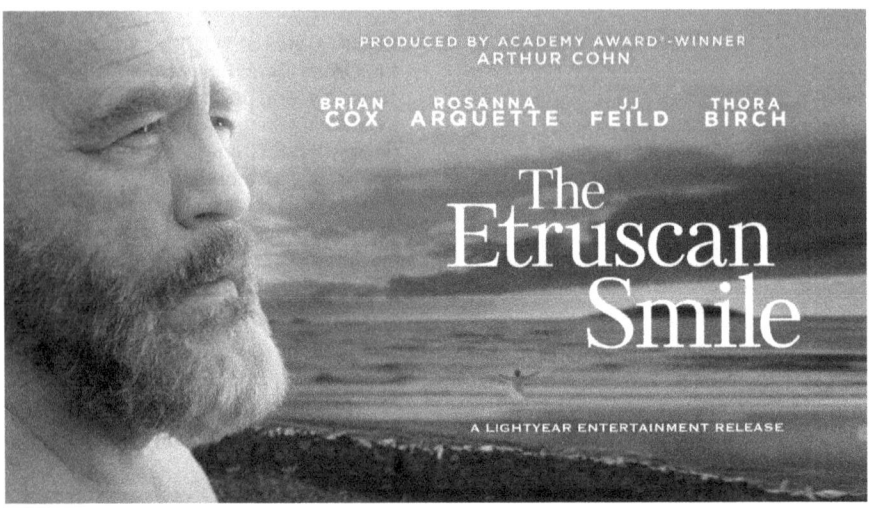

Fig. 3.8 Promotional poster for the film, *The Etruscan Smile*, 2018.

love interest, Claudia, who works at the museum, responds, 'This is how the Etruscans pictured their dead.' 'They don't look dead to me!' Rory exclaims. 'You can't die with a smile?' asks Claudia. The rhetorical comment refers to Rory's quest to live his life to the fullest – all the while battling a terminal illness. Etruscan funerary art, where banqueting, feasting and enjoying life loom large are here appropriated for their ancient life-assuring powers and their joyous views of life after death. Anyone who has read D. H. Lawrence's *Etruscan Places*, cannot help but connect Lawrence's visit to Etruscan tombs (while battling tuberculosis) with his personal and poetic reaction to their tomb painting as a life-affirming final act.[22] That there is rejoicing in Etruscan funerary art cannot be denied, in fact it is just one of the fascinating aspects of their artistic footprint. But to see how that smile can find itself in the title of an American film vis-à-vis an ancient sarcophagus may seem unexpected to many. If anything, the title of the film links the art historical term 'archaic smile', used to describe archaic Greek art (primarily sculpture) erroneously to the Etruscans. To contextualize the film more broadly, the uptake in Americans vacationing in Tuscany over the past few decades means that more Etruscan art has been seen and much of that comes in the form of banquet scenes celebrating life. Tuscan hill towns proudly advertise their Etruscan past and feature Etruscan-named restaurants where you can drink 'Etruscan' wine and enjoy 'Etruscan' olive oil. What was popular in 1970s Italian films (demonizing underworld figures for

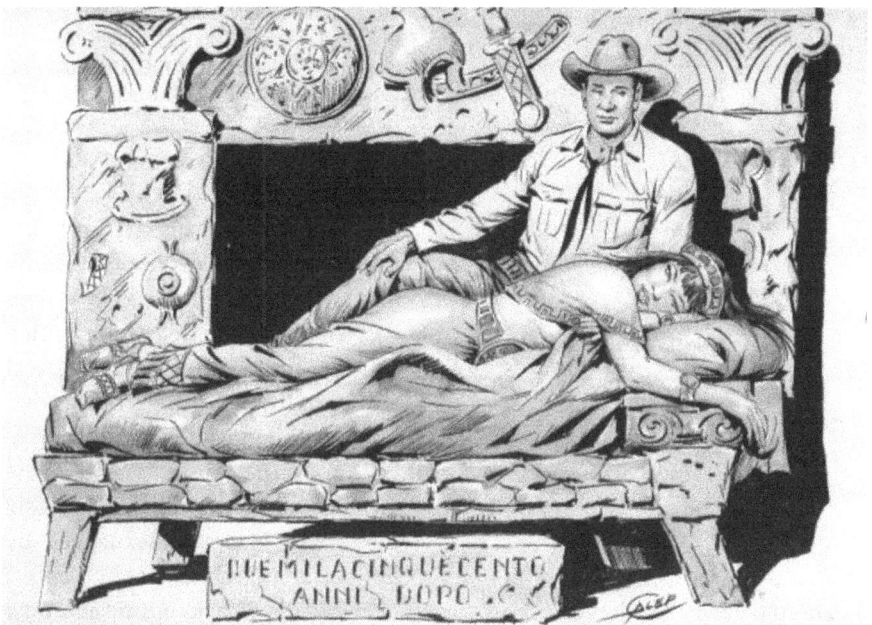

Fig. 3.9 Tex Willer by Aurelio Galleppini entitled: *2,500 Years After*.

horror films) has now been replaced for a joyous and celebratory American brand of the Etruscans. However, one could also argue that this first major American motion picture with 'Etruscan' in the title is worth celebrating simply because it brings the Etruscan name to the masses.

One of the most curious and radical re-imaginings of the Etruscans in the twentieth century has been created by the popular Italian comic series illustrator of *Tex Willer*, Aurelio Galleppini. First published in the late 1940s, the comic series became widely popular and was translated into several languages.[23] Its wide-ranging success exceeded European borders, as illustrated by its fame in South America. The series depicts the life of Tex, an American cowboy/ranger who lives in the south-west of the United States and marries a Navajo woman. In 1985 Italy celebrated the 'Year of the Etruscans' with various exhibits and conferences showcasing the Etruscan past. Galleppini was asked to contribute to the catalog for the exhibit entitled *La fortuna degli Etruschi*, and he created a cross-temporal comic-like image labeled '2,500 Years After.' It features Tex posing with either his wife dressed as an Etruscan or an Etruscan posing as his wife (Fig. 3.9).[24] The couple recline on an Etruscan banquet/funerary couch (*kline*) against the background of the Tomb of the Reliefs from ancient Caere.

Fig. 3.10 Photograph by Andres Serrano, *Sir Leonard*, 1990. Courtesy of the artist and Galerie Nathalie Obadia, Paris/Brussels.

Galleppini, who hailed from Tuscany, surely was aware of Etruscan art, history and culture (more than the American southwest for which he spent his life producing sketches) and proudly displays his iconic cowboy in a recognizable Etruscan pose. Both reclining figures gaze out at the viewer, and the woman, presumably Tex's wife, is highly sexualized by her garment and demeanor. Are we meant to believe that the American cowboy Tex has gone back in time and now reclines as a regal Etruscan aristocrat, albeit still dressed as a cowboy? Or should we instead hold the view that as the date in the title suggests, Tex was originally an Etruscan who, '2,500 years later' takes on the persona of Tex Willer? For an Italian viewer who grew up with the popular comic series, perhaps this would make perfect sense. The series romanticized 'cowboy culture' of the American West and for the 1985 print, combined it with an ancient Italian – or to be more precise: an Etruscan twist. Two worlds from diverse continents and temporalities merge in fascinating and certainly unpredictable ways – Italian viewers, I imagine, might find this contrast an amusing but recognizable sight. The Tex Willer comic series never featured an encounter with Etruscans, but oddly the Egyptians did appear in the 1979 edition entitled, *La piramide misteriosa*. There are, in fact, a few Italian comic series that do mention the Etruscans – the first being *Il Vittorioso* from 1955/56 which titled one edition *Rasena* (the name the Etruscans called themselves). It was such a success that it was published in French in 1959.[25]

I will conclude this brief encounter of Etruscans in unexpected places by way of casting light on a fascinating image from the late twentieth century, namely, a photograph by the provocative artist Andres Serrano.[26] His 1990 project, *Monumental, Heroic and Homeless: Nomads*, was a studio style approach to capturing images of those overlooked in American society.[27] It was a tribute to and a highlighting of the homeless in America, who take up residency and spaces in very

Fig. 3.11 Detail of the belt buckle in the photograph of *Sir Leonard* by Andres Serrano, Sir Leonard, 1990. Courtesy of the artist and Galerie Nathalie Obadia, Paris/Brussels.

public places like street corners, alleys and subways, yet go unnoticed by the general public. Serrano photographed people in-situ in the New York subway, but the images themselves look like grandiose portraits done in a professional studio. Serrano achieved this by bringing in backdrops and professional lighting to the subway. The results were enormous portraits of homeless people who were photographed without props – simply with the clothes they were wearing. In fact, Serrano claims he gave no instructions to those he photographed other than to look left or right.[28] Regardless, the studio backdrop as well as professional lighting add a deep chiaroscuro effect to the overall studio-like aesthetic – contributing, one could argue, controversial and exploitative aspects of the photographer's gaze. Thus, we are visually introduced to Sir Leonard (Fig. 3.10), as he sits for a portrait in a New York city subway. The close-up range of the photograph allows for the monumentalized nature of Sir Leonard's face. The overall image, however, does not show the context of poverty and the suffering of the homeless – only the torn clothes do (but one need look carefully). The viewer observes details which create an ambiguous and complex visual – grandiosity and poverty combine in complicated ways. The majestic expression of Sir Leonard, partially shaded by his hat, is juxtaposed by his clothing – two scarfs and two jackets, one of them torn. He proudly holds up a shiny belt buckle literally as if it is an honorary medal (Fig. 3.11). The belt-buckle features a relief of the Etruscan Chimaera of Arezzo – inscriptions float above and below the hybrid creature. Sir Leonard literally frames the buckle with his gloved hands and gazes at the viewer with pride. The words 'In Denim We Trust' and 'Quality Garments for Quality People,' surround the mythical creature. Serrano's late twentieth century portrait of a man holding a portrait-like image of the ancient Etruscan

Chimaera certainly requires some unpacking. For starters, issues of temporality within these interlocking portraits loom large. Is Serrano, as Laurie Schneider Adams suggests, comparing Sir Leonard to the mythic hero Bellerophon, who rode the winged Pegasus and slayed the chimaera?[29] If so, is the camera (as a machine with a distinct gaze) asking us to see Sir Leonard as a tragic hero – a homeless refugee in an urban myth?[30] Or is Seranno visually commenting on the marginalization of peoples, both past and present – an Etruscan work of art in the hands of an American homeless man? The belt buckle's inscriptions and the Chimaera align the hybrid aspects of the photo itself making an overall compelling image. 'By Parasuco' is written below the Chimaera and refers to the Italian-Canadian designer, Salvatore Parasuco who celebrates his Italian roots with the image of the Etruscan Chimaera (he proudly appropriated the image as his logo for his successful clothing line).[31] Thus, the Etruscan Chimaera on Sir Leonard's buckle becomes a twentieth-century international symbol of denim, promising to uphold trust to whomever garners the Parasuco brand; and, the Etruscan Chimaera is now a negotiator of 'quality garments for quality people'. The backstory regarding why Sir Leonard held up the belt buckle or even how he came to own it, is lost to us and perhaps not even necessary for understanding the photograph. What makes the object Sir Leonard so proudly displays so full of Etruscan import, are the thousands of years of history, art and culture which are here condensed in a modern belt buckle, showcased proudly by one of America's many homeless.

What do these examples of Etruscans in unexpected places tell us? For starters, despite the stronghold of Greece and Rome on the history and culture of the ancient Mediterranean, there is an awareness, curiosity and certainly pride and agency in Etruscan art and culture throughout the ages – even now. The visual programs of the Etruscans retain a special place in the popular imagination and contemporary responses and reverberations of their past propagate in fascinating and often complicated ways. The sheer diversity in artistic media, namely in film, sculpture, funerary architecture, comics, modern fashion and photography reveals a wide-ranging engagement with and conversation about the Etruscans. It also uncovers an attempt to demystify the Etruscans in ways that challenge their traditional categorization as 'other'. If anything, we can see how the conventional and popular reuse of the past determines what is understood as expected or unexpected when deciding what aspects of the Etruscans to replicate, fabricate, invent, highlight and mediate. Of course, one could argue that the examples I have underscored here add to the well-known tropes associated with Etruscans, as these examples may be seen as tokenizing snippets of a great Etruscan past. But I would argue otherwise. From an Etruscologist's point of view, it is refreshing, in fact, encouraging and exciting to see the temporality and agency of Etruscans throughout space, place and time.

Notes

1. The title of this chapter is inspired by Philip Deloria's book: *Indians in Unexpected Places* (Lawrence: University Press of Kansas, 2004).
2. Charlotte R. Potts and Christopher J. Smith, 'The Etruscans: Setting New Agendas', in *Journal of Archaeological Research* (Open Access, 2021); *An Etruscan Affair: The Impact of Early Etruscan Discoveries*, Judith Swaddling (ed.) (London: British Museum, 2018); Francesco De Angelis, 'The Reception of the Etruscan Culture: Dempster and Buonarroti', in *The Etruscan World*, Jean Turfa (ed.) (New York: Routledge, 2013).
3. For more on the topic of 'otherness' in the ancient world see Erich Gruen, *Rethinking the Other in Antiquity*, Series: Martin Classical Lectures (Princeton: Princeton University Press, 2010); Maria Beatrice Bittarello, 'The Construction of Etruscan "Otherness" in Latin Literature', in *Greece and Rome*, vol. 56 no. 2 (2009), pp. 211-233.
4. Lisa C. Pieraccini, 'An Egyptian Tomb, an Etruscan Inscription and the Funerary Monument of an American Civil War Officer', in *An Etruscan Affair*, pp. 188-194; Chase Viele, 'America's Pyramid on-the-Hudson: West Point's Viele Tomb Echoes Ancient Protype on Egypt's Nile', in *Assembly*, vol. 32 no. 3 (1973), pp. 20-35.
5. For more on early American cemeteries and appropriation of Greco-Roman and Egyptian architecture, see Elizabeth Macaulay-Lewis, 'Entombing Antiquity: A New Consideration of Classical and Egyptian Appropriation in the Funerary Architecture of Woodlawn Cemetery, New York City', in *Housing the New Romans: Architectural Reception and Classical Style in the Modern World*, Katharine T. von Stackelbery and Elizabeth Macaulay-Lewis (eds) (Oxford: Oxford University Press, 2017).
6. Chase Viele, 'America's Pyramid-on-the-Hudson'; Lisa C. Pieraccini, 'An Egyptian Tomb, an Etruscan Inscription and the Funerary Monument of an American Civil War Officer'.
7. It was reported that Viele installed a buzzer inside his sarcophagus so that when he woke after death, he could ring the caretaker on the West Point grounds and exit the tomb. His preoccupation with his own resurrection can also be seen in the electric light constantly turned on inside the tomb from 1902 until wartime mandated blackouts were imposed after Pearl Harbor was bombed in 1941. See Chase Viele, 'America's Pyramid on-the-Hudson'; Lisa C. Pieraccini, 'An Egyptian Tomb, an Etruscan Inscription and the Funerary Monument of an American Civil War Officer'.
8. For more on the inscription, see Alexander Crawford, *Etruscan Inscriptions* (London: J. Murray, 1872).
9. *Ibid*.
10. See Lisa C. Pieraccini, 'An Egyptian Tomb, an Etruscan Inscription and the Funerary Monument of an American Civil War Officer'; Chase Viele, 'America's Pyramid on-the-Hudson'.
11. For Viele's superstitious tendencies, as reported by his family, see Chase Viele, 'America's Pyramid on-the-Hudson'.
12. Grandiose tombs inspired by an ancient, often Greco-Roman past, were status symbols with the nineteenth and early twentieth century American elite, seen in such cemeteries as the Woodlawn Cemetery in New York; see Elizabeth Macaulay-Lewis, 'Entombing Antiquity'. Often Egyptian and Greco-Roman styles were combined in fascinating ways, but the Viele tomb is unique for merging Egyptian and Etruscan styles in highly innovative and unique ways.
13. For more on Patricia Cronin and her work, see Cronin's website: http://www.patriciacronin.net/memorial.html. (Accessed May 2023).
14. See: Balasz Takac, 'The Importance of Patricia Cronin's Memorial to a Marriage' in *Widewalls* (26 February 2021); AJ, 'Almost 20 Years of Patricia Cronin's Memorial to a Marriage' in *AfterEllen* (19 October 2021); Laura Bauld, 'The Power of Patricia Cronin's "Memorial to a Marriage"' in *Art UK* (1 February 2021).
15. For a Greek view see Theompompus, *Histories* 115 FGr Hist F 204, in Athenaeus 517d-518a; for Roman views of Etruscans see Maria Beatrice Bittarello, 'The Construction of "Otherness" in Latin Literature'.
16. See Marjatta Nielsen, 'Common Tombs for Women in Etruria: Buried Matriarchies?' in *Acta Instituti Romani Finlandiae* vol. 22, p. 116, Table 1 type 6 relates to tomb complex from Chiusi and Perugia indicating female tombs, kin or non-kin.

17. Crispino and Argento even worked together on the 1968 Italian film, *Commandos*. For more on the Etruscans in horror film, see Julie Labregere, 'The Infernal Image of the Etruscans in Fantasy and Horror Film,' in *Antikenrezeption im Horror*, Michael Kleu (ed.), (Essen: Oldib-Verlag, 2023), pp. 197-223.
18. One need only think of the American blockbuster film, *Raiders of the Lost Ark* (1984) or the earlier 1981 Italian film *Burial Ground* (a zombie movie where a scholar studying the Etruscans resurrects the dead).
19. For more on Tuchulcha see Nancy Thomson De Grummond, *Etruscan Myth, Sacred History and Legend* (Philadelphia: The University of Pennsylvania Museum of Archaeology and Anthropology, 2006) and Ingrid Krauskopf, 'The Grave and Beyond in Etruscan Religion', in *The Religion of the Etruscans*, Nancy Thomson De Grummond and Erika Simon (eds) (Austin: Texas University Press, 2006), pp. 66-89; Isabella Bossolino, 'Break on through to the Other Side: The Etruscan Netherwold and its Demons', in *Imagining the Afterlife in the Ancient World*, Juliette Harrison (ed.) (London: Routledge, 2018), pp. 52-68.
20. For general descriptions, see Alessandro Naso, *La pittura etrusca* (Rome: L'Erma di Bretschneider, 2005) and Stephan Steingräber, *Abundance of Life: Etruscan Wall Painting* (Los Angeles: J. Paul Getty Publications, 2006).
21. The film was based on the novel written by Jose Luis Sampedro *La Sonrisa etrusca* (1985). Etruscan funerary art holds a special place in the popular imagination and contemporary responses and reverberations of their funerary culture have continued throughout the centuries, even today.
22. D. H. Lawrence, *Etruscan Places* (Siena: Nuova Immagine, 1986).
23. Franco Lai, 'Le avventure di Tex Willer. Narrazioni, luoghi, paesaggi', *Lares*, vol. 85 no. 2 (2019), p. 271.
24. For more on this image and its Etruscan context, see Michael Vickers, 'Imaginary Etruscans: Changing Perceptions of Etruria Since the Fifteenth Century', in *Hephaistos*, vol. 7 (1986).
25. For more on Etruscans in comic series, see Giuseppe Pucci, 'Gli Etruschi nei fumetti', in *Gli Etruschi nella cultura e nell'immaginario del mondo moderno*, Giuseppe M. Della Fina (ed.) (Rome: Quasar, 2017).
26. *Andres Serrano, Works 1983-1993* (Philadelphia, University of Pennsylvania Institute of Contemporary Art, 1994). I thank Andres Serrano for allowing me to publish the photograph of Sir Leonard.
27. See Andres Serrano's website: https://andresserrano.org/series/nomads. (Accessed May 2023).
28. Liza Strelka, https://blog.phillipscollection.org/2013/11/04/monumental-heroic-homeless-andres-serranos-nomads-sir-leonard/. (Accessed May 2023).
29. Laurie Schneider Adams, *A History of Western Art* (New York: McGraw-Hill Education, 2004).
30. *Ibid.*
31. See Parasucco's website: https://www.parasuco.com/en-us/page/about/. (Accessed May 2023).

The Demonisation of the Etruscans: From Alfred Grünwedel to German Schoolbooks

Martin Miller

Over the past decades, several highly successful exhibitions about the Etruscans have been organised in Germany, including the exhibition *Die Etrusker und Europa* ('The Etruscans and Europe') in 1993 in Berlin[1] and the *Die Etrusker. Weltkultur im antiken Italien* ('The Etruscans. World Culture in Ancient Italy') in 2017-18 in Karlsruhe.[2] In the same period popular science books on Etruscan topics sold well, yet the Etruscans remained remarkably absent from German literature and culture at large. Despite the high level of scientific attention to the Etruscans in Germany, in contrast to Italy, Great Britain or France, there was (and still is) only very limited creative reception and adaptation of Etruscan art and culture.

In the eighteenth and nineteenth century, German travellers on their way to Rome and southern Italy crossed Tuscany, ancient Etruria, but paid little attention to Etruscan antiquities. In their writings, Greek and Roman antiquities are considered in longer sections, whereas references to the Etruscans are quite rare, if they appear at all. During their visits to Florence and Rome, the academically educated Germans frequently met Italian scholars. Johann Caspar Goethe (1710-1782), for example, during his trip to Italy in 1740,[3] met the archaeologist and Etruscologist Anton Francesco Gori (1691-1757)[4] in Florence. Johann Wolfgang Goethe's father also knew the relevant literature. On a visit to Viterbo, he recalls the figure of Annio da Viterbo (1432-1502),[5] a fifteenth century scholar who, combining Old Testament tradition and Greco-Roman history, relocated the ancestry of the Etruscans to the beginnings of the world and cited as evidence a few sources he had forged himself.[6] Goethe also copies several Latin inscriptions from the town hall of Viterbo. Apart from this reference, Goethe describes only medieval and contemporary buildings on his journey from Rome to Florence, with stops in Storta, Bracciano, Monterosi, Ronciglione, Montagna di Viterbo, Viterbo, Montefiascone, Radicofani, Siena, Livorno, Pisa, Lucca and Pistoia. In Florence, he visits the city's ducal gallery and mentions the Arezzo

Chimaera and the bronze statue of Arringatore, which he considers to be an Etruscan ruler or Scipio Africanus.[7]

In 1786 his son Johann Wolfgang von Goethe (1749-1832) also travelled to Italy, from where he did not return until 1788. According to his diaries, it was not until 1813 to 1817 that he wrote and published an account of this journey free of any too personal comments (yet it was still an autobiographical text).[8] Although, on the outward journey, Goethe passed through Florence (to continue for Rome via Arezzo, Perugia, Assisi, Spoleto, Foligno, Terni and Civita Castellana) and visited Florence again on the return journey (travelling via Civita Castellana and Siena), he never mentioned either the Etruscans or Etruscan works of art. In Assisi he was only interested in the so-called Minerva Temple in the city centre, 'I left with aversion the immense substructures of the Babylonian towering churches where St. Francis rests'.[9] Apparently, however, Goethe only became interested in the remains of Roman times in Rome: 'The Roman antiquities are also beginning to make me happy. History, inscriptions, coins, about which I didn't want to know before, everything is pressing up. How I fared in natural history is the same here. Because in this place the whole history of the world is connected, and I am counting a second birthday, a true rebirth, from the day I entered Rome'.[10]

Barely two months after Goethe's return to Germany, his older friend Johann Gottfried Herder (1744-1803) also left for Italy. Unlike Goethe, however, Herder was rather disappointed. In Italy, he found neither Goethe's 'Arcadia' nor personal enrichment. Herder never published an account of his journey,[11] but his experiences in Italy can be reconstructed through personal letters and diary entries from 1788 and 1789. Herder first travelled south from Bologna along the Adriatic coast to cross the Apennines between Ancona and Foligno. Then the route went via Spoleto, Terni and Civita Castellana to Rome. On the return journey he then travelled to Florence via Siena and Pisa. Herder does not describe Etruscan antiquities, even though he seems to have met a few archaeologists during his journey.

The fourth traveller who came through Etruria was Johann Gottfried Seume (1763-1810). His *Spaziergang nach Syrakus im Jahre 1802* ('Walk to Syracuse in 1802')[12] took him on the outward journey along an itinerary similar to Herder's, via Foligno, Spoleto, Terni, Narni, Otricoli, Nepi and Civita Castellana to Rome. The return journey to Florence via Viterbo, Montefiascone, Bolsena, Acquapendente and Siena also followed a route often taken by travellers: the medieval Via Francigena.[13] Seume's account of his journey is very different from the academic works of its predecessors in that it is highly subjective and contains many political and critical observations. Seume does visit churches, palaces and libraries, but Etruscan antiquities do not appear in this account.

August Wilhelm Schlegel (1767-1845), poet, literary historian and translator of English, Italian, Spanish and Portuguese literature, accompanied the Geneva-born francophone writer Anne-Louise-Germaine Baroness von Staël-Holstein to Italy from December 1804 to June 1805 and then again from September 1815 to February 1816.[14] While the first trip led them to Naples from Lyon via Turin, Milan and Rome, the second trip had Florence as their final destination, as de Staël's daughter Albertine wanted to marry Victor de Broglie in Pisa. Unlike Goethe, Herder or Seume, Schlegel did not keep a travel diary and only sporadically wrote letters to relatives and friends. The direct impact of the journey on his literary and scientific work is actually very limited. During the first trip, he wrote the elegy *Rome*, a lengthy poem about the origins and the ancient history of the city. The city walls of Romulus are described as 'square hewn according to Etrurian standard'.[15] August Wilhelm Schlegel was appointed professor of Indology at the University of Bonn in 1818, the first chair in this field in Germany,[16] and in 1822 he held a lecture entitled *Antiquitates Etruscae*,[17] apparently at the request of colleagues and friends. In this lecture, as he emphasised several times, he was guided by his own views or conversations with Italian scholars like Giovanni Battista Zannoni (1774-1832),[18] Francesco Inghirami (1772-1846)[19] or Sebastiano Ciampi (1769-1847).[20] Unfortunately, the lecture has never been fully written out in a text, and the partial version that has been preserved deals only with the origin and the topography. It becomes clear that many of the large Etruscan cities such as Luni, Vetulonia, Vulci, Veji or Falerii had not even been located at the time of Schlegel. As regards the origin of the Etruscans, Schlegel discusses all theories known from ancient sources, including the origin from the north, mentioned only in Livy. Schlegel dismisses the theory that the Etruscan origins lay in the Orient.

The gaps in knowledge that still existed in Schlegel's time were largely closed in the course of the nineteenth century. German scholars and intellectuals interested in antiquity also played a large part in this. Research and excavations helped locate the Etruscan cities known from ancient literature. This research also involved Germans living in Italy, especially in Rome, like the diplomat August Kestner (1777-1853) and Baron Otto Magnus von Stackelberg (1786-1837), who explored painted graves in Tarquinia.[21] In 1823, a group of artists, scholars and other Germans living in Rome founded the Roman-Hyperborean Society, from which the Istituto di Corrispondenza Archeologica emerged in 1828, the forerunner of the German Archaeological Institute.[22] In the same year Karl Otfried Müller (1797-1840) summarised all the available knowledge on the Etruscans in his book *Die Etrusker*, which became a classic in archaeological literature.[23] Eduard Gerhard (1795-1867), one of the co-founders of the Roman

Institute, set up an Etruscan cabinet as an 'Archäolog bei dem Museum' (archaeologist at the museum) in Berlin in 1844, in which the Etruscan antiquities that had been acquired for the royal museums were exhibited.[24]

At the end of the nineteenth century, a German colony also emerged in Florence. This institute comprised writers, painters, sculptors, doctors and other intellectuals like the writer Isolde Kurz (1853-1944),[25] her brother, the doctor Edgar Kurz (1853-1904),[26] the sculptors Adolf von Hildebrand (1847-1921)[27] and Paul Peterich (1864-1937),[28] the painter Arnold Böcklin (1827-1901)[29], the classical philologist Theodor Heyse (1803-1884)[30], the writers Karl Hillebrand (1829-1884)[31] and Theodor Däubler (1876-1934)[32] and the publisher Jakob Hegner (1882-1962).[33] In 1899, they built holiday homes in Forte dei Marmi, which was in fact the origin of the seaside resort.[34] Most of the references to Italy can be found in Isolde Kurz's work. However, her stories either take place in the Florentine Renaissance[35] or have clearly autobiographical features.[36] In the works of the writers based in Florence, there seems to be no place for ancient history and certainly not for the Etruscans. Only in Isolde Kurz's story *Solleone*, does the archaeologist Dr. Karl Johannsen, who takes part in a hike to Monte Giovi near Pontassieve east of Florence, walk in the footsteps of the Etruscans. But the figure of Dr. Johannsen and his profession play no real role in the plot of the story.[37] At the time the story was written, Isolde Kurz could of course not have known that Etruscan finds were actually being made on Monte Giovi in 1972.[38] Eckart Peterich (1900-1968),[39] the son of the sculptor Paul Peterich, lived in Italy for a long time and wrote a travel guide that was widely used in Germany.[40] In 1926 he took part in the first national Etruscan congress in Florence.[41] However, he made no reference to the Etruscans[42] in either his Guide to Italy or in his poetic work[43]. An *Exkurs über die Etrusker* ('Excursus about the Etruscans')[44] in a longer treatise on *Rom und die Geschichte Italiens*[45] remained unpublished during his lifetime. The Germans living in Florence evidently stayed mostly within their own community; there seem to be no real contacts with Italian writers like Gabriele D'Annunzio (1863-1938) around the turn of the century or with Curzio Malaparte (1898-1957) in the interwar period[46] – to name only two writers who incorporated Etruscan culture and history in some of their works.[47]

This lack of interest in the Etruscans by German poets and writers is perhaps due to the way in which German scientists, in particular, dealt with the Etruscans and other ancient civilizations. The nineteenth and early twentieth centuries were the time of positivism, the philosophical and epistemological theory according to which 'genuine' knowledge (i.e. knowledge on any subject that is not true by definition) is exclusively derived from the observation of natural phenomena and their properties and relations. This principle was widely applied in many scientific disciplines, including archaeology, and for the study of Etruscan culture this meant that there was a strong focus on the creation and careful description of numerous corpora of individual types of finds like inscriptions, Etruscan mirrors, coins and so on.[48] Little space is given to speculative interpretations that go beyond the mere findings. An analysis of the contributions by German archaeologists in the most important Etruscan journal, *Studi Etruschi*, reveals that this situation continues to dominate until the 1930s. One will find fewer, culturally and historically relevant interdisciplinary articles, but will instead find material templates for individual art objects or detailed analyses.[49] Works, for example, on a comprehensive analysis of the origins of Roman portrait art or the structure of ancient Italian sculpture,[50] as presented by Guido Kaschnitz von Weinberg (1890-1958),[51] are more of an exception. This sober approach of the Etruscans apparently offered little nourishment for the imagination of poets to make use of Etruscan culture in their works.

It is therefore not surprising that the Nazi ideologist Alfred Rosenberg took a completely different view of the Etruscans and their cultural-historical classification – a view that he presented as a scientific claim (although it was completely devoid of scientific basis).[52]

In the first chapter of his work *Der Mythus des 20. Jahrhunderts. Eine Wertung der seelisch-geistigen Gestaltenkämpfe unserer Zeit* ('The Myth of the Twentieth Century. An Evaluation of the Spiritual-Intellectual Confrontations of Our Age'),[53] Rosenberg deals with the history of ancient Greece and Italy and their culture, focussing on the Etruscans in the third section of the chapter. First, a contrast is built up between the Romans belonging to a 'Nordic wave of peoples' ('nordischen Völkerwelle'), who would have mixed with the still pure, indigenous Mediterranean race, and the 'foreign, Near Eastern' Etruscans ('fremden, vorderasiatischen'), who would have been in constant battle with one another.[54] However, even the most formidable representatives of Roman culture, like Cato,[55] Sulla[56] or Augustus[57] were not able to cope with the 'immigration of a foreign race' ('fremdrassigen Zuzug') to Rome. Rosenberg sees the roots of the decline of the patrician (i.e., 'Nordic' ('nordischen')) Romans, on the one hand, in the mixing with the plebeians (permission for marriage between plebeians and patricians, access for plebeian families to state and priestly offices[58]) and, on the other hand, in the negative influence of Etruscan culture.[59] The suppression of Carthage and the conquest of the Orient are portrayed as a 'racial struggle' ('Rassenkampf'). However, this only ended successfully in the case of Carthage.[60] The historical picture of the Romans, who came from the north, corresponds completely to the National Socialist conception of European cultures having spread over the continent from the north, the alleged original home of the Teutons.

The Etruscan image of Rosenberg and the conclusions drawn from it for the further course of history must be examined in greater detail here. The Etruscan being is characterised by two types: 'the divine hetaera' ('die göttliche Hetäre'), the 'great whore of Babylon' ('Große Hure von Babylon'), whom he sees personified in the 'goddess priestess' ('Göttin-Priesterin') Tanaquil, and the 'magical priest' ('zauberstarken Priester'), the haruspex who also holds witchcraft linked with pederasty, masturbation, murder of boys, magical appropriation of the manna of the slaughtered by the priestly murderer, and prophecies derived from the excrements and the piled up entrails of the victims.[61] The Etruscans are said to have perverse and obscene cult practices, including Satanism and a penchant for belief in witches – Rosenberg always speaks of 'witch mania' ('Hexenwahn') or 'witchcraft' ('Hexenwesen'). Great phalloi always play a role in their cults and myths. The creature resulting from the union of Tanaquil and Haruspex is also a decaying phallus. The murdered boy becomes a 'little goat' ('Böckchen'), the origin of the 'goat-headed devil' ('bockköpfigen Teufels').[62] When performing this ritual – the ritual union of the hetaera and the priest, the birth of the boy and his assassination – 'the power of the murdered boy is supposed to pass to the priest, who is the representative of the "Chosen" (Rasna, Rasena), as the Etruscans – like the Jews – called themselves'.[63] In summary, he says: 'The Etruscans present us with an unequalled example of the way in which the Greek religion and way of life afforded them neither progress nor spiritual elevation. Like other near eastern peoples, the Etruscans had encountered at one point the Atlantic Nordic Myths, which were by then embodied in Greek tradition, and they imitated Greek plastic and pictorial art as best they could, even appropriating the Hellenic pantheon. They succeeded only in corrupting everything they touched and turning each attribute into its opposite'.[64] And a little later: 'The Etruscans, to be sure, have left a record of obscene practices and monuments, but nothing which would permit us to assume any creative spiritual faculties.'[65]

In his remarks, Rosenberg relies on the thoughts of Albert Grünwedel, which he had formulated in his 1922 publication *Tusca*.[66] In Grünwedel (1856-1935), a renowned Indologist and Tibetologist who had organised two of the four German Turfan expeditions before the First World War, we read 'the preconceived interpretation increasingly took precedence over philology,'[67] that is, he did not always distinguish between reality and illusion. Scientists of the time criticised Grünwedel's books, sometimes in explicit terms, but further damage to the figure of Grünwedel could be averted by the fact that science remained silent. Scientists knew that Grünwedel was untrustworthy and a bad scholar but stayed silent about it thus avoiding a major scandal.[68] The Berlin papyrologist Wilhelm Schubart, the reviewer of both Gustav Herbig's *Geheimsprache der Etrusker*[69] and Grünwedel's *Tusca*, advised as early as 1924 that Grünwedel's book 'for the sake of the author and for the sake of German science should be forgotten as quickly as possible.'[70] The Tibetologist Johannes Schubert (1896-1976)[71] goes even further in his criticism: 'With no regard for all the Etruscan research – and deliberately! – a completely new solution to the problem is offered, a so-called magic unveiling of the best-known and most important Etruscan written monuments, which admittedly shows the whole culture of this people in a terrible light.'[72] However, Schubert decidedly refuses to describe Grünwedel's condition as 'pathological' ('pathologisch') in his final years.[73] Albert Grünwedel was convinced that he could understand the Etruscan language through Egyptian. He had fully translated all longer Etruscan texts from the *Liber Linteus Zagrabiensis* to the Cippus of Perugia to the Tablet from Capua and identified gruesome rituals with human sacrifices and phallic symbols throughout. Even the inscriptions of the 'Golini Tombs', which mainly consist of names, become texts in this sense in Grünwedel. Grünwedel had already started his studies on the *Liber Linteus Zagrabiensis* in the spring of 1916. He had allegedly found the original Egyptian texts on which the bands were based, with which he could compile an Etruscan-Egyptian dictionary. By this he meant that he could translate any inscription. In May 1916, he describes the results of his work in a letter to his teacher Ernst Kuhn (1846-1920)[74]: 'I don't know whether I'll translate the mummy texts. The content is such a shameful mockery of all human rights that I cannot find the necessary expressions in any language on earth. And the Greek, which alone could express such things, I would not like to pollute with such faeces'.[75] However, Grünwedel's transcriptions of Egyptian texts with a vocalisation that was completely new in research, as well as the translations obtained from them, are viewed with scepticism by his teacher Kuhn, who for this reason does not support the idea of having Grünwedel's writings published by the Bavarian Academy of Sciences.[76] Apparently, Grünwedel was completely self-taught in the field of Egyptology, as his teacher Ernst Kuhn was actually a specialist in Indian languages: from 1877 to 1917 he was a full professor at the university of Munich, initially of Aryan philology and comparative Indo-European linguistics and, from 1909, he was professor of the newly founded chair for comparative Indo-European linguistics.[77] His predecessor Ernst Trumpp (1828-1885) also taught Semitic languages and literature, and not Egyptology.[78] After Grünwedel's death, the former officer and apparently esotericist Otto Ilzhöfer[79] assembled a never-published work from further notes by Grünwedel in which he sought to prove the connections between Etruscans and Jews.[80]

In particular, the sections of Rosenberg's *Mythus* on the Etruscans seem to figure in the parts of his manuscript that were completed in 1925. Grünwedel's book *Tusca*, published in 1922, was relatively new at the time of writing. Rosenberg was obviously not aware of the scientific discussion – or the deliberate concealment of the book. It is doubtful whether this would have prevented Rosenberg from further disseminating Grünwedel's theses about the Etruscans, for Rosenberg saw the Etruscans and what he judged to be their reprehensible culture as the basis for papacy and belief in witches in the Middle Ages.[81] The Haruspex with its college of priests is the direct forerunner of the Pope and his cardinals.[82] The construct of the Catholic Church based on Etruscan beliefs is thus the attempt to combine anti-Semitism – including the demonisation of everything Near Eastern in general – with anti-clericalism, that is, to denounce the Middle Eastern and thus Jewish roots of the church.[83] The connection between belief in witches and the Etruscans can only be found in Rosenberg's work, even if the idea apparently once again comes from Alfred Grünwedel. In 1916, he considered the witch trials in Ulm of 1416 and in Wemding of 1628-1632 and believed he found 'Etruscan reminiscences' (etruskische Reminiscenzen') up to the Middle Ages.[84] However, these considerations, which were only expressed in a letter to Ernst Kuhn, were never published. There is no proof as to whether Rosenberg and Grünwedel knew each other personally and, if so, whether they exchanged views. In sex-magical and satanic writings from around 1900, however, witchcraft and sorcery were still regarded as pagan-Germanic and belonged to the ancient knowledge of popular belief.[85]

Despite the widespread use of Rosenberg's *Mythus des XX Jahrhunderts*, his theses on the cruel and obscene cult practices of the Etruscans and the origin of the medieval papacy, Satanism and the belief in witches are rarely picked up by other publications for scholars or for larger audiences. This thesis is only discussed in an article, written by Wilhelm Brachmann (1900-1989) and Theodor Kluge (1880-1958), about the Etruscans that appeared in the *Handbuch der Romfrage* ('Handbook of the Rome Question') published by Rosenberg.[86] Even in the schoolbooks of the time before the Second World War, Rosenberg's theses are not explicitly repeated. An examination of the curricula in schools and textbooks, especially for the subject of history, reveals a persistent negative attitude towards the Etruscans.[87] In the curriculum for the grammar schools in Prussia from 1938, the key phrase 'racial significance of Etruscanism for Rome' ('rassische Bedeutung des Etruskertums für Rom') is found for the first half of the 6th grade and then later 'the Roman Church as heir to the world empire' ('die Römische Kirche als Erbin des Weltreichs').[88] From these key phrases in the relatively cursory publication of the curricula for all subjects, one could conclude that Rosenberg's theories should be taught there. However, the textbooks that were not available until 1940 and were modified in accordance with the 1938 curriculum remained relatively cautious as regards the Etruscans. The first section of the history of Rome now has the uncontroversial title 'The Unification of Italy under Rome' ('Die Einigung Italiens unter Rom'), the first section of the chapter is entitled 'The victory of Nordic tribes over the Near Eastern Etruscans in Italy' ('Der Sieg nordischer Stämme über die vorderasiatischen Etrusker in Italien'). Although the Etruscans are consistently referred to as 'Near Eastern' ('vorderasiatisch'), the conquest of Etruria by Rome is portrayed as a struggle to keep the 'Nordic' race clean, but their culture is not further devalued, the Etruscans are even regarded as the 'masters of stone construction' ('Lehrmeister im Steinbau'). However, there are also statements that the Etruscans were cruel pirates who lived lustfully with a large group of slaves in fortified cities and who believed in terrible demons and an unpleasant afterlife. They protected themselves against these threats by interpreting the signs pointing into the future through augurs and *haruspices*[89]. In Dietrich Klagges' (1891-1971)[90] handbook for teachers, the history of the 'Nordic colony' ('nordischen Kolonie') of Rome is presented very similarly.[91] The Etruscans, who are also 'Near Eastern' ('vorderasiatisch') here, tend to be dangerous rivals for supremacy in Italy, and not a people of obscene cults and effeminate customs.[92] Only the Tarquins disrupted the 'basic features of the Old Nordic constitution' ('Grundzüge altnordischer Verfassung') and abused 'the king's right to lead Near Eastern despotism' ('das Führerrecht des Königs zu vorderasiatischer Despotie'). The annihilation of the Etruscans had been completed 'without any significant intermingling of the two races'.[93] Even the chapter on 'the Roman Church as heir to the world empire' ('die Römische Kirche als Erbin des Weltreichs') is not presented in the textbook in the manner of Rosenberg. The thesis about the roots of the papacy among the priests of the Etruscans is not repeated.[94] Consequently, by 1945 only a few teachers would have included Rosenberg's *Mythus des 20. Jahrhunderts* in preparation for their lessons.[95]

After the Second World War, the aim was to free schoolbooks from all Nazi ballast. The terms of race and consequently also the racial struggle between oriental Etruscans and Carthaginians against Nordic – Aryan – Romans were no longer allowed to be used.[96] As the forerunners of the Romans, however, the Etruscans remained present in schoolbooks until recently, even if they are actually described or dealt with to an ever lesser extent.[97] In many schoolbooks, however, certain stereotypes are repeated, such as the origin from Asia Minor, the Etruscans as the builders of the first permanent cities in Italy, fortune telling and the dark and gruesome aspects of their religion, at the centre of which is always the thought of death and the afterlife.[98]

The oriental origin of the Etruscans is only questioned in some schoolbooks from the mid-1960s onwards. Both the work *Menschen in ihrer Zeit* ('People in their Time')⁹⁹ and the new edition of *Kletts geschichtlichem Unterrichtswerk* ('Klett's History Textbook') do not consider the problem of the origin of the Etruscans. Either the origin is presented as unknown¹⁰⁰ or the 'Orient' theory and 'Autochthony' theory are placed side by side as being equally valid hypotheses.¹⁰¹ In the *Grundriss der Geschichte* ('History Outline') the question of the origin of the Etruscans is left open only in 1984.¹⁰² In all of these schoolbooks, the omission of evaluative expressions, like 'gruesome' religion, is striking. The text appears completely neutral. However, the theory that the Etruscans immigrated from the Orient at the beginning of the first millennium can also be found in relatively new history books, for example, in the 1995 edition of *Geschichte und Geschehen* ('History and Things Past')¹⁰³ and in the 1992 edition of *Europäisches Geschichtsbuch* ('European History Book'),¹⁰⁴ an initiative created by numerous European publishers under the supervision of Hachette. In *Geschichte und Geschehen*, the pupil is given a map that shows the situation on the Apennine peninsula in 264 BC, with small arrows indicating the immigration of the Etruscans (from the sea), Carthaginians, Greeks, Celts and Illyrians. However, there is no indication of when this was meant to have happened.¹⁰⁵

The demonisation of the Etruscans, as propagated by Alfred Rosenberg based on the hair-raising translations of Albert Grünwedel, continued to appear in German school books until the mid-1960s. The origin of the Etruscans from the Orient, and their gloomy and gruesome religion always focussed on death and the afterlife with their fortune tellers, contributes to this demonisation and certainly continued to dominate, at least to a certain extent, the public image of the Etruscans. While scientific research in Germany has remained rather dry and neutral since the nineteenth century, and therefore art and literature did not stimulate any reception of the Etruscans, the Etruscans are still perceived as 'dark' and 'mysterious' by the general public. Certain popular science books also contributed to this until the 1970s.¹⁰⁶

Eckart Peterich (1900-1968), who grew up in the German colony in Florence and Forte dei Marmi and also spent most of his later life in Italy, included a diary entry on 31 May 1960 that reflected the public perception of the Etruscans in his lifetime:

> The impressive images on the Etruscan sarcophagi represent the individual soul, since the Etruscans apparently had a very precise idea of the survival of the individual soul after death. They must have been good psychologists. This psychological is supplemented with them by the exuberant demonology: formation of the unconscious. The Babylonians, whose astrology is religious psychology, just as the Etruscan soul science appears to be reli-

giously conditioned, were also unsurpassable experts and performers of demons. The 'oriental' with the Etruscans may therefore be their knowledge of the soul paired with knowledge of ghosts and spook: connections that can only be recognised if we succeed in developing a 'stylistic science' based on the history of religion.[107]

Notes

1. Staatliche Museen zu Berlin, *Die Etrusker und Europa*, Katalog der Ausstellung Altes Museum Berlin 28 February – 31 May 1993 (Milan: Fabbri, 1992). The exhibition was visited by 190.000 visitors: https://www.berlin.de/chronik/index.php?-date=1993-02-28. (Accessed December 2021).
2. Badisches Landesmuseum Karlsruhe, *Die Etrusker. Weltkultur im antiken Italien*, Katalog der Ausstellung 16 December 2017 – 17 June 2018 (Darmstadt: Badisches Landesmuseum Karlsruhe, 2017).
3. Johann Caspar Goethe, *Viaggio per l'Italia fatto nel anno MDCCXL ed in XLII Lettere descritto da J.C.G. (Reise durch Italien im Jahre 1740. Viaggio per l'Italia).* Herausgegeben von der Deutsch-Italienischen Vereinigung e.V. Frankfurt am Main. Aus dem Italienischen übersetzt und kommentiert von Albert Meier unter Mitarbeit von Heide Hollmer. Illustrationen von Elmar Hillebrand (Munich: Deutscher Klassiker Verlag, 1986), pp. 355-356. Carlo Knight, 'Il Viaggio per l'Italia (1740) del padre di Goethe', *Rendiconti dell'Accademia di Archeologia, Lettere e Belle Arti*, vol. 76 (Naples: Giannini, 2011-2013), pp. 185-226.
4. Fabrizio Vannini, 'Gori, Anton Francesco', in *Dizionario Biografico degli Italiani*, vol. 58 (Rome: Treccani, 2002).
5. 'Viterbo, which [...] is also the hometown of the deceitful Dominican monk and historian Giovanni Annio' ('Viterbo, das [...] zugleich die Vaterstadt des verlogenen Dominikanermönchs und Geschichtsschreibers Giovanni Annio ist'). Johann Caspar Goethe, *Reise durch Italien im Jahre 1740. Viaggio per l'Italia.* p. 318. About Annio da Viterbo: Mauro Cristofani, 'Der "etruskische Mythos" zwischen dem 16. und 18. Jahrhundert', in *Die Etrusker und Europa*, Katalog der Ausstellung Altes Museum Berlin 28.02. – 31.05.1993, Massimo Pallottino and Irma Wehgartner (eds) (Milan: Fabbri, 1993); Riccardo Fubini, 'Nanni, Giovanni', in *Dizionario Biografico degli Italiani*, vol. 77 (Rome: Treccani, 2012). All translations from the German quotes in this contribution are by Martin Miller.
6. *Antiquitatum variarum voluminia XVII a venerando et sacrae theologiae et praedicatorii ordinis professore Ioanni Annio* (Rome: Eucharius Silber, 1498).
7. Johann Caspar Goethe, *Reise durch Italien im Jahre 1740. Viaggio per l'Italia*, p. 350.
8. Johann Wolfgang von Goethe, *Italienische Reise* (Tübingen: Cotta, 1816-1817).
9. '[...] die ungeheuren Substruktionen der babylonisch übereinander getürmten Kirchen, wo der heilige Franziskus ruht, ließ ich links mit Abneigung...'. Johann Wolfgang Goethe, *Italienische Reise*, mit vierzig Zeichnungen des Autors, Herausgegeben und mit einem Nachwort versehen von Christoph Michel (Frankfurt: Insel-Verlag, 1976), p. 153.
10. 'Auch die römischen Altertümer fangen mich an zu freuen. Geschichte, Inschriften, Münzen, von denen ich sonst nichts wissen mochte, alles drängt sich heran. Wie mir's in der Naturgeschichte erging, geht es auch hier. Denn an diesem Ort knüpft sich die ganze Geschichte der Welt an, und ich zähle einen zweiten Geburtstag, eine wahre Wiedergeburt, von dem Tage, da ich Rom betrat'. *Ibid.*, p. 194.
11. Johann Gottfried Herder, *Italienische Reise. Briefe und Tagebuchaufzeichnungen 1788-1789*, herausgegeben, kommentiert und mit einem Nachwort versehen von Albert Meier und Heide Hollmer (Munich: Dtv, 1988).
12. Johann Gottfried Seume, *Spaziergang nach Syrakus im Jahre 1802* (Brunswick and Leipzig: Vieweg, 1803).
13. Thomas Szabo, 'Via Francigena', in *Lexikon des Mittelalters*, vol. 8 (Munich: LexMa, 1997), col. 1610-1611.
14. Sabine Gruber, 'Rom und Italien', in *August Wilhelm Schlegel. Aufbruch ins romantische Universum*, Claudia Bamberg and Cornelia Ilbrig (eds) (Frankfurt: Göttinger Verlag der Kunst, 2017), pp. 126-135 (p. 130). During his first trip to Italy

(December 1804 – June 1805) Schlegel saw Etruscan antiquities, for example in Rome (February – May 1805) and Florence (May 1805). During his second trip to Italy (September 1815 – February 1816), he visited mainly Pisa and Florence, where Albertine de Staël married on 20 February 1816. Schlegel definitely visited Florence, Volterra and Carrara.

15. '[…] viereckig gehaun nach etrurischem Richtmaaß'. August Wilhelm Schlegel, *Rom. Elegie* (Berlin: Unger, 1805).
16. Jürgen Hanneder, 'August Wilhelm Schlegel und die Begründung der Indologie in Deutschland', in *August Wilhelm Schlegel. Aufbruch ins romantische Universum*, pp. 192-195.
17. August Wilhelm Schlegel, *Antiquitates Etruscae* (SLUB Dresden, Sign. Mscr.Dresd.e, 90, XLII, 2); Eduard Böcking, *Opuscula quae Augustus Guilelmus Schlegelius latine scripta reliquit* (Leipzig: Weidmannos, 1848), pp. 115-286. A critical edition with comments by Martin Miller and Sabine Gruber and a translation by Michael Braunger is being prepared by Georg Braungart in the series 'August Wilhelm Schlegel: Kritische Ausgabe der Vorlesungen', ed. by Georg Braungart, vol. 5-6 (Bonner Vorlesungen [1818–1845]) (in preparation).
18. URL: https://siusa.archivi.beniculturali.it/cgi-bin/pagina.pl?TipoPag=prodpersona&Chiave=48491 (Accessed December 2021).
19. Ève Gran-Aymerich, *Les chercheurs de passé* (Paris: CNRS Éditions, 2007), p. 887.
20. Domenico Caccamo, 'Ciampi, Sebastiano', in *Dizionario biografico degli italiani*, vol. 25 (Rome: Treccani, 1981).
21. Anna Viola Siebert, *August Kestner, Etrurien und die Etruskologie*, Museum Kestnerianum, 14 (Hannover: Museën für Kulturgeschichte, 2010).
22. Giovanna Colonna, 'Das romantische Abenteuer', in Staatliche Museen zu Berlin, *Die Etrusker und Europa*, (Berlin: SMPK Fabbri Editori, 1993) pp. 322-337; Anita Rieche, 'Eduard Gerhard und die frühe Geschichte des "Instituto di corrispondenza archeologica"', in *Dem Archäologen Eduard Gerhard 1795-1867 zu seinem Geburtstag*, Henning Wrede (ed.), Winckelmann-Institut der Humboldt-Universität zu Berlin 2 (Berlin: Arenhövel, 1997), pp. 35-42.
23. Karl Otfried Müller, *Die Etrusker* (Breslau: J. Max, 1828); Wolfhart Unte and Helmut Rohlfing, *Quellen für eine Biographie Karl Otfried Müllers (1797-1840). Bibliographie und Nachlaß* (Hildesheim: Olms, 1997).
24. Gertrud Platz-Horster, 'Eduard Gerhard und das Etruskische Cabinet im Alten Museum', in *Die Etrusker und Europa* (Berlin, Staatliche Museen zu Berlin, 2020), pp. 362-365.
25. Marion Ónodi, *Isolde Kurz. Leben und Prosawerk als Ausdruck zeitgenössischer und menschlich-individueller Situation von der Mitte des 19. bis zur Mitte des 20. Jahrhunderts* (Frankfurt: Peter Lang, 1989); Sibylle Lewitscharoff, Jutta Bendt, Karin Schmidgall, 'In der inneren Heimat oder nirgends. Isolde Kurz (1853-1944)', *Marbacher Magazin* vol. 104 (Stuttgart: Deutsche Schillergesellschaft, 2003); Isolde Kurz, *Ein Splitter vom Paradies. Erzählungen und Erinnerungen aus dem Florenz der Jahrhundertwende*, Herausgegeben von Gisela Schlientz (Stuttgart-Leipzig: Hohenheim, 2003).
26. Isolde Kurz, 'Edgar Kurz (Ein Lebensbild)', in *Florentinische Erinnerungen*, Isolde Kurz (ed.) (Munich and Leipzig: Georg Müller, 1920) pp. 157-175; Karin Schmidgall, 'Leben und Schreiben', in Sibylle Lewitscharoff, Jutta Bendt, Karin Schmidgall, 'In der inneren Heimat oder nirgends. Isolde Kurz (1853-1944)', pp. 71-77.
27. Isolde Kurz, 'Adolf Hildebrand' (zu seinem 60. Geburtstage), in *Florentinische Erinnerungen*, Isolde Kurz (ed.), pp. 176-219; Sigrid Esche-Braunfels, *Aldolf von Hildebrand* (Munich: Deutscher Verlag Für Kunstwissenschaft, 1993).
28. Ulrich Schulte-Wülwer, *Sehnsucht nach Arkadien. Schleswig-Holsteinische Künstler in Italien* (Heide: Boyens Buchverlag, 2009) pp. 346-349.
29. Isolde Kurz, 'Von Arnold Böcklin', in *Florentinische Erinnerungen*, Isolde Kurz (ed.), pp. 220-232; Norbert Glas, 'Böcklins Biographie', in *Arnold Böcklin: eine Studie aus dem Nachlass*, Norbert Glass (ed.) (Basel: Perseus, 2012) pp. 11-29.
30. Rainer Hillenbrand, *Isolde Kurz als Erzählerin. Ein Überblick* (Frankfurt: Peter Lang, 2000), p. 10.
31. Anna M. Voci, *Karl Hillebrand. Ein deutscher Weltbürger* (Rome: Istituto Italiano di Studi Germanici, 2015).
32. Theodor Däubler, *Das Nordlicht. Florentiner Ausgabe* (Munich-Leipzig: Georg Müller, 1910); Friedhelm Kemp, 'Theodor Däubler gegen den Strich', *Marbacher Magazin*, vol. 30 (Stuttgart: Deutsche Schillergesellschaft, 1984).
33. Fritz Homeyer, *Deutsche Juden als Bibliophilen und Antiquare* (Tübingen: Mohr, 1966), pp. 22-25.
34. Isolde Kurz, 'Wir begründen ein Weltbad', in *Die Pilgerfahrt nach dem Unerreichlichen. Lebensrückschau*, Isolde Kurz (ed.) (Tübingen: Rainer Wunderlich Verlag, 1938). Eckart Peterich, 'Zwischen Meer und Marmor', in *Fragmente aus Italien. Aus dem Nachlass herausgegeben von H.*

Melchers, Eckart Peterich (ed.) (Munich: Prestel, 1969), pp. 107-128.
35. For example: Isolde Kurz, *Florentiner Novellen* (Stuttgart-Berlin: G.J. Göschensche Verlagsbuchhandlung, 1890).
36. For example: Isolde Kurz, *Florentinische Erinnerungen*.
37. 'The two of them were joined by Martin Francke's schoolfriend, the archaeologist Dr. Karl Johannsen who died a few years later during the excavations on Crete. For his sake, the friends made a long detour and walked through the Umbrian and part of the Tuscan in the footsteps of the Etruscans' ('Den Beiden schloß sich als dritter Reisekamerad noch ein Studienfreund Martin Franckes an, der Archäologe Dr. Karl Johannsen, der einige Jahre später bei den Ausgrabungen auf Kreta starb. Ihm zuliebe machten die Freunde einen starken Umweg und durchwanderten zu Fuß das Umbrische und einen Teil des Toskanischen auf den Spuren der Etrusker'). Isolde Kurz, 'Solleone', in *Der Ruf des Pan. Zwei Geschichten von Liebe und Tod*, Isolde Kurz (ed.) (Tübingen: R. Wunderlich, 1928); on the novel *Solleone*, see Rainer Hillenbrand, *Isolde Kurz als Erzählerin. Ein Überblick*, pp. 102-105.
38. Monte Giovi. *"Fulmini e saette": da luogo di culto a fortezza d'altura nel territorio di Fiesole etrusca*, Luca Cappucini (ed.), Series IdA – Insediamenti d'Altura, vol. 2 (Florence: All'insegna del giglio, 2017).
39. Johannes Hösle, 'Eckart Peterich', *Studi Germanici*, vol. 7 (1969), pp. 369-382.
40. Eckart Peterich, *Italien*, 3 vols. (Munich: Prestel Verlag, 1958, 1961, 1965).
41. Atti del Primo Convegno Nazionale Etrusco, 27 April – 4 May 1926 (Florence, 1926), pp. 175-184.
42. The following comment by Peterich on the description of the antiquities in the Museo Nazionale Etrusco di Villa Giulia is significant: 'If you disregard the few larger sculptures in the museum, we mainly wandered through a small-art-museum, which only provides real enjoyment after repeated studies, but can then inspire, even arouse passions. For the travel book writer, describing such small-art-museums is always particularly difficult, which is why I would like to ask my readers for your forbearance if my brief tour of the Museo di Villa Giulia should have bored them' ('Wenn man von den wenigen größeren Plastiken des Museums absieht, haben wir vor allem ein Kleinkunstmuseum durchwandert, das nur bei wiederholtem Studium wirklichen Genuß gewährt, dann aber begeistern, ja Leidenschaften erwecken kann. Für den Reisebücherschreiber ist die Schilderung solcher Kleinkunstmuseen immer besonders schwierig, weswegen ich denn meine Leser um Nachsicht bitten möchte, wenn meine kurze Führung durch das Museo di Villa Giulia sie gelangweilt haben sollte'). Eckart Peterich, *Italien*, vol. 2: *Rom und Latium, Neapel und Kampanien* (Munich: Prestel Verlag, 1961), p. 345; The section on the history of Umbria and Tuscany begins in the early Middle Ages: Eckart Peterich, *Italien*, vol. 1: *Oberitalien, Toskana, Umbrien* (Munich: Prestel Verlag, 1958) pp. 501-542.
43. Eckart Peterich, *Gesammelte Gedichte* (Munich: Prestel Verlag, 1967).
44. Written in 1961: Eckart Peterich, 'Exkurs über die Etrusker', in *Fragmente aus Italien. Aus dem Nachlass herausgegeben von H. Melchers*, Eckart Peterich (ed.) (Munich: Prestel Verlag, 1969) pp. 316-324.
45. Written in 1961: Eckart Peterich, 'Rom und die Geschichte Italiens', in *Fragmente aus Italien. Aus dem Nachlass herausgegeben von H. Melchers*, pp. 306-339.
46. Isolde Kurz, 'Wir begründen ein Weltbad', in *Erzählungen und Erinnerungen. Herausgegeben von Andreas Vogt*, Isolde Kurz (ed.) (Tübingen: Klöpfer & Meyer, 2012) pp. 209-211; 'Das Hildebrandthaus, das während des Krieges von einer recht unerfreulichen Persönlichkeit, dem Schriftsteller Curzio Malaparte, erworben worden war, ist vor einigen Jahren abgerissen worden' ('The Hildebrandt house, which was bought during the war by a rather unpleasant personality, the writer Curzio Malaparte, was demolished a few years ago'): Eckart Peterich, 'Zwischen Meer und Marmor', in *Fragmente aus Italien. Aus dem Nachlass herausgegeben von H. Melchers*, pp.115-116.
47. Gabriele D'Annunzio, *Forse che si, forse che no* (Milan: Treves, 1910); Gabriele D'Annunzio, *Vielleicht, vielleicht auch nicht*, translated by Karl Gustav Vollmoeller (Leipzig: Matthes & Seitz Berlin, 1910); Alessia Dei, *Volterra nel romanzo Forse che sì forse che no di Gabriele D'Annunzio* (Pisa: Il Campano, 2008); Maurizio Harari, 'Gabriele D'Annunzios beunruhigde Antike', in *Ruinen in der Moderne. Archäologie und die Künste*, ed. by Eva Koszisky (Berlin: Reimer, 2011), pp. 261-272; Curzio Malaparte, *Maledetti Toscani* (Rome Milan: Aria d'Italia, 1956); Curzio Malaparte, *Those Cursed Tuscans* (Athens, Ohio: Ohio University Press, 1964). Sabine Witt, *Curzio Malaparte (1898-1957). Autobiographisches Erzählen zwischen Realität und Fiktion*, Series Grundlagen der Italianistik, vol. 8 (Frankfurt: Peter Lang, 2008).

48. Filippo Delpino, 'Das Zeitalter des Positivismus', in Staatliche Museen zu Berlin, *Die Etrusker und Europa*, pp. 340-347.
49. Martin Miller, 'Archeologi e linguisti tedeschi e l'Istituto di Studi Etruschi prima della Seconda Guerra Mondiale', in *La construction de l'étruscologie au début du XXe siècle*, Marie-Laurence Haack and Martin Miller (eds) (Bordeaux: Ausonius Édition, 2015) pp. 107-119, doi: http://books.openedition.org/ausonius/5448. (Accessed May 2023). See also Massimo Pallottino's remarks on the need to combine data-driven historical scholarship with enthusiasm and passion in 'Scienza e poesia dell'Etruria', *Quaderni dell'Associazione Culturale Italiana*, 24 (1957), pp. 5-22 (p. 21); the article has been published in English as 'In Search of Etruria: Science and the imagination', in D. H. Lawrence, *Etruscan Places* (Siena: Nuova immagine, 1986), pp. 11-28.
50. Guido Kaschnitz von Weinberg, 'Studien zur etruskischen und frühromischen Porträtkunst', *Römische Mitteilungen*, vol. 41 (1926), pp. 133-211. Guido Kaschnitz von Weinberg, 'Bemerkungen zur Struktur der altitalischen Plastik', *Studi Etruschi*, vol. 7 (1933), pp. 135-196.
51. Wulf Raeck and Claudia Becker, *Guido von Kaschnitz-Weinberg: Gelehrter zwischen Archäologie und Politik* (Frankfurt: Societäts Verlag, 2016).
52. Martin Miller, 'Alfred Rosenberg, die Etrusker und die Romfrage', in *La construction de l'étruscologie au début du XXe siècle*, pp. 81-94.
53. The first edition appeared in 1930; the quote comes from the second edition: Alfred Rosenberg, *Der Mythus des 20. Jahrhunderts. Eine Wertung der seelisch-geistigen Gestaltenkämpfe unserer Zeit* (Munich: Hoheneichen-Verlag, 1931); English translation: Alfred Rosenberg, *The Myth of the 20th Century* (La Vergne, 2017), URL: https://archive.org/details/TheMythOfThe20th-Century. (Accessed December 2021).
54. Alfred Rosenberg, *Der Mythus des 20. Jahrhunderts*, p. 59.
55. 'Als Prätor von Sardinien, als Konsul von Spanien, dann als Zensor in Rom kämpfte er gegen Bestechung, Wucher und Verschwendungssucht. Die schmutzige Menschenflut aus Afrika und Syrien einzudämmen, schien ihm aber unmöglich. Da ging der rotblonde, große Mann von Eisen hin und stürzte sich ins Schwert'. ('As praetor of Sardinia, consul in Spain, and finally censor in Rome, he fought against corruption, usury and extravagance. In this he resembled Cato the elder who, after a fruitless struggle to stem the utter decay of the state, threw himself upon his own sword'). *Ibid.*, pp. 60-61.
56. 'Der blauäugige gewaltige Sulla' ('The powerful, blue eyed Sulla'), *Ibid.*, p. 61.
57. 'Der rein nordische Kopf des Augustus' ('The pure Nordic head Augustus'). *Ibid.*, pp. 31, 61.
58. *Ibid.*, pp. 60-62.
59. *Ibid.*, pp. 65-72.
60. 'Die Zerstörung Karthagos war eine rassengeschichtlich ungeheuer wichtige Tat: dadurch wurde auch die spätere mittel- und westeuropäische Kultur von den Ausdünstungen dieses phönizischen Pestherdes verschont. Die Weltgeschichte hätte auch sonst vielleicht einen anderen Gang genommen, wenn gleich der Niederlegung Karthagos auch die Zerstörung aller anderen syrischen und vorderasiatischen semitisch-jüdischen Zentralen vollkommen gelungen wäre. Die Tat des Titus kam jedoch zu spät: der vorderasiatische Schmarotzer saß nicht mehr in Jerusalem selbst, sondern hatte bereits seine stärksten Saugarme von Ägypten und ‚Hellas' aus gegen Rom ausgestreckt. Und er wirkte auch schon in Rom!' ('The destruction of Carthage was a deed of superlative import in racial history: by it even the later cultures of central and Western Europe were spared the infection of this Phoenician pestilence. World history might well have taken a very different course had the obliteration of Carthage been accompanied by a total annihilation of all the other Semitic Jewish centres in the near east. The act of Titus came too late. By then, the near eastern parasite was no longer centered in Jerusalem, but had already spread its thickest tentacles from Egypt and Hellas to Rome itself, to which city everyone possessed of ambition and greedy for profit was drawn. And he already worked in Rome!'). *Ibid.*, p. 60.
61. *Ibid.*, pp. 66-67.
62. *Ibid.*, pp. 67-68.
63. '[…] die Kraft des Ermordeten auf die Priester über, die Vertreter der "Auserwählten" (Rasna, Rasena), wie die Etrusker sich, ähnlich den Juden, zu nennen beliebten'. *Ibid.*, p. 68.
64. 'Die Etrusker bieten ein typisches Beispiel dafür, dass für sie die griechische Glaubens- und Lebensform keinen Fortschritt, keine mögliche Veredelung bildeten. Ebenso wie die anderen Vorderasiaten hatten sie einst atlantisch-nordische Mythen vorgefunden, sie werden dann zwar auch von griechischer Kultur überzogen, sie ahmten, so gut sie konnten, griechische Plastik und Zeichnung nach, sie eigneten sich auch den hellenischen Olymp an, und doch ist alles das entartet, in sein Gegenteil verwandelt worden'. *Ibid.*, p. 65.

65. 'Weiter haben uns die Etrusker zwar einen Haufen obszöner Gebräuche und Denkmäler hinterlassen, aber auch nicht einen Ansatz, der schöpferische seelische Fähigkeiten vermuten ließe'. *Ibid.*, p. 134.
66. Albert Grünwedel, *Tusca*. 1. Die Agramer Mumienbinden. 2. Die Inschrift des Cippus von Perugia. 3. Die Pulena-Rolle. 4. Das Bleitäfelchen von Magliano. 5. Die Leber von Piacenza. 6. Das Golini-Grab I. 7. Die Inschrift von Capua. Unter Zuziehung anderen sachlich zugehörigen archäologischen Materials übersetzt (Leipzig: Hiersemann, 1922).
67. '[…] die vorgefasste Interpretation zunehmend Vorrang vor der Philologie', Albert Grünwedel, *Briefwechsel und Dokumente, Asien- und Afrikastudien*, vol. 9, Hartmund Walravens (ed.) (Wiesbaden: Harrassowitz Verlag, 2001), p. X.
68. Ernst Waldschmidt, 'Albert Grünwedel', *Ostasiatische Zeitschrift*, N.S. 11 (1935), pp. 215-219; Johannes Schubert, 'Albert Grünwedel und sein Werk', *Artibus Asiae*, 6 (1936), pp. 124-142; Hemut Hoffmann, 'Grünwedel, Alfred', *Neue Deutsche Biographie*, vol. 7 (Berlin: Duncker & Humblot, 1966), pp. 204-205; Hartmut Walravens, 'Albert Grünwedels Briefwechsel. Eine neue Quelle zur Vorgeschichte des Museums für Indische Kunst', *Jahrbuch Preußischer Kulturbesitz*, 25 (1988), pp. 125-150; Albert Grünwedel, *Briefwechsel und Dokumente, Asien- und Afrikastudien*, vol. 9, pp. IX-XI; Werner Sundermann, 'Grünwedel, Albert', in *Encyclopaedia Iranica*, vol. 11, *Giōni-Harem I* (New York: Encyclopaedia Iranica Foundation, 2003), pp. 377-378; Hartmut Walravens, 'Albert Grünwedel – Leben und Werk', in *Turfan revisited. The first Century of Research into the Arts and Cultures of the Silk Road*, Monographien zur Indischen Archäologie, Kunst und Philologie, ed. by Desmond Durkin-Meisterernst and others, vol. 17 (Berlin: Reimer, 2004), pp. 363-370; Caren Dreyer, *Albert Grünwedel: Zeichnungen und Bilder von der Seidenstraße im Museum für Asiatische Kunst* (Berlin: EB-Verlag, 2011), pp. 2-31; Caren Dreyer, 'Albert Grünwedel (1856–1935). Ein Leben für die Wissenschaft', in *Auf Grünwedels Spuren. Restaurierung und Forschung an zentralasiatischen Wandmalereien*, ed. by Toralf Gabsch, Ausstellung des Museums für Asiatische Kunst – Staatliche Museen zu Berlin (Leipzig: Koehler & Amelang, 2012) pp. 14-29.
69. Gustav Herbig, *Die Geheimsprache der Etrusker*, Philosophisch-philologische und historische Klasse, (Munich: Verlag der Bayerischen Akademie der Wissenschaften, 1923), pp. 1-25.
70. '[…] um des Verfassers willen und um der deutschen Wissenschaft willen'. Wilhelm Schubart, 'Grünwedel, Albert: Tusca – Herbig, Gustav: Die Geheimsprache der Etrusker', *OLZ*, vol. 27 (1924), col. 179-180; *Studien zum Mythus des XX. Jahrhunderts*, Amtliche Beilage zum Kirchlichen Anzeiger für die Erzdiözese Köln (Köln, 1934), pp. 9-10.
71. Eberhardt Richter and Manfred Taube, *Asienwissenschaftliche Beiträge Johannes Schubert in memoriam*, Veröffentlichungen des Museums für Völkerkunde, vol. 32 (Berlin: Akademie Verlag, 1978). Johannes Schubert was not a student of Albert Grünwedel, as Caren Dreyer assumed: Caren Dreyer, 'Albert Grünwedel (1856–1935). Ein Leben für die Wissenschaft', p. 28.
72. 'Ohne jegliche Rücksicht auf die gesamte etruskologische Forschung – und das absichtlich! – wird eine völlig neue Lösung des Problems u. sw. eine sogenannte magische Entschleierung der bekanntesten und hauptsächlichsten etruskischen Schriftdenkmäler geboten, die freilich die ganze Kultur dieses Volkes in einem fürchterlichen Lichte zeigt'. A few pages later, Johannes Schubert somewhat toned down his criticism, citing Emil Vetter: Johannes Schubert, 'Albert Grünwedel und sein Werk', *Artibus Asiae*, vol. 6 (1936), pp. 134, 136-137; Emil Vetter, 'Der gegenwärtige Stand der etruskischen Sprachforschung', in: *Verhandlungen der 57. Versammlung Deutscher Philologen und Schulmänner zu Salzburg vom 25. bis 28. September 1929* (Leipzig-Berlin, 1930).
73. Letter from Dr. Johannes Schubert at Leipzig to Otto Ilzhöfer 11 January 1942: Albert Grünwedel, *Briefwechsel und Dokumente, Asien- und Afrikastudien*, vol. 9, Hartmund Walravens (ed.), pp. 198-199. Theodor Kluge used the term '*pathological*' in 1941 in his report on Otto Ilzhöfer's Grünwedel -bibliography: *Ibid.*, p. 197.
74. Hanns Oertel, 'Ernst Kuhn. Zu seinem 70. Geburtstag (7. Februar 1916), in *Aufsätze zur Kultur- und Sprachgeschichte vornehmlich des Orients. Ernst Kuhn zum 70. Geburtstag am 7. Februar 1916 gewidmet von Freunden und Schülern*, Lucian Shermann and C. Bezold (eds) (Breslau: Marcus, 1916), pp. IX-XI; Friedrich Wilhelm, 'Kuhn, Ernst', *Neue Deutsche Biographie*, vol. 13 (Berlin: Duncker & Humblot, 1982), p. 257.
75. 'Ob ich die Mumientexte übersetze, weiß ich nicht. Der Inhalt ist eine so schandvolle Verhöhnung aller menschlichen Rechte, dass ich in keiner Sprache der Erde die nötigen Ausdrücke finden kann. Und die griechische, die allein solche Dinge ausdrücken könnte, möchte ich mit solchem Kot nicht beschmutzen', Letter from Albert

Grünwedel to Ernst Kuhn May 31, 1916: Albert Grünwedel, *Briefwechsel und Dokumente, Asien- und Afrikastudien*, vol. 9, ed. by Hartmund Walravens, pp. 97-98 no. 109; Hartmut Walravens, 'Albert Grünwedels Briefwechsel. Eine neue Quelle zur Vorgeschichte des Museums für Indische Kunst', *Jahrbuch Preußischer Kulturbesitz*, 25 (1988), pp. 144-145. Another letter about the work on the Etruscan texts: Letter from Albert Grünwedel to Ernst Kuhn, 27 June 1916: Albert Grünwedel, *Briefwechsel und Dokumente, Asien- und Afrikastudien*, vol. 9, Hartmut Walravens (ed.), pp. 100-101 (letter no. 111).

76. Letter from Albert Grünwedel to Ernst Kuhn 22 June 1918 and letter from Ernst Kuhn to Albert Grünwedel 23 June 1916: *Ibid.*, pp. 98-100 (letter no. 110); Hartmut Walravens, 'Albert Grünwedels Briefwechsel. Eine neue Quelle zur Vorgeschichte des Museums für Indische Kunst', pp. 144-145.

77. Hanns Oertel, 'Ernst Kuhn. Zu seinem 70. Geburtstag', p. IX.

78. Eugen Härle and Otto Conrad, 'Prof. Dr. Ernst Trumpp (1828–1885)', in *Ilsfeld in Geschichte und Gegenwart. Ein Heimatbuch für Ilsfeld, Auenstein und Schozach* (Ilsfeld: Gemeinde Ilsfeld, 1989), pp. 602-605.

79. Albert Grünwedel, *Briefwechsel und Dokumente, Asien- und Afrikastudien*, vol. 9, Hartmut Walravens (ed.), p. 181 note 186.

80. O. Ilzhöfer and Albert Grünwedel, *Palaio-Tuscoiudaica. Etruskertum-Judentum, oder: Der zusammenbrechende Saustall nach Albert Grünwedels bisher völlig unbekanntem, urtextlichen Belastungs- und Beweismaterial zum Problem der Magie, des Zauberwesens und Hexentums* (Munich, Deutsches und lateinisches Typoskript in der Staatsbibliothek München, 1939). There are widespread anti-Jewish remarks in Grünwedel's letters and private notes. The word 'Jude' (Jew) is often used as a swear word to refer to someone as an illiterate, unscientific and arrogant parvenu: Albert Grünwedel, *Briefwechsel und Dokumente, Asien- und Afrikastudien*, vol. 9, Hartmut Walravens (ed.), pp. IX-X.

81. Barbara Schier, 'Hexenwahn und Hexenverfolgung. Rezeption und politische Zurichtung eines kulturwissenschaftlichen Themas im Dritten Reich', in *Bayerisches Jahrbuch für Volkskunde*, (Munich: Institut für Volkskunde, 1990), pp. 49-57.

82. Alfred Rosenberg, *Der Mythus des 20. Jahrhunderts*, pp. 70-71.

83. Miloslav Szabó, 'Rasse, Orientalismus und Religion im antisemitischen Geschichtsbild Alfred Rosenbergs', in *Antisemitische Geschichtsbilder, Antisemitismus: Geschichte und Strukturen 5*, Werner Bergmann and Ulrich Sieg (eds) (Essen: Klartext, 2009), pp. 212, 222-223.

84. Letter from Albert Grünwedel to Ernst Kuhn 27 June 1916: Albert Grünwedel, *Briefwechsel und Dokumente, Asien- und Afrikastudien*, vol. 9, Hartmut Walravens (ed.), pp. 100-101 (letter no. 111); Hartmut Walravens, 'Albert Grünwedels Briefwechsel. Eine neue Quelle zur Vorgeschichte des Museums für Indische Kunst', p. 145.

85. Felix Wiedemann, *Rassenmutter und Rebellin. Hexenbilder in Romantik, völkischer Bewegung, Neuheidentum und Feminismus* (Würzbug: Königshausen & Neumann, 2007), pp. 174-175; Felix Wiedemann, 'Altes Wissen oder "Fremdkörper im deutschen Volksglauben"? Hexendeutungen im Nationalsozialismus zwischen Neuheidentum, Antiklerikalismus und Antisemitismus', in *Die völkisch-religiöse Bewegung im Nationalsozialismus. Eine Beziehungs- und Konfliktgeschichte*, Schriften des Hannah-Arendt-Instituts für Totalitarismusforschung, Uwe Puschner and Clemens Vollnhals (eds), vol. 47 (Göttingen: Vandenhoeck & Ruprecht, 2012), pp. 444-445.

86. Alfred Rosenberg, *Handbuch der Romfrage*, vol. I (A - K) (Munich: Hoheneichen, 1940), pp. 394-409; Martin Miller, 'Alfred Rosenberg, die Etrusker und die Romfrage', in *L'étruscologie au XXe siècle: Les Étrusques au temps du fascisme et du nazisme*, Marie-Laurence Haack and Martin Miller (eds) (Bordeaux: Ausonius Éditions, 2016), pp. 89-92, doi:10.4000/books.ausonius.10620. (Accessed May 2023).

87. Raffaella Da Vela, 'L'immagine degli Etruschi nell'educazione scolastica in Italia e in Germania (1928–1945)', *L'étruscologie au XXe siècle: Les Étrusques au temps du fascisme et du nazisme*, pp. 17-66.

88. Reichs- und Preußisches Ministerium für Wissenschaft, Erziehung und Volksbildung, *Erziehung und Unterricht in der Höheren Schule. Amtliche Ausgabe des Reichs- und Preußischen Ministeriums für Wissenschaft, Erziehung, und Volksbildung* (Berlin: Weidmann, 1938), pp. 91-93; Stefan Bittner, 'Die Entwicklung des Althistorischen Unterrichts zur Zeit des Nationalsozialismus', in *Antike und Altertumswissenschaft in der Zeit von Faschismus und Nationalsozialismus*, ed. by Beat Näf, Kolloquium Universität Zürich 14.-17. Oktober 1998 (Mandelbachtal–Cambridge: Edition Cicero, 2001) pp. 285-303; Johann Chapoutot, *Le national-socialisme et l'Antiquité* (Paris: PUF, 2014), pp. 95-98.

89. Walther Gehl, *Geschichte. 6. Klasse. Oberschulen/Gymnasien und Oberschulen in Aufbauform.*

Von der Urzeit bis zum Ende der Hohenstaufen (Breslau: Verlag Ferdinand Hirt, 1940), pp. 72-74; Marie-Laurence Haack and Martin Miller, 'Une Antiquité sélective: La disparition des Étrusques dans les manuels française et italiens du XXème siècle', in *Anabases. Traditions et Réceptions de l'Antiquité*, vol. 31 (2020), pp. 63-64.
90. Holger Germann, *Die politische Religion des Nationalsozialisten Dietrich Klagges. Ein Beitrag zur Phänomenologie der NS-Ideologie* (Frankfurt: Peter Lang, 1994); Eckhard Schimpf, *Heilig. Die Flucht des Braunschweiger Naziführers auf der Vatikan-Route nach Südamerika* (Brunswick: Appelhans, 2005).
91. Dietrich Klagges, *Geschichtsunterricht als nationalpolitische Erziehung* (Frankfurt: Verlag Moritz Diesterweg, 1937), pp. 279-286.
92. *Ibid.*, p. 281.
93. '[…] ohne dass eine beträchtliche Vermischung beider Rassen erfolgt wäre'. *Ibid.*, p. 283.
94. Walther Gehl, *Geschichte. 6. Klasse. Oberschulen/Gymnasien und Oberschulen in Aufbauform. Von der Urzeit bis zum Ende der Hohenstaufen*, pp. 115-121.
95. The first schoolbooks, written according to the 1938 curriculum, did not appear until 1940: *Ibid.* Until then, some books from the Weimar Republic were still used; see Johann Chapoutot, *Le national-socialisme et l'Antiquité*, p. 96.
96. The first post-war edition of the textbook *Grundriss der Geschichte* still contains a chapter 'Racial history of mankind' ('Rassengeschichte der Menschheit'), but the text emphasises that the question of the biological evolution of the human body has no significance for historical-cultural development: Karl Leonhardt, *Grundriss der Geschichte für die Oberstufe der Höheren Schulen, Ausgabe A, Band. I, Geschichte der Alten Welt. Von den Anfängen der Menschheit bis zum Verfall des Römischen Reiches* (Stuttgart, 1954), pp. 8-10.
97. Marie-Laurence Haack and Martin Miller, 'Une Antiquité sélective: La disparition des Étrusques dans les manuels française et italiens du XXème siècle', pp. 62-67.
98. Margarete Kirsten-Noé and Hermann Pinnow, *Geschichtliches Unterrichtswerk für die Mittelklassen. Band I, Geschichte des Altertums* (Offenburg-Stuttgart, 1951), pp. 97-98.
99. Friedrich J. Lucas and W. Hilligen, *Menschen in ihrer Zeit. Arbeitsbuch für den Geschichtsunterricht an Realschulen, Band II, Im Altertum* (Stuttgart: Klett, 1965).
100. *Ibid.*, p. 66.
101. Emil Stöckl and Otto Seis, *Kletts geschichtliches Unterrichtswerk, Ausgabe C, Band I, Urzeit und Altertum* (Stuttgart: Ernst Klett, 1965), p. 98.
102. Andreas Mehl, Helmut G. Walther and Volker Dotterweich, *Tempora. Grundriss der Geschichte, Sekundarstufe II, Band I, Altertum-Mittelalter-Frühe Neuzeit* (Stuttgart: Anbieter medimops, 1984), p. 14.
103. Ulrich Hammer, 'Rom – vom Stadtstaat zum Weltreich', in *Geschichte und Geschehen, Oberstufe, Ausgabe A, Band I* (Stuttgart: Ernst Klett, 1992) 58.
104. Frédéric Delouche, *Das europäische Geschichtsbuch: von den Anfängen bis heute* (Stuttgart: Klett-Cotta, 1992), p. 48.
105. Ulrich Hammer, 'Rom – vom Stadtstaat zum Weltreich', p. 61.
106. Sybille von Cles-Reden, *Das versunkene Volk. Welt und Land der Etrusker* (Innsbruck: Margarete Friedrich Rohrer Verlag, 1948); Werner Keller, *Denn sie entzündeten das Licht. Geschichte der Etrusker – die Lösung eines Rätsels* (Munich: DroemerKnaur, 1970); Martin Miller, 'Wissenschaft für Laien – Laien machen Wissenschaft. Populärwissenschaftliche Literatur über die Etrusker im deutschsprachigen Raum', in *L'étruscologie dans l'Europe d'après-guerre*, Marie-Laurence Haack and Martin Miller (eds) (Bordeaux, Ausonius Éditions, 2017) pp. 209-231; Marie-Laurence Haack, 'Sibylle von Cles et l'Europe des Étrusques', in *L'étruscologie dans l'Europe d'après-guerre*, pp. 233-244.
107. 'Die eindrucksvollen Bildnisse auf den etruskischen Sarkophagen stellen das Einzeln-Seelische dar, da die Etrusker offenbar vom Fortleben der Einzelseele nach dem Tode eine sehr genaue Vorstellung hatten. Sie müssen gute Psychologen gewesen sein. Dieses Psychologische wird bei ihnen durch die üppige Dämonologie ergänzt: Gestaltwerdung des Unbewußten. Auch die Babylonier, deren Astrologie religiöse Psychologie ist, wie ja auch die etruskische Seelenkunde religiös bedingt erscheint, waren ebenfalls unübertreffliche Kenner und Darsteller der Dämonen. Das "Orientalische" bei den Etruskern mag darum ihre mit Geister- und Gespensterwissen gepaarte Seelenkunde sein: Zusammenhänge, die nur erkannt werden können, wenn es uns gelingt, eine religionsgeschichtliche "Stilkunde" zu entwickeln'. Eckart Peterich, 'Aufzeichnungen und Tagebuchblätter – Italienisches Tagebuch II – Volterra, 31. Mai', in *Fragmente aus Italien. Aus dem Nachlass herausgegeben von H. Melchers*, Eckart Peterich (ed.) (Munich: Prestel, 1969), p. 106.

Mr Lawrence and Lady Larthia: D. H. Lawrence as an Apprentice Etruscologist

Marie-Laurence Haack

The study I am going to present is not that of a literary scholar,[1] but one of an etruscologist who chose to give serious consideration to *Etruscan Places* by D. H. Lawrence, a book he later called *Sketches of Etruscan Places* or *Etruscan Sketches*[2]. As indicated by the final title of *Etruscan Sketches*, Lawrence did not see the volume as a comprehensive survey on the Etruscans, instead he wished to offer the reader a series of subjective, personal impressions on the Etruscans. Therefore, modern and contemporary specialists of the Etruscans did not study these texts, quoted them unfrequently,[3] thought poorly of them[4] and many, no doubt, did not even read them. A careful reading of the text, however, demonstrates that the deliberate negligence exhibited by the author sharply contrasts with the extensive and thorough preparatory reading Lawrence did on the Etruscans. Lawrence spent several years familiarising himself with Etruscan culture, he read the main studies published by the etruscologists of his time and his opinion on their work is consistent with the precise time when etruscology was becoming an academic and scientific subject. Lawrence gave his friend Earl Brewster an outline of his project: he intended to write a book on the Etruscans, as attested to by a letter written on 25 April 1926 ('[…] doing a book on the Etruscans', *Letters*, V, 3693).[5] Interestingly, the letter was written two days before the first Convegno nazionale etrusco in 1926 (27 April – 4 May), organised by a Comitato permanente per l'Etruria created in 1925 by Italian Etruscan specialists. Before the end of the symposium, Lawrence had appropriated this subject: 'my Etruscans', he wrote twice in a letter to Dorothy Brett dated 28th April 1926: '[…] I wander about to my Etruscans. […] But I suppose I shall only go round and find my Etruscans for a bit' (*Letters*, V, 3698). Lawrence visited the sites of Cerveteri, Tarquinia, Vulci, Volterra in 1927, the year when the first journal entirely devoted to the Etruscans, *Studi Etruschi*, was published in Florence. The essays were then published in *World Today* precisely in the period the first Congresso internazionale etrusco took place in Florence and Bologna, that is from

27 April – 5 May 1928.⁶ This concomitant interest enables us to assess Lawrence's original point of view on the Etruscans. Lawrence, relying on his first experience of writing a history handbook, first carried out significant preparatory work: he read at least some recently published reviews on the Etruscans and gathered images of funereal drawings. This documentation gave Lawrence the possibility to distance himself from established science and to produce his own interpretation of some sites, of the people and in particular of the Etruscan woman.

Lawrence had no specific qualifications to write on the Etruscans. Although he attended a university course, in college he did not study in detail either ancient history or archaeology, still less the Etruscans, and he never claimed to be working as an Etruscologist. The *incipit* of *Etruscan Places* dismisses from the outset the idea that the text would offer a comprehensive survey on the Etruscans: 'The Etruscans, as everyone knows, were the people who occupied the middle of Italy in early Roman days […]'.⁷ Rather than providing an introduction on Etruscan civilisation, its historical and geographical context and its material culture, Lawrence – as shown by the expression 'as everyone knows' – chose to summarise the available knowledge on the Etruscans in a conveniently abridged form, without going any further into the different positions and avenues of research. Lawrence clearly did not want to compete with people like Pericle Ducati[8] or Antonio Minto,[9] the most famous Etruscologists of his time, but rather chose to pass on existing knowledge and continue the academic traditions of his time, including the speculations about the question of Etruscan origins.

However, Lawrence did not limit himself to taking up the ideas of established Etruscologists of his time. *Etruscan Sketches*, whatever we may say, is a history book, that is, a book whose perspective is historical, seeking to help readers understand the history of a people unknown to most. Lawrence was not alone in making a sudden start on a historical investigation. He cut his teeth by writing a history handbook, *Movements in European History,* published in 1921 and, until *Sketches of Etruscan Places* in 1927, Lawrence developed a vision of history and the Etruscans that took him from a European understanding of history to a local one, from a factual history to a transfigured vision of a time, from a school textbook to a guide for adults.

Lawrence's taste for history[10] had nothing to do with his training. We do not know if Lawrence studied history at Beauvale Board School, or later at Nottingham High School.[11] At Nottingham university college, where history was one of many subjects in the academic programme, Lawrence got the best marks of the exam session for the year 1908. A gifted student, he seemingly did not have a great deal of appreciation for the teaching skills of the teachers in his time. Once he became a teacher at Croydon's Davidson Road School, he attempted to introduce teaching methods that were original for his time.[12] According to his wife Frieda, he had his pupils play historical battles: 'In English history for instance he did not only expound the battle of Agincourt, but arranged the boys in two sides and they *fought* the battle of Agincourt over school forms and all'.[13] No doubt he wanted to avoid in turn becoming a boring teacher like the narrator of the *Schoolmaster poems*, which he had started writing in 1909, where he lashed out at 'a quarry of knowledge they hate to hunt' in 'Last Lesson of the Afternoon' (v. 4).[14]

More than in secondary education and at the university, Lawrence became versed in history through independent reading. He was interested in all periods, did not manifest any particular predilection for antiquity[15] and read, without establishing a hierarchy, local history publications as well as broad overall syntheses. The reading of Griseleia in Snotingscire *An Illustrated History from the Earliest Times and from Reliable Sources of the Parish Church of Greasly and Priory of Beauvale*, by Rodolph von Hube.,[16] Published in 1901, it offered a history of Greasley parish which inspired Lawrence's description of Beauvale Priory in *A Fragment of Stained Glass*, the first versions of which date from 1907.[17] Furthermore, in *The First Women in Love* the description of St Mary's church, in Greasley, with its tombstones of the Barber family, was also partly inspired by *Griseleia*.

This interest in history grew when Vere Henry Gratz Collins, editor of a series of school manuals for Oxford University Press, helped Lawrence, who was short of money after *The Rainbow* was banned in 1915. Sometime between July 1918 and May 1919, Vere Henry Gratz Collins offered Lawrence 50 pounds to write a textbook on European history: 'Struck by the knowledge he showed of history, I suggested to him that he might consider the idea of writing an elementary text-book for junior forms in grammar, or in upper forms in primary, schools, of European history. […] I suggested that Lawrence should not attempt to write a formal, connected, textbook, but a series of vivid sketches of movements and people'.[18] Vere Henry Gratz Collins's recommendations on the form of the book obviously made an impression on Lawrence. Not only can the expression 'series of vivid sketches of movements and people' be applied to *Etruscan Places* but it is used in a title of the book *Sketches of Etruscan Places*. To write the Oxford University Press textbook, Lawrence carried out intense documentation work. Many of the reference books used by Lawrence were in all likelihood supplied by the publishing house: Suetonius, Plutarch's *Lives*, the translation of Tacitus' *Annals* by Alfred J. Church and William J. Brodribb (1906) and *A History of Europe* by Arthur J. Grant (1906). Facing difficulties in writing,[19] Lawrence followed his sources very closely:[20] each chapter required efforts to be at the same time faithful to history and free to find its meaning. 'I am going on with the history. I have only one more chapter. Every chapter, I suffer before I can begin, because I do loathe the broken pots of historical facts. But once I can get hold of the thread of the developing significance, then I am happy, and get ahead [...]. But you'll see, when you get these 4 last chapters, the book does expand nicely and naturally. I am rather pleased with it. There is a clue of developing meaning running through it: that makes it real to me'.[21] In fact, Lawrence gained a clear idea on the way he wished to explain history. In the introduction to the book, he distinguished between good and bad history: 'The old history is abolished. The old bad history consisted of a register of facts. It drew up a chart of human events, as one might draw up a chart of the currants in a plum-pudding, merely because they happen promiscuously to be there. No more of this. The new history is different. It is [...] either graphic or scientific. Graphic history consists of stories about men and women who appear in the old records, stories as vivid and as personal as may be'.[22] Clearly, Lawrence placed his textbook on the side of good history: he did not wish to present a simple register of facts or events but rather to flesh out events by presenting 'stories as vivid and as personal as may be'.

Lawrence sought characters, without establishing a hierarchy between the past and his own time, in the seven volumes of *Decline and Fall of the Roman Empire* by Edward Gibbon,[23] published in 1776. In a letter to Cecil Gray on 18 April 1918, he wrote: 'I am reading Gibbon. I am quite happy with these old Roman Emperors – they were so out-and-out, they just did as they liked, and vogue la galère, till they were strangled. I can do with them'.[24] In his letter of 28 April 1918 to Mark Gertler, he added: 'I found a great satisfaction in reading Gibbon's *Decline and Fall of the Roman Empire* – the emperors are all so indiscriminately bad. But unfortunately, I only had the first vol. in the *Oxford Classics* – and there are seven such vols. – I must borrow the work from somewhere'.[25] In Gibbon, however, Lawrence found little information on the Etruscans, for Gibbon's focus was on the Empire and not on the Republic. Nevertheless, the few contradictory ideas expressed by Gibbon seem to have resonated with his own interests in the *Etruscan Sketches*. Whereas in the first volume of *Decline and Fall of the Roman Empire*, the Etruscans are depicted as one of Italy's peoples who brought civilisation to the Romans,[26] the fourth volume laments the influence of Etruscan immorality (a term that alludes at homosexuality) on the first Romans.[27] In a note, to lend support to his idea of Etruscan lust, Gibbon quoted well-known Greek literary sources, that all underlined Etruscan *truphè*.[28] We do not know if Lawrence took over the idea of Etruscan indecency from Gibbon, as it is so much part of the set of commonplaces that were included in any study on the Etruscans. In any case, this subject appeared very early in Lawrence's work, in the poem *Cypresses* devoted to the Etruscans and written in Fiesole in 1920, that is, one year after reading at least the first book of *Decline and Fall of the Roman Empire*: 'men of Etruria, / Whom Rome called vicious [...] Evil-yclept Etruscan? / For as to the evil / We have only Roman word for it'[29] and it was used by Lawrence to capture the reader's attention at the very beginning of *Etruscan Sketches*: 'Besides, the Etruscans were vicious. We know it, because their enemies and exterminators said so.'[30] Gibbon's point of view on the Etruscans fits in with a general vision of antiquity which also influenced *Etruscan Sketches*. Gibbon put forward the idea of the fragility and the end of civilisations,[31] of danger and barbarism from the north, and he criticised the destruction of the classic mind by the victory of the Church.[32] The picture that Gibbon painted of the 2nd century AD as a golden age thanks to the enlightened policies of moderate rulers, that subsequently fell victim to barbarity and religious doctrine[33] is not without similarities with the idyllic Etruria described by D. H. Lawrence in his *Etruscan Sketches*: a peaceful and prosperous country forcefully eliminated by barbaric hordes. More fundamentally, as Gibbon attributed the fall of the Roman Empire to cyclical causes so that the empire was supposed to be a victim of a natural cycle in which the beginning, childhood and maturity were followed by death, the Etruscan civilisation, according to Lawrence, after a period of maturity, was supposed to have slowly degenerated.

With Gibbon, however, Lawrence did not have an extensive, well-informed and original secondary source on the Etruscans. To write his *Etruscan Sketches*, Lawrence therefore turned to the method of *Movements in European History,* making use of the major historians of the Roman Republic and of scholars of Etruscology.

The main reference in Roman history at his time was the Prussian historian Theodor Mommsen, whose work D. H. Lawrence could read in the original language, and whom he turned into a foil. Yet, the historians he was most interested in were not Romanists (as they were deemed partisans of their subject), but Etruscologists, who in principle were less suspected of contempt towards the Etruscans. While seemingly praising Mommsen in his *Etruscan Places*, Lawrence presented this 'great scientific historian'[34] ironically and as a caricature. Mommsen was called a 'Prussian' whose affinities with the Romans rested on the 'Prussian' element in Roman history: 'The Prussian in him was enthralled by the Prussian in the all-conquering Romans.'[35] Lawrence blamed Mommsen for not giving to the Etruscans their rightful place in history.[36] In fact, in his *Römische Geschichte,* Mommsen devoted just one page to the Etruscans, with judgements clearly based on Greek and above all Roman biases. According to Mommsen, the Etruscans' defeat by the Romans should be explained by their intrinsic, physical, religious and moral inferiority. He took for granted ancient

Roman sources accusing the Etruscans of licentiousness, irrationalism and disunity and he linked the three phenomena, the political and military Etruscan decline being explained by their lack of morality. Lawrence, who considered Etruscan indecency as a quintessential Etruscan feature, could not but disagree with Mommsen and blame him for his hostility towards the Etruscans: 'Their existence was antipathetic to him. […]. He didn't like the idea of them. That was enough for a great scientific historian'.[37]

By opposing Mommsen at the very beginning of the book, Lawrence chose an original angle, unknown to most of his readers. He left official history and took the side of the vanquished. To gather information on those unconventional people, pursuing sensuous pleasures, Lawrence turned to a German-speaking Etruscologist, Fritz Weege.[38] Lawrence may have found the title of Weege's book, *Etruskische Malerei* in the two volumes of a compilation named *Etruria antica*, first published in 1925, in which the author, Pericle Ducati, mentioned the first 1921 edition of Weege's book. In his book, Ducati harshly criticised Weege's point of view, in particular on Etruscan migration from Asia Minor,[39] presenting his hypothesis as an isolated opinion.[40] Given Lawrence's hostility towards Pericle Ducati, these attacks could not but arouse his curiosity and interest.

In fact, in his letters, Lawrence expressed several times his desire to get hold of Weege's book. When preparing his visit of several Etruscan sites, he asked his sister-in-law, Else Jaffe, to check the quality of the reproductions in the book.[41] Lawrence probably acquired Weege's book, but we do not know the date, surely in 1929, when he set to work on the final version of the essays. Indeed, he made several formal criticisms of the book.

Although he appreciated the effort made by Weege to gather iconographic documentation and he seems to have made great use of Weege's reproductions when he wrote his commentaries on the frescoes, Lawrence explicitly criticised Weege in his *Etruscan Places*. For example, he took exception to the quality of the reproduction of a section of frescoes in the 'Tomb of the Triclinium.'[42] While he acknowledged the good quality of the drawing, he listed its defects: spots on a rabbit, a squirrel and flowers in a shrub. Above all, he lashed out at the mania of some scholars like Weege to discuss and interpret the frescoes according to their own aesthetic standards, or rather according to the standards of previous generations heavily inspired by Greek classical art. Now, according to Lawrence, Etruscan art was original and had its own aesthetic qualities that most scholars failed to detect.

Lawrence criticised and poked fun at established Etruscologists like Fritz Weege, because of their failure to understand the Etruscans with their scientific and historical methods. For him, the Etruscans were an experience, not the product of science. He opposed any attempt to create a system. For him, the diversity of the Etruscans made it impossible to create a theory applicable to all and he used on purpose the trivial metaphor of the omelette:

> Why must all experience be systematised? Why must even the vanished Etruscans be reduced to a system? They never will be. You break all the eggs, and produce an omelette which is neither Etruscan nor Roman not Italic nor Hittite, nor anything else, but just a systematised mess. Why can't incompatible things be left incompatible? If you make an omelette out of a hen's egg, a plover's, and an ostrich's, you won't have a grand amalgam or unification of hen and plover and ostrich into something we may call 'oviparity'. You'll have that formless object, an omelette.[43]

This aversion was aimed at museums as well as books, because both in the former and the latter, Lawrence found a system. Thus, Lawrence was dissatisfied with his visit to the reconstructed 'Inghirami Tomb' in the gardens of the archaeological museum in Florence. Although the tomb had been restored to its original state, Lawrence blamed Italian archaeologists for moving the tomb and removing the objects it contained. Indeed reconstruction implies creating order, Lawrence indicated that the urns were classified clockwise, from the most ancient to the most recent, the will is thus to show and instruct ('object-lessons') which irritated Lawrence.

To him, museums were like picture books, arranged by a curator imposing a point of view, a history, a meaning. At the end of his essay on Volterra, although he appreciated his visit to the archaeological museum, he declared peremptorily: 'A museum is not a first-hand contact: it is an illustrated lecture. And what one wants is the actual vital touch. I don't want to be "instructed"; nor do many other people.'[44] This unfortunate experience was not specific to the museum in Volterra. It was the very principle of museums that upset Lawrence: 'And the experience is always spoilt. Museums, museums, museums, object-lessons rigged out to illustrate the unsound theories of archaeologists, crazy attempts to coordinate and get into a fixed order that which has no fixed order and will not be coordinated! It is sickening!'[45] The Etruscans cannot be reduced to a few information panels; they cannot be found in the museums. '[…] [I]n the cut-and-dried museum sense, there never were.'[46]

Lawrence preferred immediacy over any form of mediation, over intellectual reconstruction he preferred what he called 'the actual vital touch', a direct contact, an experience. In fact, Lawrence generally identified two types of expression: a principle of culture expressed in art in an impulsive manner and a principle of civilisation expressed theoretically in religion and science.[47] He privileged contact with Etruscan art endowed with a carnal, lively quality: 'the peculiar physical or *bodily*, lively quality'.[48] His visit to the 'Regolini-Galassi Tomb' in Cerveteri, for example, gave him the opportunity to experience the past directly. And yet, this tomb, situated away from the necropolis of the Banditaccia in the necropolis of the Sorbo when he visited it in 1927, was deprived of most of the archaeological material.[49] Lawrence, who deplored this absence, was forced to describe the state of the tomb when it was discovered in 1836. He did so using the present: according to him, the first chamber – or rather the oval cell on the right – sheltered the remains of a warrior's bronze armour in which the body had turned to dust, whereas the central chamber – in fact, the back chamber – contained earrings and golden bracelets on a stone bed reserved for a woman. Starting from this evidence found in his readings[50] rather than on-site seeing, Lawrence imagined the owner's identity. He translated the words engraved on a silver vase found in the tomb 'Mi Larthia'[51] by 'Here is Larthia' and wondered if the 'noble Lady of close to three thousand years ago' was not called Larthia. The Lady buried in the tomb, however, was not called Larthia, for proper names of persons engraved on objects are generally written in the genitive, in the form of a meaningful speaking formula 'I am the vase of'. Furthermore, Larthia is generally considered as a shortened form of *larthial*, genitive of the male Etruscan first name Larth.[52] This Lady Larthia of the tomb, wife of a warrior with an evanescent body, is a fiction, created by the evocative power of Etruscan art and undoubtedly influenced by Lawrence's concerns at the time. While beginning to gather documentation on the Etruscans, indeed Lawrence finished between October 1926 and February 1927 two versions of *Lady Chatterley's lover*, a novel described to his friends as 'improper' and that after his visit of Etruscan sites, on August 1927, he said he wanted to extend with a sequel. Although he was very much hampered by the tuberculosis he suffered from, when Lawrence carried out his project to go and see the Etruscans on site, where they lived, in April 1927, he thus found himself in an in-between where ideas on the Midlands and Cerveteri were mingled with images of an English Lady and an Etruscan princess. Lady Larthia reminds us of another solitary lady, naked and primitive in her own way, on whom, during the same period, Lawrence kept a watchful eye: Lady Chatterley, seeking the darkness of an isolated and narrow cabin, to shelter her love affair with a 'warrior' other than her husband, the gamekeeper.

With *Etruscan Sketches*, Lawrence did not engage in an ordinary travelogue, since what he described was rather an itinerary in the past more than a series of excursions. To let himself be led on the twists and turns of Etruscan history and into the maze of tombs, Lawrence used the method he tested when he wrote *Movements in European History*. He carried out extensive documentation work, increased the number of readings, of historical books as well as scholarly guides, but, in his readings, he only remembered a few facts, a few images which served as a support to a constantly active imagination. So, when he visited the 'Regolini-Galassi Tomb', bare, without furniture, and saw at the Museo Gregoriano Etrusco pieces of furniture snatched from the tomb he was led to imagine a Lady Larthia, who had many common features with the lady Chatterley of his novel he had completed two versions of just before his trip to Etruria. While being well informed on the state of historical and archaeological research of his time, Lawrence broke away from the dry narratives of many professional historians and managed to produce 'stories about men and women'.

Notes

1. Some highly interesting literary analyses of Lawrence's texts can be found in Stefania Michelucci, 'D. H. Lawrence Discovey of the Etruscans: A Pacific Challenge Against Imperialism', in *Moving the Borders*, Marialuisa Bignami and Caroline Patey (eds) (Milan: Unicopli, 1996), pp. 374-381; Ead., 'L'espace perdu: D. H. Lawrence's Travel Writings', *Studies in Travel Writing*, vol. 8 (2004), pp. 35-48; Ead., 'La Toscana etrusca e quella romana di D. H. Lawrence', in *Una sconfinata infatuazione. Firenze e la Toscana nelle metamorfosi della cultura anglo-americana 1861-1915*, Serena Cenni and Francesca di Blasio (eds) (Florence: Consiglio regionale Toscana, 2012), pp. 369-390; Ead., 'A Means of Non-Verbal Communication: D. H. Lawrence and Popular Dance', in *Lake Garda: Gateway to D. H. Lawrence's Voyage to the Sun*, Nick Ceramella (ed.) (Newcastle Upon Tyne: Cambridge Scholars, 2013), pp. 295-313; Ead., 'A Challenge to all Authorities: D. H. Lawrence's Provocative Remote South', *Journal of Language and Literary Studies*, vol. 24 (2018), pp. 85-93; Ead., 'D. H. Lawrence's Etruscan Seduction', *Etruscan Studies*, vol. 22, 1-2 (2019), pp. 1-14, doi: https://doi.org/10.1515/etst-2018-0030. (Accessed May 2023).
2. Hereafter quotations from *Etruscans Places* will refer to D. H. Lawrence, *Sketches of Etruscan Places and other Italian Essays*, Simonetta De Filippis (ed.) (Cambridge: Cambridge University Press, 1992).
3. Massimo Pallottino was the only one, in the twentieth century, to pay attention to D. H. Lawrence's work. Cf. Massimo Pallottino, *Etruscologia* (Milan: Hoepli, 1984), p. 22; Id., 'La Grande Bretagne: l'Étrurie de Huxley et de Lawrence', in *Les Étrusques et l'Europe, exposition Galeries nationales du Grand Palais, Paris 15th September-14th December 1992, Altes Museum, Berlin 25th February-31st May 1993* (Paris-Milan: Réunion des musées nationaux, 1992), pp. 450-452. Pallottino's observations were taken up by Giovannangelo Camporeale, 'La Gran Bretagna e gli Etruschi', in *Seduzione etrusca. Dai segreti di Holkham Hall alle meraviglie del British Museum*, Exhibition catalogue, Cortona, 21st March – 31st July 2014, Paolo Bruschetti and others (eds) (Milan: Skira, 2014), pp. 19-35 (p. 32-33).
4. See, for example, in *Latomus*, 17, January-March 1958, pp. 145-147, the critical remarks by Marcel Renard in his account of Alain Hus's book, *Le peuple secret*: 'M. Hus a beaucoup lu, mais il abuse peut-être des citations. Celles de D. H. Lawrence, en particulier, même si elles sont pittoresques, ne sont guère des références sérieuses'. The same Marcel Renard in 'La question étrusque', *L'Antiquité classique*, vol. 9, no. 1 (1940), pp. 77-111 (pp. 90-91), underlined the interest of a vast audience for the Etruscans after the publication of *Etruscan Places* by a gifted author.
5. Hereafter quotations from D. H. Lawrence's works and letters will be referenced through an abbreviation of the Cambridge Edition's title followed by the volume number, and by the line number. Where necessary, the line number has also been mentioned in the footnotes.

6. These essays were published in the Londonian magazine, *World Today* in February and May 1928: 'City of the Dead at Cerveteri', in *World Today*, February 1928, pp. 280-288; 'Sketches of Etruscan Places, Tarquinia', in *World Today*, March 1928, pp. 389-398; 'Sketches of Etruscan Places, Painted Tombs of Tarquinia', in *World Today*, April 1928, pp. 552-566; 'Sketches of Etruscan Places, Volterra', in *World Today*, May 1928, pp. 662-674.
7. *Etruscan Places*, vol. 9, pp. 1-2.
8. On Pericle Ducati, cf. Nicola Parise, 'Pericle Ducati', in *Dizionario biografico degli Italiani*, XLI (Rome: Treccani, 1992), pp. 727-730; Giambattista Cairo, *Pericle Ducati. Il carteggio ritrovato* (Bologna: Ante Quem, 2012); Marie-Laurence Haack, 'Introduction: l'étruscologie de la période du fascisme et du nazisme', in *Les Étrusques au temps du fascisme et du nazisme*, ed. by Marie-Laurence Haack & Martin Miller (Bordeaux: Ausonius Éditions, 2016), p. 11; Enrico Benelli, 'La linguistica etrusca in Italia: 1928-1942', in *Les Étrusques au temps du fascisme et du nazisme*, pp. 231-234, p. 237; Vincenzo Bellelli, 'Le ricerche sulla religione etrusca fra la prima e la seconda guerra mondiale, con particolare riferimento alla situazione italiana', in *Les Étrusques au temps du fascisme et du nazisme*, pp. 264-265; Sarah Rey, 'Les étruscologues français à l'heure des régimes autoritaires', in *Les Étrusques au temps du fascisme et du nazisme*, pp. 279-280; Marie-Laurence Haack, 'Introduction. L'Européisation des Étrusques après la Seconde Guerre mondiale', *L'étruscologie dans l'Europe d'après-guerre*, Marie-Laurence Haack and Martin Miller (eds) (Bordeaux: Ausonius Éditions, 2017), p. 9 and note 3.
9. On Antonio Minto, cf. Anna Patera, 'Antonio Minto', in *Dizionario biografico dei Soprintendenti Archeologi (1904-1974)* (Rome-Bologna: Ministero per i beni e le attività culturali– Bononia University Press, 2012), pp. 503-514; Marie-Laurence Haack, 'De la veine au crâne. L'étruscologie entre éclatement et ouverture: le cas des sciences naturelles', in *La construction de l'étruscologie au début du XXe siècle*, Marie-Laurence Haack and Martin Miller (eds) (Bordeaux: Ausonius Éditions, 2015), pp. 165-184.
10. Cf. Gamini Salgado, 'Lawrence as Historian', in *The Spirit of D. H. Lawrence. Centenary Studies*, G. K. Das, Gamini Salgado and Raymond Williams (eds) (London: Macmillan, 1988), pp. 234-247.
11. The school transcripts presented by Lewis Spolton, 'D. H. Lawrence-Student and Teacher', *British Journal of Educational Studies*, vol. 14, no. 3 (1966), pp. 18-35, especially. note 3, p. 20, for the first term of the 1898-1899 school year, does not mention history.
12. On this experience, cf. Keith Cushman, 'Self and Sequence: Lawrence's *The Schoolmaster*', *Études Lawrenciennes*, 47 (2016), doi: http://journals.openedition.org/lawrence/254. (Accessed October 2018).
13. Letter from Frieda to Amy Lowell of 15 April 1938, cf. John Worthen, *D. H. Lawrence: The Early Years 1885 – 1912* (Cambridge: Cambridge University Press, 1991), p. 208; *The Letters of D. H. Lawrence & Amy Lowell, 1914-1925*, E. Claire Healey and Keith Cushman (eds) (Santa Barbara, CA: Black Sparrow Press, 1985), p. 132.
14. Cf. D. H. Lawrence, *Complete Poems*, Vivian de Sola Pinto and Warren Roberts (eds) (London: Penguin Classics, 1977), p. 74.
15. On D. H. Lawrence's readings, cf. Rose Marie Burwell, 'A catalogue of D. H. Lawrence's Reading from Early Childhood', *The D. H. Lawrence Review*, vol. 3, no. 3 (1970), pp. III, V-VI, 193-330.
16. See William Latta, 'Lawrence's Debt to Rudolph, Baron von Hube', in *The D. H. Lawrence Review*, vol. 1, no. 1 (1968), pp. 60-62.
17. We also find allusions to the book in the play *The Merry-Go-Round* written in 1910, in *The Rainbow* (Harry T. Moore, *The Intelligent Heart: the Story of D. H. Lawrence* (London: Penguin, 1955), p. 59). Cf. William Latta, 'Lawrence's Debt to Rudolph, Baron von Hube': Lawrence created the character of Baron Skrebensky from baron Hube and multiplied parallelisms between the two, in particular between the two men's parishes and the dedications of their book (*The Rainbow*, p. 22).
18. Cf. Edward Nehls, *D. H. Lawrence: A Composite Biography, Volume One, 1885-1919* (Madison: University of Wisconsin Press, 1957), p. 471.
19. Cf. *Letters*, III, 1671 to Katherine Mansfield of 10th December 1918: 'Somehow I hate doing that *European History* for the Oxford Press. Curse it – why shouldn't one do as one likes'.
20. The result was a success. *Movements in European History* was released under a fictitious name, Lawrence H. Davidson, in 1921, with 2000 copies printed; then, an illustrated edition was published in 1925. Critics nevertheless accused D. H. Lawrence of plagiarising. Lawrence, indeed, organised his paragraphs by source: a source or a passage of a source corresponded to each paragraph and was reproduced almost literally.
21. Cf. *Letters*, III, 1690 to Nancy Henry of 23 January 1919, p. 322.

22. Cf. *Movements in European History D. H. Lawrence*, Philip Crumpton (ed.) (Cambridge: Cambridge University Press, 1979), p. 7.
23. On Edward Gibbon, cf. Arnaldo Momigliano, 'Gibbon's Contribution to Historical Method', in *Studies in Historiography*, Arnaldo Momigliano (ed.) (New York: Harper & Row, 1966), pp. 40-55; *Edward Gibbon and the Decline and Fall of the Roman Empire*, ed. by Glen W. Bowersock, John Clive, Stephen Graubard (Cambridge, MA: Harvard University Press, 1977); José Antonio Dabdab Trabulsi, 'Edward Gibbon, du Déclin et Chute aux Mémoires et vice versa', *Dialogues d'histoire ancienne*, vol. 32, no. 1 (2006), pp. 101-120; Roy Porter, *Gibbon: Making History* (New York: Palgrave Macmillan, 1989); Charlotte Roberts, *Edward Gibbon and the Shape of History*, (Oxford: Oxford University Press, 2014).
24. *Letters*, III, 1984, no. 1555, p. 233. No doubt it should be read: Yoruban.
25. Cf. *Letters*, III, no. 1656, p. 239.
26. Edward Gibbon, *The Decline and Fall of the Roman Empire*, vol. I (London: Methuen & Co, 1896), p. 21: 'The middle part of the peninsula, that now composes the duchy of Tuscany and the ecclesiastical state, was the ancient seat of the Etruscans and Umbrians; to the former of whom Italy was indebted for the first rudiments of a civilised lif'. See also *ibid.*, p. 37 'The ancient dialects of Italy, the Sabine, the Etruscan, and the Venetian, sunk into oblivion'.
27. Cf. *Ibid.*, vol. IV (London: Methuen & Co, 1898), p. 504: 'I touch with reluctance, and despatch with impatience, a more odious vice, of which modesty rejects the name, and nature abominates the idea. The primitive Romans were infected by the example of the Etruscans and Greeks'.
28. Cf. *Ibid.*, p. 504, note 196: '[Timon (l. i.) and Theopompus (l. xliii. apud Athenaeum, l. xii. p. 517) describe the luxury and lust of the Etruscans. About the same period (A. U. C. 445) the Roman youth studied in Etruria (liv. ix. 36.)]'. It should be underlined that Gibbon immediately stressed in the same note the intellectual contribution brought by the Etruscans to the Romans during the same period.
On the notion of *truphè*, cf. Yves Liébert, *Regards sur la truphè étrusque* (Limoges: Presses Universitaires de Limoges, 2006).
29. Cf. D. H. Lawrence, *Complete Poems*, Vivian de Sola Pinto and Warren Roberts (eds), pp. 296-298.
30. *Etruscan Places*, vol. 9, pp. 29-30.
31. Cf. Edward Gibbon, *The Decline and Fall of the Roman Empire*, vol. VI (London: Methuen & Co, 1914), chapter XXXVIII, pp. 173-174: 'The rise of a city, which swelled into an empire, may deserve, as a singular prodigy, the reflection of a philosophic mind. But the decline of Rome was the natural and inevitable product of immoderate greatness. Prosperity ripened the principle of decay: the causes of destruction multiplied with the extent of conquest; and as soon as time or accident had removed the artificial supports, the stupendous fabric yielded to the pressure of its own weight'.
32. 'In the revolution of ten centuries, not a single discovery was made to exalt the dignity or promote the happiness of mankind. Not a single idea has been added to the speculative systems of antiquity, and a succession of patient disciples became in their turn the dogmatic teachers of the next servile generation. Not a single composition of history, philosophy, or literature, has been saved from oblivion by the intrinsic beauties of style or sentiment, of original fancy, or even of successful imitation' (Edinburgh, 1811, X, pp. 161-162).
33. Cf. Edward Gibbon, *The Decline and Fall of the Roman Empire*, vol. I (London: Methuen & Co, 1896), chapter XV, p. 431: 'I have described the triumph of barbarism and religion'.
34. *Etruscan Places*, vol. 9, p. 22.
35. *Ibid.*, pp. 24-25.
36. Cf. 'And a great scientific historian like Mommsen hardly allows that the Etruscans existed at all'. *Ibid.*, pp. 22-23; 'he almost denies the very existence of the Etruscan people'. *Ibid.*, pp. 25-26.
37. *Ibid.*, pp. 23-27.
38. On this Etruscologist, cf. *Kürschners Deutscher Gelehrten-Kalender 1940/41*, 7, ed. by Gerhard Lüdtke (Berlin: De Gruyter, 1941), col. 1041; Gerhard Lüdtke, 'Necrologia Fritz Weege', *Studi Etruschi*, 19 (1946), p. 397; Eugen von Mercklin, 'Fritz Weege', *Gnomon*, 23 (1951), pp. 117-118; *Deutsche Biographische Enzyklopädie*, 10 (1999), p. 371; URL: https://www2.catalogus-professorum-halensis.de/weegefritz.html. (Accessed May 2023).
39. Cf. Pericle Ducati, *Etruria antica*, vol. I (Turin: Paravia, 1926), p. 36.
40. Cf. *Ibid.*, p. 46.
41. Cf. *Letters* V, 3725 to Else Jaffe of 26 May 1926: '[…] Have you seen F[ritz] Weege's Etruskische Malerei.1921? If there is a copy in one of your libraries, I wish you'd look at it and tell me if it has good reproductions. […]'.
42. Cf. 'It is interesting to see, in Fritz Weege's book *Etruskische Malerei*, a reproduction of an old water-colour drawing of the dancers on the right

wall. It is a good drawing, yet as one looks closer, it is quite often out, both in line and position. The Etruscan paintings, not being in our convention, are very difficult to copy. The picture shows my rabbit all spotted, as if it were some queer cat. And it shows a squirrel in the little tree in front of the piper, and flowers, and many details that have now disappeared. But it is a good drawing, unlike some that Weege reproduces, which are so Flaxmanised and Greekified and made according to what our great-grandfathers thought they *ought* to be, as to be really funny, and a warning forever against thinking how things *ought* to be, when already they are quite perfectly what they are'. *Etruscan Places*, vol. 52, p. 4.
The plate he alluded to is the twentieth of Fritz Weege's volume, p. 23.

43. *Etruscan Places*, vol. 171, pp. 7-15.
44. *Ibid.*, pp. 19-21.
45. *Ibid.*, pp. 3-7.
46. *Ibid.*, vol. 175, pp. 5-6.
47. *Ibid.*, pp. 9-14.
48. *Ibid.*, vol. 178, p. 27.
49. On the tomb's archaelogical furniture, cf. Giovanna Bagnasco Gianni, *Oggetti iscritti di epoca orientalizzante in Etruria* (Florence: Olschki 1996), pp. 77-81; Maurizio Sannibale, 'La Principessa Etrusca della Tomba Regolini-Galassi', in *"Principesse" del Mediterraneo all'alba della Storia, Catalogo della mostra* (Athens, *Museum of Cycladic Art,* 2012*)*, Nicholas Stampolidis (ed.) (Athens, 2012), pp. 306-321; Id., 'Les mobiliers funéraires; la tombe Regolini-Galassi', in *Les Étrusques et la Méditerranée: La cité de Cerveteri*, Françoise Gaultier and Laurent Haumesser (eds) (Paris: Somogy, 2013), pp. 104-106.
50. Cf. George Dennis, *The Cities and Cemeteries of Etruria*, 3rd edition, vol. I (London: John Murray, 1888), pp. 264-270 and Wolfgang Helbig, *Führer durch die öffentlichen Sammlungen klassischer Altertümer in Rom*, 3rd edition, 1912-1913, who devotes a section to the Vatican Etruscan museum, no. 523, pp. 321-323, in which he reminds us of the discovery, the date and the precise composition of the tomb and p. 390, no. 707, indicating the presence of two small silver vases with the inscription Milarthia. We note that Weege contributed to the edition of Wolfgang Helbig's guide. D. H. Lawrence corrected Dennis's mistake, who presented the tomb under the name of Grotta Regulini-Galassi, but he took up the main features of his description and his interpretation.
51. In fact, two inscriptions on the tomb silver vases provide this text. These inscriptions are listed in *Etruskische Texte. Editio minor*, vol. II, Gerhard Meiser (ed.) (Hamburg: Baar-Verlag, 2014), Cr 2.13 and 2.14.
52. Cf. Giovanna Bagnasco Gianni, *Oggetti iscritti di epoca orientalizzante in Etruria*, p. 84, nos 52, 54; Francesco Buranelli and Maurizio Sannibale, 'La Tumba Regolini-Galassi', in *Principes etruscos. Entre Oriente y Occidente,* Catálogo de la exposición en Caixaforum, Madrid, Anna Mura Sommella (ed.) (Madrid: Fundation la Caixa, 2008), p. 96, no. 36.

Etruscan Studies and the Infernal Landscape in Vincenzo Cardarelli's prose d'arte

Gennaro Ambrosino

Introduction

In a passage from 'Vita delle tombe etrusche', published in *Il cielo sulle città* (1939), the Italian poet and journalist Vincenzo Cardarelli (1887-1959), describing a fresco in the 'Tomba della caccia e della pesca' (located in Tarquinia, discovered in 1873 and dating from the VI century BC) he writes:

> The only exciting episode, among so many gay and bloodless scenes, is that of a madman who dives from a very high cliff into the sea in order to cause a bit of confusion in a group of fishermen who were watching the incredible dive from afar. Except that the madman is an accomplished swimmer, an expert diver, driven to madness. And nothing could better express the fury of a spring in Maremma than this miraculous episode.[1]

The painting the author is referring to is the famous 'Diver'. The scene and the atmosphere Cardarelli reconstructs are based on the observation of the painting, but an imaginative element takes over and attaches new and deeper nuances to the modern perception of ancient Etruscan culture. The writer continues: 'What I tried to summarise, omitting an infinite number of very graceful details, is the faithful representation, albeit imaginative and burlesque, of one of the most beautiful days in my homeland.'[2] The life of the Etruscan fresco is in Cardarelli's imagination: everything he describes is a product of his fancy, as it emerges clearly from the previous passage: paradoxically, the representation is at once 'faithful', 'imaginative' and 'burlesque'. The same happens when he writes about Etruscan sepulchres or tombs: first, he pays attention to the archaeological data and then shifts to the imaginative dimension. Moreover, when describing the paintings, Cardarelli superimposes the old Etruscan civilisation and the modern inhabitants of Tarquinia, underlining their inextricable genealogical linkage:

> The funeral dancers, so frequent in these frescoes, are nothing more than ancient tarantella dancers and the inevitable tibicino with its long stride and magical fingers, the mystic citaredo [...], seem to me almost like natural predecessors of those fanatical musicians who, in the days of my childhood, turned the people and the municipality upside down with their band tantrums and rivalries.[3]

The link between the past and the present, or rather, between the ancient past of the Etruscans ('danzatrici funebri' e 'il mistico citaredo') and the author's personal past ('quei fantastici musicanti [...] al tempo della mia infanzia') is a rhetorical element that runs through Cardarelli's entire production and constitutes an important motif in the literary representation of the Etruscans.

This chapter analyses how Vincenzo Cardarelli translates concrete archaeological data about the Etruscans in his *prosa d'arte* and his literary representation of this ancient civilisation. The works that will be examined are: *Favole e memorie* (1925), *Il sole a picco* (1929), *Il cielo sulle città* (1939), and *Il viaggiatore insocievole* (1953). The prose texts included in these collections had already been published in the newspapers and journals Cardarelli collaborated with over the years and were later reorganised in edited volumes. I will discuss what the Etruscans meant for Cardarelli and how he depicted them in his writings using recurring metaphors and drawing on existing stereotypes. To do so, I will begin with the analysis of the relationship between the writer and his native village, Corneto/Tarquinia, which is an essential starting point to understand his attachment to the Etruscans. Then, I will focus on two central elements in the rhetoric on the Etruscans: the metaphor of the 'strata' and the influence of Dante's *Inferno*.

Prosa d'arte is a fluid category, a certain way of writing and a literary taste that is associated with different genres (like the *elzeviro*, travel writing, autobiographical memories) and that became very popular in Italy after the First World War. *La Ronda* (1919), an influential literary periodical that counted Cardarelli among its founders, called for a return to Leopardi's and Manzoni's model as opposed to the radical renewal of the avant-gardes. The defence of tradition, and the call for a *retour à l'ordre* were ideas shared by many authors of *prosa d'arte*, as well as by many a figurative artist.[4] *Prosa d'arte* favours the use of a poetical and highly personalised style and tends to be short and fragmentary in form. The meandering language and loosely structured forms of the *prosa d'arte* are perfectly suited to treat the theme of the Etruscans: at the time, archaeologists still had very few certainties about their language, their origins and the nature of their art, which was considered barbaric and odd. The fragmentary nature of *prosa d'arte* writing seems to be perfectly in tune with the fragmented knowledge about the Etruscans.[5] At the same time, the suggestive tone, the lyrical patina, the sense for nuance and the open structure of the *prosa d'arte* play a fundamental role in the mythological and fable-like evocation of the Etruscans and respond to the aura of mystery surrounding this subject.

Indeed, Etruscan studies had been a loosely organised area of studies and interests for decades, before they were methodologically codified and institutionally recognised as a separate branch of archaeology and ancient history.[6] The years in which Cardarelli wrote his *prose d'arte* were central for the debate on Etruscan civilisation and its relationship with the Roman conquerors, especially with the rise of Fascism. Although it reaches its peak in that period, the debate on the Etruscan 'nation' has more remote origins and it had been a central aspect since the eighteenth and nineteenth centuries. In the course of the eighteenth century, enthusiasm for archaeological discoveries led to the spread of the so-called 'Etruscheria', and sparked an almost obsessive curiosity about the origins, language and customs of the Etruscans.[7] During the nineteenth century, Etruscology had acquired an increasingly significant role largely because of new archaeological excavations. Representative figures of these excavations were Prince Luciano Bonaparte, who was very active in the fief of Canino (today Vulci) and Marquis Giovanni Pietro Campana, who was active in Cerveteri.[8] As pointed out by De Francesco[9] and Barsotti,[10] many of these studies on the Etruscans have to be situated within the political and patriotic context, as they were influenced by the general ideological framework of the Risorgimento (and contributed in turn to that ideology). Both De Francesco and Barsotti start their analysis from the work of Vincenzo Cuoco, entitled *Platone in Italia* (1804-1806) and highlight the fundamental role played by Giuseppe Micali's *Storia degli antichi popoli italiani*. Whereas Barsotti reconstructs the development of concepts as 'nation' and 'race' during the Risorgimento years, De Francesco concentrates mainly on the political myth of the Etruscans and on the Roman/Etruscan dichotomy, which will later feed into the fascist racist doctrines.[11]

Nevertheless, as mentioned before, the years that contributed most to the revival of the study of Etruscan history and art were between 1909 and 1936, especially after the discovery of the Apollo of Veii (see Chiara Zampieri's essay in this book). The fact that the debate on the Etruscans has deep historical roots, which have inspired not only archaeological research but also political ideologies, accounts for the different representations of the Etruscans, the stratified motives and stereotypes associated with their culture and the aura of mystery that surrounded them.

The reason for this particular connotation is that first-hand, written accounts by the Etruscans are scarce, even to this day, and they are often limited in size and scope. We only have some funerary inscriptions but no extensive or discursive written sources. Because knowledge of the Etruscans is mediated by Greek and Roman sources and the vast majority of archaeological findings are related to necropolises and tombs, the Etruscans have been associated with the underworld. These aspects stirred the imagination of intellectuals and writers: concrete archaeological data were used as a starting point, offering the possibility to move from a purely scientific approach to a literary one through lexical/semantic and metaphorical networks that are linked to mystery.[12] Although we don't have written texts, the Etruscans left to posterity numerous cave paintings that were used to elaborate and spread stereotypes regarding their lifestyle, their religion and their attitude. For instance, in the same text quoted at the beginning of the chapter, Cardarelli wrote: 'The *obesus etruscus* is no legend. It's the Maremman belly, which is quite rare among city people and very common among so-called country merchants, it grows on horseback, in the open air'[13].

Cardarelli and Tarquinia

Some biographical elements influenced Cardarelli's representation of the Etruscans in his works. As mentioned above, he was born in Corneto Tarquinia, an old Etruscan city, near Viterbo in Northern Latium. Like other authors of the Italian modernist period (e.g. Curzio Malaparte, Giovanni Papini) who were born in territories once belonging to Etruria, Cardarelli considers Etruscan culture as his cultural heritage and the Etruscans as his ancestors. This link was accentuated by the fact that the poet never met his mother and his stepmother died when he was very young: 'Fate, after taking my mother away from me, gave me a golden-hearted stepmother […] All this happiness did not last long, just three years.'[14] Moreover, in 1905, one year after he moved to Rome, his father also died. Therefore, he was deprived of the parental figures, which he tried to project in the Etruscan civilisation thanks to his genealogical lineage. In Rome, he began his career by collaborating with newspapers and magazines like *Avanti!*, *Il Marzocco*, and *La Voce*. His close link with Tarquinia is evident in a prose text entitled 'Il mio paese' and published in *Il sole a picco*: 'The village where I was born, where I spent my childhood and part of my youth and where I met my first love, was once called Corneto Tarquinia.'[15]

Thus, the relationship between Cardarelli and Tarquinia is complicated and has to be understood in the light of his move to Rome: the loss of his primitive and native place created a literary myth which takes Leopardi's Recanati as a model. In Cardarelli's texts, Tarquinia is fixed in a timeless dimension where everything is idyllic and stationary: it is represented as an old Etruscan city. The modern inhabitants often become protagonists of his works and are described with physical and behavioural traits that recall the Etruscans. What I would like to point out is that it is only after his separation from his genealogical roots that Cardarelli was able to start translating them into literary forms. As Christine Wampole observes in her work on the root metaphor, the fear of decontextualisation and abstraction leads to a search for roots: 'Rootedness matters most when it is threatened.'[16] Cardarelli thus creates his literary, idealised, timeless, imaginary Tarquinia while living in Rome.

This element is also linked to the creative writing of the *strapaese* movement, which defended the rural character of the Italian people against modern fashions and foreign ways of thinking.[17] The most relevant contribution by Cardarelli to the *strapaese* movement is the *prosimetro* entitled *Il sole a picco*. Nevertheless, his relationship with Tarquinia often turned out to be negative: every time he went back to his village, he suffered and felt trapped, discovering that the reality was quite different from his memories as demonstrated by several letters written between 1945 and 1949: 'The cemetery is a stone's throw away, I don't want to die in Corneto, and yet I don't see how I can get out of this *trap* I've fallen into.'[18] Thus, the author is able to appreciate his native village only from a distance:

> Years pass before I go back to my fabulous village. And I do nothing but dream of it and sigh for it as if it were at the end of the world; more satisfied, one would say, with the privation I impose on myself by staying away from it; more satisfied with the memory and the image I carry with me, than with the pleasure I would feel seeing it again.[19]

The same village that is described in the letters as a 'trap' from which it is impossible to escape is called 'favoloso' in the *prosa d'arte* and is perceived as a place detached from time, in which the different historical eras easily overlap and merge. The reference to Giacomo Leopardi's complicated relationship with his home town in the Marche is evident: Tarquinia is depicted as a new Recanati. In addition to this, however, Tarquinia has been one of the main cities of ancient Etruria. The evocation of his childhood and adolescence spent at Tarquinia overlaps with the historical past that involves the Etruscans. Therefore, in his texts, the writer's individual past and the collective past of humanity intertwine:

> 'I will always remember my village, with the desolate poetry of those peripheral places, near the castle walls […]. Here the Etruscan laughed, one day, lying down, with his eyes on the ground, looking at the sea. And he welcomed in his eyes the multiform and silent splendour of the flourishing and young land, of which he had taken the mystery gaily, without disgust and fear, sinking his hands and face'.[20]

In this prose fragment, which is titled 'Terra' ('Earth') (and we will see how important the Earth is in Cardarelli's rhetoric about the Etruscans) this overlap is evident: he starts from his personal experience and memories and then moves to Etruscan history.[21] Cardarelli projected his childhood in the Etruscan antiquity, reproducing the same structure used by Leopardi and analysed by Fabio Camilletti in his *Leopardi's Nymphs*.[22] As Jacques Lacan suggested, 'home' is a familiar place connected to infancy and origin; more than a physical space it is an affective perimeter which is always connected to individual memory.[23] The poetic memory of his 'home' and his origins leads to a return to the past: the journey is not physical but mental, and the correspondence between 'children' and 'ancients' once again recalls Leopardi.

Moreover, the particular historical period in which Cardarelli lived, spurred him to face the problem of origins. In fact, during the fascist period, Etruscan studies were caught up in the broader and more widespread public discourse about the 'origins' of Italianness, a discourse with obvious connections to nationalism, patriotic rhetoric and racist propaganda[24] and marked by overt tensions between different positions.[25] Antonino De Francesco explains how Romanism endorsed the core value of the unified state and rejects every reading of Italian identity which did not fit in the idea of complete uniformity associated with Roman civilisation,[26] yet this dominant idea did not eradicate the awareness of Italy's history of plurality, mainly because of the publications of Massimo Pallottino. With respect to the topic of Italy's plural identity, Cardarelli has an ambiguous position: while an author like Savinio in *Dico a te, Clio* (1939) firmly maintains the position of the Etruscans describing the Romans as conquerors and murderers,[27] Cardarelli does not address the violent Roman conquest; rather, he uses a vocabulary to try to mitigate the historical conflict between the two ancient civilisations.²⁸ In 'Elegia etrusca' he affirms:

> Rome surprised the Etruscans while they were working without any suspicion, as always; and went along the lament [...]. Today, of this mysterious and overwhelmed population who stands at the origins of our civilisation, coming from who knows where, perhaps from the sea, but facing upstream, there remains only the corrupt mould of its image on earth, where it lay dying.²⁹

He tries to integrate into a coherent system two civilisations that in the narrative of those years were seen as in conflict. In *Il viaggiatore insocievole* the point of view changes and the violent conquest is represented: 'The Etruscan people were truly strangled, rather than slaughtered, by the Gauls, Greeks and Romans together, and the information that remains of them is that which was handed down to us by their enemies.'³⁰ This portrait of the Etruscans as victims of a coalition of several peoples allows the author to justify the stereotypes that accompany the Etruscan literary representation: 'Historians tell us that Etruscan women used to prostitute for their dowry [...], the dark religion, certain very cruel systems of thought.'³¹ Nevertheless, in a passage from *I Villanoviani*, the author praises the Etruscans for what he sees as their role in spreading civilisation across the Italic territory: 'What are the Etruscans, after the Indo-European whirlwind, if not the restorers of the pristine Mediterranean civilisation which they brought to its greatest perfection? It is through the Etruscans that Rome became Mediterranean in many ways, but above all by assuming that character of a commercial city which, according to the most authoritative historians, distinguished it from any other Latin city from the very beginning.'³² In these statements and in other passages of these *prose d'arte*, a veiled racist undertone slips into Cardarelli's discourse on culture and civilisation. In fact, in some passages Cardarelli seems to introduce a hierarchy among the primitive Italic populations, assigning the highest position to the Etruscans: 'A more evolved type of man, which would be that of the Majella and of the Olmo grotto, near Arezzo, replaced this first semi-monkey element in Italy and it is to him that we like to refer as our distant and direct progenitor. [...] He is the progenitor of a breed that is called Mediterranean or Ligurian-Sicilian. [...] I will only say that Tuscany seems to have been one of the regions where the Siculi worked most thoroughly.'³³ Genealogy, political discourse and personal recollections here combine and merge into an idea of racial superiority which ties in with fascist propaganda.

The Metaphor of Stratification

Within the general framework that was highlighted in the previous section of this chapter, Cardarelli also uses some specific representations of the Etruscans. I will focus on the metaphor of 'stratification'. First, it is important to stress that Cardarelli had direct experience and knowledge of Etruscan archaeology and excavations, as he often emphasises himself in his prose writings:

> When I was a boy I was witness to some excavations in the Etruscan necropolis of my village. They were looking for chamber tombs, sarcophagi of nenfro or coloured stone, gold, bronze, bucchero vases, precious decorated amphorae. But most of the time, after so much effort, when they lifted up a slab of tuff, all that was found was a bowl full of burnt bones and, in the midst of that shredding of arid white bones, something that glittered.[34]

And again:

> For some time now, out of love for Italy and for my birthplace, I have given myself over to archaeology and palaeontology. I like to know how and by whom the Italian land was inhabited when the islands were still attached to the continent, but already the gaps that are now filled by the sea must have been difficult to access, because the Italic man appears, earlier than elsewhere, on the nascent peninsula and seems to cling to the shores.[35]

The concrete archaeological data were elaborated through the use of a vocabulary and a set of metaphors creating a sense of mystery. This is evident in 'Elegia etrusca' ('Etruscan elegy'): 'What do I know about the Etruscans? Only what I can imagine, since I was born, one might say, in the midst of their graves.'[36] Here, the author once again underlines his identity of being a 'native' to the place, since he was born 'among their tombs' ('in mezzo alle loro tombe'), and highlights how his reimagining of the archaeological sites is spurred by the lacunae in the archaeological record as well as by his strong personal connection with the area.

As pointed out by Sascha Colby,[37] during the early twentieth century the archaeological site becomes a magnetic site, as it drew widespread public and literary interest and assumes numerous connotations and metaphorical meanings. Some of the fundamental themes include 'the auratic importance of the archaeological relic, the parallel between archaeological regression and dreams, the reclamation of the lost pantheistic landscape.'[38] These motifs are present in

'Villa Tarantola', a prose text included in the 1952 edition of *Il sole a picco*. The aura of mystery given by the archaeological relic, and more generally by the archaeological site, is emphasised several times by the author:

> I seldom went as far as that strange, uninhabited villa, called Villa Tarantola, which already sees the cemetery and was then for me a mysterious, enigmatic site, evoking, in its name, the poisonous spiders of San Vito's festivity […]. Nor did I ever hear voices or see a living soul while poking around in there. The appearance of this solitary cottage was impeccable, and the terror or rather astonishment it inspired in me every time I pried through the bars, that had a quality well known to readers of Edgar [Allan] Poe.[39]

The vocabulary of mystery, darkness and terror and the intertextual reference to Poe enhance the gothic and spectral aura that characterises the archaeological site. The parallel between the archaeological site and dreams is highlighted by the narrated episode of the young woman who falls into a state of 'imbambolamento' (to quote the author), due to the bite of a tarantula:

> They were taking her to the hospital in a cart, and she was standing there, enchanted, overwhelmed, beautiful. Her white face shone like that of a saint in ecstasy. In the light of a summer sunset, in that landscape, I could not have had a more moving and, I dare say, significant encounter, with regard to the effects that a spider inhabiting such macerated and deadly lands can produce. But science does not believe in the mysterious ailments attributed to the tarantula. And these are only the impressions and fantasies of a *layman*.[40]

It is very interesting to notice how these 'fantasie di un profano', which refer to themes of dream and ecstasy, are inspired by an Etruscan archaeological site, which thus becomes a privileged place for the emergence of these tensions towards the occult and the mysterious. Finally, we find the motif of the lost paradise, already analysed above, and re-proposed by Cardarelli in this *prosa d'arte*:

> Ever since I was a boy, I have loved distance and solitude. Going out of the gates of my village and looking at it from the outside, like something lost, was one of my most regular pleasures.[41]

These elements are further developed in the metaphor of the 'strata' which is based on the idea that archaeological stratification corresponds to the archaeology of the self and of the unconscious.[42] The connection between archaeology and psychoanalysis was famously made by Sigmund Freud, who used an archaeological terminology to substantiate the scientific character of the new discipline. Freud imagined the human mind as an archaeological site which hides in depth the richest treasures:

> We may expect that the analysis of dreams will lead us to a knowledge of man's archaic heritage, of what is psychically innate in him. Dreams and neuroses seem to have preserved more mental antiquities than we could have imagined possible; so that psychoanalysis may claim a high place among the sciences which are concerned with the reconstruction of the earliest and most obscure periods of the beginnings of the human race.[43]

As Julian Thomas has pointed out: 'Like an archaeological site, the mind is stratified, and the deeper layers, more removed from everyday perusal, are connected with the past of the individual and the human species.'[44] The archaeologist digs deep into the ground exploring the origins of humanity which bear similarities to the origins of the individual; the analyst, instead, digs deep into the patient's self, trying to explore his unconscious (only in this way can the therapist heal the patient). This metaphor reinforces the value of the previous reasoning about Tarquinia as 'paradise lost' and affective place in which the individual and collective pasts overlap. In 'Il mio paese', this metaphor finds its clearest application:

> In the cavernous and shattered ground, at least three civilisations lie on top of each other, stratified; the more a man digs, the more he realises that the time in which he dates his presence in these places, confuses itself with the age of the earth, that time is much older than his memory.[45]

This passage clearly shows how the distinction between human time and historical time is blurred through the metaphors of stratification and digging. The stratification of Tarquinia evokes reflections on memory, and the same process is present in the prose text 'Italia preistorica' (from *Il viaggiatore insocievole*): 'The history of mankind is confused, over an endless succession of centuries, with that of the earth's crust. It is pure geology.'[46] This indissoluble link between man and earth will be explored further in the next section on the presence of Dante in Cardarelli's writings on the Etruscans.

Dante and the Infernal Landscape

As already explained in the introduction to this chapter, Etruscan heritage consists mainly of necropolises and tombs, which explains why Etruscans evoke images of death and of the underworld. Cardarelli describes archaeological finds with an infernal lexicon as if everything belonged to another dimension. In 'Elegia etrusca' he affirms: '[The Etruscans] exasperated this myth of the Inferno so much that they created, of its gigantic gods, the fiercest and most ardent among them'.[47] Cardarelli uses an infernal lexicon to describe Etruscan graves, as Gabriele D'Annunzio did in his novel *Forse che sì forse che no*.[48] The substantial difference is that in the genre of the novel, the evocation of infernal landscapes and death is expressed through the voice and the actions of the characters. In *prose d'arte* the reference is less explicit and is filtered through the use of specific words and rhetorical figures. The Etruscans were seen as the creators of the *Inferno* because of their care for the dead, the enormous necropolises and numerous paintings representing demons and frightening creatures. The literary sources Cardarelli draws on in his descriptions of Hell range from the Homeric poems to Virgil and Dante.

In 'La tomba del guerriero', Cardarelli compares the journey to the underworld with the work of the archaeologist:

> As he went down to retrieve it, our gentleman made, without realising it, the journey of Ulysses to the Underworld. He found himself thrown into another time, in an indefinable place, where everything 'spoke' the great language of the Etruscans, in its more direct and emotional forms.[49]

Cardarelli expresses the idea that the underworld is a quintessentially Etruscan place, and the archaeologist exploring a necropolis finds himself in another temporal era where finally everything speaks 'the great Etruscan language' ('il grande linguaggio degli Etruschi'): that is, the language of death. This civilisation, which is silent on the earth's surface, only speaks in the place it is most strongly connected to: the underworld. The uses of this vocabulary and the images of the underworld surfaces in 'Il mio paese'. In this case Dante's *Inferno* is explicitly named:

> It seems that once, around my country, however vast the territory be, it was all a patch of dogwood; forest, curly, bristly, and dense [...] where the pilgrim who went to Rome, entered with fear. The seat of beasts and brigands. Thus, Dante represented this country or rather its barren countryside[50].

The lexical elements of the 'selva', 'pellegrino', 'fiere' and the atmosphere of fear, mystery, darkness directly recall the first Canto of Dante's *Inferno*. Cardarelli also refers to *Canto XIII* of *Inferno* in which Dante mentions Corneto and its countryside: 'Non han sì aspri sterpi né sì folti/ quelle fiere selvagge che 'n odio hanno/ tra Cecina e Corneto i luoghi colti' (*Inf.* XIII, 6-9). Moreover, in his *Solitario in Arcadia* Cardarelli dedicated a prose to Dante as the author of *Convivio* and *De Vulgari Eloquentia*, highlighting the importance of Dante for Italy from the linguistic point of view. In this description of Dante's method, he uses a vocabulary which directly refers to the primitiveness and purity that recalls the descriptions of the Etruscans:

> [The words] for him never have an imposed or conventional meaning, but always original or, may we say, supreme. He seeks its first root and that distant purity and virginity of meaning that lies buried and often unrecognisable under the tyranny of use.[51]

Therefore, it is interesting to notice that this rhetoric of primitiveness, which may have a link with the *retour à l'ordre* typical of the arts of the 1920s, is present also in prose writings in which the Etruscans are not directly involved (even if Dante could be considered 'Etrusco' for geographical and historical reasons).[52]

On the one hand, the tombs are associated to an 'infernal' underworld, but on the other they are also closely associated with the 'earth' and the 'ground'. This relation is paradigmatic in the two English terms used before to refer to the sepulchres: 'under-world' and 'under-ground'. By exploring the graves, the archaeologist enters in another 'world' which is physically placed 'under the ground'. Therefore, as pointed out by Martina Piperno,[53] it is possible to rehash Vico's etymology connecting the words '*homo*', '*humanus*' with '*humus*' ('ground') and '*humare*' ('to bury'): humanity is on the same line of the ground and of the idea of death. This correlation is also present in Cardarelli's 'Gli Etruschi':

> If they were attached to the land in such a way that history does not know a more steadfast, more *rooted* people, it was only because in them the love for the land was confused with the religion of the dead. Because of this fact mainly, out of consideration for the dead, whom they wanted to bury intact, as if hoping for a slow regeneration, they became fond of the land that guarded them; and everything the Etruscans did was, essentially, nothing more than a great work of recognition and consecration of the Italian soil.[54]

Also in 'La tomba del guerriero', the author continues with this assimilation:

> And by now the debris will have filled it [the tomb], or it will be one of the many suspicious holes found in that land made of clay and tuff, that the Tarquinian people call, because of the many mounds scattered all over it, the Monterozzi.[55]

Cardarelli's gaze often stands on archaeological finds which are intermingled with the everyday life of Tarquinia, revealing, on the one hand, a mixture between ancient and modern times (see the second paragraph in this contribution) and on the other hand a sense of decay: 'It is not rare to find in a vineyard, in a garden, an Etruscan or Roman sarcophagus reduced to the use of a tub to wash herbs.'[56] In 'I Villanoviani' a newly found tomb is described in a similar vein:

> Since the miserable bowl was hidden in the hollow of a large tuff or terracotta jar, which, carefully unearthed, was usually placed in the corner of a garden, and could become if necessary a convenient vase to plant flowers or an orange or lemon tree.[57]

As can be seen from the preceding passages, the link between human beings, earth and the realm of death is very tight, which results in the use of the infernal model. Dante's model becomes even more central in *Il cielo sulle città*, which is a travel prose: the author's journey to the land that was once inhabited by the silent, infernal Etruscans runs parallel to Dante's journey to the underworld.

Etruschi Moderni

Cardarelli's *prose d'arte* represent Etruscan civilisation through a wide range of images, associations and metaphors which have been analysed throughout this chapter, from the metaphor of stratification to the association with the *inferno* and the close link with the earth. Nevertheless, several of his prose texts do not mention explicitly Etruscan civilisation but evoke its characteristics referring to the same themes, such as primitiveness, vulgarity, and the occult. Indeed, my point is that in Cardarelli's *prose d'arte*, 'the Etruscan character' ('il carattere etrusco') amounts to a certain way of relating to nature, cosmos and humanity, a certain way of connecting with the earth. It is a 'type' of civilisation which survives in Tuscans of centuries and millennia later but always with a genealogical and/or geographical relationship with the Etruscans. This idea is present also in prose texts in which Cardarelli recalls his travels across Italy. *Etrusco* is, in 'La vita quotidiana', the river Tiber which he describes as 'argilloso' (made of clay) and clay is a material which art historians attribute specifically to the Etruscans: 'And in the way that its [= the Tiber's] clayey waters, shaded with green, remind me of the Etruscan land'.[58] *Etruschi* are Dante, Michelangelo and Machiavelli, not only because of their geographical affinity to the Etruscan area but for their particular characteristics:

> And if you want to get an idea of Etruria […] think of Tuscany, the Orcagna frescoes, Dante's geology. Etruscan is Leonardo in his necromantic familiarity with nature. Etruscan is Machiavelli's mind, an unexplored cave.[59]

The fact that Leonardo was 'Etruscan' by virtue of his 'necromantic familiarity' suggests that there is a certain continuity between life and death. It is as if the descendants of the Etruscans were bequeathed the ability to contact the world of the dead in a simple, intuitive and familiar way. Therefore, everything may be considered 'etrusco' if it has some kind of 'contact' with ancient Etruria (landscape, being born in Tuscany, etc.) and possesses the established qualities and characteristics pointed out by Cardarelli. This perspective also informs Maurizio Harari's analysis of D'Annunzio *Forse che sì forse che no*,[60] in which he stresses how an Etruscan aura is predominant in different points of the novel, even in passages where there is no explicit mention of the Etruscans and their culture. The settings of Volterra and the Museo Guarnacci, as well as Tarquinia and the river Tiber, for Cardarelli, contributed to realise this impression and to call to memory the Etruscan civilisation.

Furthermore, as briefly mentioned above, descriptions of modern inhabitants of Tarquinia as Etruscans are very frequent within his works. The constant connections and even overlaps between past and present finds its personification in the highly burlesque character of 'Re Tarquinio', a modern citizen, who is known by the name of the ancient Roman-Etruscan king: 'a distant and fabulous character, as old as the cliffs of my village.'[61] Aside from the name that already refers to the Etruscans, it is interesting to note that 'Re Tarquinio' seems to be part of a temporal flow which unites the inhabitants of that village since ancient times (also the Villanovans, older than the Etruscans, are part of this temporal flow). 'Sor Ettore' as well, the protagonist of the prose 'Soggiorno in Toscana', has these characteristics:

> Sor Ettore was a stonemason by profession and, of course, a man of few words, but he spoke like a Tuscan god of a good race, he represented the facts and the men of history as if he had lived among them, with a spirit that is completely confidential [...] I learned from sor Ettore to understand the Etruscan character and that slow, energetic way of speaking that is typical of some old Tuscans.[62]

Here, too, the rusticity and the primitiveness of Sor Ettore are highlighted. In the examples, there is always a strong relationship of spatial and temporal contiguity with ancient Etruria: the author seems to delineate a direct genealogical correspondence between the ancient and the modern inhabitants of those lands, which are linked by 'Tuscan-ness'.

Conclusion

This overview of Cardarelli's *prose d'arte* has highlighted a number of themes and motifs that are often associated with the Etruscans, especially during the first decades of the twentieth century, but which in the case of Cardarelli take on a particular slant, because of their connection with Tarquinia, a place in which 'silence and solitude have a superhuman touch'[63], with words that clearly echo Leopardi's *Infinito*. The literary myth of the fabulous and timeless Tarquinia occupies centre stage in many of the prose texts on the Etruscans. Tarquinia is the place where the poet's personal memory meets the ancient memory of the Etruscans, where tombs and necropolises evoke scenarios of death and the afterlife and where archaeological remains mix with the everyday utensils of the modern inhabitants. In his prose works, Cardarelli constructs an image of himself as a writer genealogically linked with the ancient Etruscans who once inhabited Tarquinia. Starting from his personal experience, connecting the idea of death with that of the ground and using an infernal vocabulary taken from Dante's *Inferno* to describe tombs and necropolises, the author constructs a trans-historical idea of the *Etrusco* that can be applied to the modern and ancient inhabitant of *Etruria*.

Notes

1. 'Il solo episodio emozionante, fra tante scene gaie e incruente, è quello di un forsennato che da un'altissima rupe si butta in mare per mettere un po' di scompiglio in un gruppo di pescatori che assistono da lontano all'incredibile tuffo. Se non che il forsennato è un nuotatore provetto, un campione del salto in acqua, a cui la primavera ha dato alla testa. E nulla potrebbe valere meglio di questo miracoloso episodio a esprimere il furore d'una primavera in Maremma'. Vincenzo Cardarelli, *Opere*, Clelia Martignoni (ed.) (Milan: Mondadori, 1981), p. 534. All translations and emphases are by Gennaro Ambrosino.
2. 'Questa che ho cercato di riassumere, tralasciando infiniti altri particolari leggiadrissimi, è la rappresentazione *fedele*, benché *fantasiosa* e *burlesca*, di una delle più belle giornate della mia terra'. *Ibid.*
3. 'Le danzatrici funebri, così frequenti in questi affreschi, non sono che antichissime ballerine di tarantella e l'immancabile tibicino dal passo lungo e dalle magiche dita, il mistico citaredo [...], mi sembrano quasi naturali predecessori di quei fanatici musicanti che al tempo della mia infanzia misero sossopra il popolo e il comune con le loro bizze e rivalità bandistiche'. *Ibid.*, p. 536.
4. Charles Burdett, *Vincenzo Cardarelli and his Contemporaries. Fascist Politics and Literary Culture* (Oxford: Oxford University Press, 1999), p. 7.
5. Regarding this genre see Caroline Zekri, 'L'"espace autobiographique" de Vincenzo Cardarelli entre prose et poésie: une anthologie de l'escriture de soi', *Revue des études italiennes*, 56 (2010), pp. 31-56.
6. See Massimo Pallottino, *Etruscologia* (Milan: Hoepli, 1984); and Antonino De Francesco, *The Antiquity of the Italian Nation: The Cultural Origins of a Political Myth in Modern Italy, 1796-1943* (Oxford: Oxford University Press, 2013).
7. 'The prevailing interest in an antiquity rooted in Tuscan territory [...] led many scholars to an inadequately supervised exercise of historical research in the local area, and gave rise to that particular strand of eighteenth-century antiquarianism, exasperatingly parochial and reckless to the point of consciously falsifying archaeological or epigraphic data, which is usually defined as *Etruscheria* or *Etruscomania*" ('L'interesse prevaricante per un'antichità radicata in territorio toscano [...] condusse non pochi eruditi a un esercizio insufficientemente sorvegliato della ricerca storica di ambito locale, e originò quel particolare filone dell'antiquaria settecentesca, esasperatamente campanilistico e avventuroso fino alla cosciente contraffazione del dato archeologico o epigrafico, che viene usualmente definito etruscheria o etruscomania'). Gilda Bartoloni, *Introduzione all'etruscologia* (Milan: Hoepli, 2012), p. 7.
8. Lucy Shipley, *The Etruscans: Lost Civilizations* (London: Reaktion Books, 2017).
9. Antonino De Francesco, *The Antiquity of the Italian Nation: the Cultural Origins of a Political Myth in Modern Italy, 1796-1943*.
10. Edoardo M. Barsotti, *At the Roots of Italian Identity: 'Race'and 'Nation'in the Italian Risorgimento, 1796–1870* (New York: Routledge, 2021).
11. This rhetoric had different development. For an in-depth analysis see De Francesco and Barsotti; regarding the literary sphere see Martina Piperno, *L'anitchità "crudele". Etruschi e Italici nella letteratura italiana del Novecento* (Rome: Carocci, 2020).
12. Martina Piperno, *L'antichità "crudele". Etruschi e Italici nella letteratura italiana del Novecento*.
13. 'L'*obesus etruscus* non è una leggenda. Ma la pancia maremmana, piuttosto rara fra la gente di città e frequentissima invece nei cosiddetti mercanti di campagna, cresce a cavallo, all'aria aperta'. Cardarelli, *Opere*, p. 536.
14. 'Il destino, dopo avermi tolto la madre mi aveva regalato in compenso una matrigna, tutta d'oro, dal cuore alle mani. [...] Tutta questa felicità durò poco, tre anni appena'. *Ibid.*, pp. 257-258
15. 'Il paese dove nacqui, dove ho trascorso la mia infanzia e parte della giovinezza, e conobbi il mio primo amore, si chiamava una volta Corneto Tarquinia'. *Ibid.*, p. 373
16. Christy Wampole, *Rootedness: The ramifications of a metaphor* (Chicago: University of Chicago Press, 2016), p. 24.
17. For a more in-depth look at the *strapaese* movement, see Charles Burdett, *Vincenzo Cardarelli and his Contemporaries: Fascist Politics and Literary Culture*, p. 138.
18. 'Il cimitero è qui a due passi, io non voglio morire a Corneto, e non veggo, d'altra parte, in che modo potrò uscire da questa *trappola* in cui sono cascato'. Cardarelli, *Opere*, p. 915.
19. 'Lascio passare gli anni prima di rimettere piede in questo mio favoloso paese. E non faccio che sognarmelo e sospirarlo come se fosse in capo al mondo; più soddisfatto, si direbbe, dalla privazione che m'impongo standone lontano, più pago del ricordo e dell'immagine che ne porto con me, che non del piacere che proverei rivedendolo'. Cardarelli, *Opere*, pp. 249-250. *Ibid.*, p. 388.

20. 'Sempre ricorderò del mio paese, la deserta poesia di quei luoghi fuori mano, presso alle mura castellane […]. Qui rise l'Etrusco, un giorno, coricato, cogli occhi a fior di terra, guardando la marina. E accoglieva nelle sue pupille il multiforme e silenzioso splendore della terra fiorente e giovane, di cui aveva succhiato il mistero gaiamente, senza ribrezzo e senza paura, affondandoci le mani e il viso'. *Ibid.* pp. 249-250.
21. Martina Piperno, *L'anitchità "crudele". Etruschi e Italici nella letteratura italiana del Novecento*, pp. 59-60.
22. Fabio Camilletti, *Leopardi's Nymphs: Grace, Melancholy, and the Uncanny* (New York: Routledge, 2013).
23. *Ibid.*, p. 112.
24. See Edoardo M. Barsotti, 'Race and Risorgimento: An unexplored chapter of Italian history', *Journal of Modern Italian Studies*, vol. 25 (2020), pp. 273-294.
25. Martina Piperno, *L'anitchità "crudele". Etruschi e Italici nella letteratura italiana del Novecento*, pp. 70-72.
26. Antonino De Francesco, *The Antiquity of the Italian Nation: the Cultural Origins of a Political Myth in Modern Italy, 1796-1943*, pp. 181-188.
27. 'The Etruscans are our romantic fathers. The fury that Rome put into dispersing the Etruscans, destroying their civilisation, silencing their language, was inspired by her naive repugnance for all sorts of romanticism. The struggle between the Romans and the Etruscans was more than a war of religions: it was a war of souls' ('Gli Etruschi sono i nostri padri romantici. L'accanimento che Roma pose a disperdere gli Etruschi, a distruggere la loro civiltà, ad ammutolire la loro lingua, le era ispirato dalla sua ingenita ripugnanza per ogni sorta di romanticismo. La lotta fra Romani ed Etruschi fu più che una guerra di religioni: fu una guerra di anime'). Alberto Savinio, *Dico a te, Clio* (Milan: Adelphi, 1992), p. 94.
28. Martina Piperno, *L'anitchità "crudele". Etruschi e Italici nella letteratura italiana del Novecento*, pp. 70-71.
29. 'Roma sorprese gli Etruschi mentre stavano lavorando senza sospetto, come sempre; e ne andò lungo il lamento […]. Oggi, di questo popolo misterioso e sopraffatto che siede alle origini della nostra civiltà, venuto non si sa dove, dal mare forse, ma rivolto a monte, non ci rimane che lo stampo corrotto della sua immagine sulla terra, là dove s'è coricato morendo'. Cardarelli, *Opere*, p. 392.
30. 'Il popolo etrusco fu veramente *strozzato*, più che abbattuto, da Galli, Greci e Romani riuniti, e le notizie che di esso ci rimangono sono quelle che ci hanno tramandato i suoi *nemci*' *Ibid.*, p. 653.
31. 'Narrano dunque gli storici che le donne etrusche solevano prostituirsi per farsi la dote […], [seguissero] la religione tenebrosa, certi sistemi di pena crudelissimi'. *Ibid.*
32. Che cosa sono gli Etruschi, dopo il turbine indoeuropeo, se non i restauratori della prisca civiltà mediterranea ch'essi condussero, in sostanza, alla massima perfezione? È attraverso gli Etruschi che Roma, se mai, si mediterraneizza in tanti modi, ma soprattutto assumentosi quel carattere di città commerciale che, secondo i più autorevoli storici, la distingue, fin dall'inizio, da ogni altro abitato latino'. *Ibid.*, p. 666.
33. 'Un tipo d'uomo più evoluto, che sarebbe quello della Majella e della grotta dell'Olmo, vicino ad Arezzo, si sostituì in Italia a questo primo elemento semiscimmiesco ed è a lui che noi amiamo rifarci come al nostro lontanissimo e diretto progenitore. […] è il capostipite di una razza che si dice mediterranea o altrimenti ligure-sicula. […] Dirò solo che la Toscana sembra essere stata una delle regioni dove i Siculi operarono più a fondo'. *Ibid.*, pp. 657-658.
34. 'Da ragazzo ho assistito a qualche scavo nella necropoli etrusca del mio paese. Si cercavano tombe a camera, sarcofaghi di nenfro o di pietra colorata, ori, bronzi, vasi di bucchero, preziose anfore istoriate. Ma il più delle volte, dopo tante fatiche, alzata una lastra di tufo, non si scopriva che una ciotola colma di ossa bruciate e, in mezzo a quel tritume di ossetti bianchi ed aridi, qualche cosa che luccicava'. *Ibid.*, p. 662.
35. 'Da qualche tempo, per amore dell'Italia e del mio natale, mi sono dato all'archeologia e alla paleontologia. Mi piace sapere come e da chi fu abitata la terra italiana quando le isole erano ancora attaccate al continente, ma già gl'intervalli che ora sono colmati dal mare dovevano essere difficilmente praticabili, perché l'uomo italico appare, prima che altrove, sulla nascente penisola e sembra aggrapparsi alle rive'. *Ibid.* p. 657.
36. 'Che so io degli Etruschi? Quel tanto solo che m'è dato immaginare, essendo nato, si può dire, in mezzo alle loro tombe'. *Ibid.*, p. 391.
37. Sacha Colby, *Stratified Modernism: The Poetics of Excavation from Gautier to Olson* (London: Peter Lang, 2009).
38. *Ibid.*, p. 39.
39. 'Di rado mi spingevo fino a quella strana, disabitatissima villa, chiamata Villa Tarantola, che vede già il camposanto ed era allora per me un sito misterioso, enigmatico, evocante, nel suo nome, i velenosi ragni che danno il ballo di San Vito […]. Né mai mi avvenne di udire voci o scorgere

anima viva curiosando là dentro. L'aspetto di questa solitaria villetta era irreprensibile e il terrore o piuttosto stupore ch'essa m'inspirava, tutte le volte che io ficcassi il naso fra quelle sbarre, d'una qualità ben nota ai lettori d'Edgardo Poe'. Cardarelli, *Opere*, p. 393.

40. 'La portavano all'ospedale col carretto, e lei stava in piedi là sopra, incantata, trasumanata, bellissima. La sua bianca faccia splendeva come quella di una santa in estasi. Nella luce d'un tramonto d'estate, in quel paesaggio, non potevo fare un incontro più commovente e oserei aggiungere significativo, per quel che riguarda gli effetti che può produrre un ragno abitatore di terre così macerate e mortifere. Ma la scienza non crede ai misteriosi malori che si attribuiscano alla tarantola. E queste mie non sono che impressioni e fantasie di un *profano*'. *Ibid.*, p. 396.

41. 'Fin da ragazzo ho amato le distanze e la solitudine. Uscire dalle porte del mio paese e guardarlo da di fuori, come qualche cosa di perduto, era uno dei miei più abituali diletti'. *Ibid.*, p, 393.

42. See Sasha Colby, *Stratified Modernism: The Poetics of Excavation from Gautier to Olson*.

43. Sigmund Freud, *The Interpretation of Dreams* (Toronto: McClelland & Stewart, 2020), p. 588.

44. Julian Thomas, 'Sigmund Freud's archaeological metaphor and archaeology's self-understanding' in *Contemporary Archaeologies: Excavating Now*, Cornelius Holtorf and Angela Piccini (eds) (London: Peter Lang, 2009), pp. 49-50.

45. 'Nel suolo cavernoso e sconquassato, tre civiltà, per lo meno, giacciono, l'una sopra l'altra, stratificate, e piú l'uomo scava più s' accorge che il tempo da cui data la sua presenza in questi luoghi si confonde con l'età della terra, è piú antico assai della sua memoria'. Cardarelli, *Opere*, p. 374.

46. 'La storia dell'umanità si confonde, per una sterminata successione di secoli, con quella della crosta terrestre. È geologia pura'. *Ibid.*, p. 656.

47. 'Questa razza di bonificatori […] portò a cottura *il mito dell'Inferno* e creò forse, dei suoi giganteschi numi, i piú infuocati e rossi'. *Ibid.*, p. 392.

48. Martina Piperno, *L'antichità "crudele". Etruschi e Italici nella letteratura italiana del Novecento*; Maurizio Harari, 'Non si va senza duca in questo Inferno. D'Annunzio e il mito etrusco', in *Velathri Volterrae. La città etrusca e il municipio romano*, Atti del convegno di studi (Volterra, 21-22 september 2017), vol. I, Marisa Bonamici and Elena Sorge (eds) (Rome: Bretschneider Giorgio, 2001), pp. 239-251.

49. 'Scendendo a recuperarlo il nostro gentiluomo fece, senza saperlo, il viaggio di Ulisse all'Inferno. Egli si trovò sbalzato in un altro tempo, in un luogo indefinibile, dove tutto parlava il grande linguaggio degli Etruschi, nelle forme piú commoventi e dirette'. Cardarelli, *Opere*, p. 524.

50. 'Pare che una volta, attorno al mio paese, per quanto è vasto il territorio, fosse tutta una macchia di cornioli; selva, riccia, ispida e fitta […] dove il pellegrino che andava a Roma si addentrava con paura. Albergo di fiere e di briganti. Così Dante rappresentò questo paese o piuttosto le sue incolte campagne'. *Ibid.*, pp. 373-374. 'L'Inferno' is also the title of one of his prose d'arte in *Prologhi*. In that case there is no reference either to Dante or to Tarquinia.

51. '[Le parole] per lui non hanno mai un significato imposto o convenzionale, ma sempre *originario* o, se vogliamo dire, supremo. Ne ricerca la *prima radice* e quella *lontana purità* e *verginità* di senso che giace *sepolta* e spesso irriconoscibile sotto la tirannia dell'uso'. *Ibid.*, p. 363.

52. See Martina Piperno, *L'antichità "crudele". Etruschi e Italici nella letteratura italiana del Novecento*, pp. 25-55.

53. *Ibid.*, p. 64.

54. 'Se ci si attaccarono in modo che la storia non conosce un popolo più fermo, più *radicato*, fu soltanto perché in loro l'amore per la terra si confondeva con la religione dei morti. Per questo fatto principalmente, per riguardo ai morti, che essi miravano a seppellire intatti, come per una lenta rigenerazione, si affezionarono alla terra che li custodiva; e tutto quello che fecero gli Etruschi non fu, in sostanza, che una grande opera di ricognizione e consacrazione del suolo italiano'. Cardarelli, *Opere*, p. 530.

55. 'E ormai i *detriti* l'avranno colmata [la tomba], o sarà una delle tante buche sospette che s'incontrano per quella terra *argillosa* e *tufacea* che i tarquiniesi chiamano, a cagione dei molti tumuli di cui è sparsa, li Monterozzi'. *Ibid.*, p. 526.

56. 'Non è raro trovare in una vigna, in un orto, un sarcofago etrusco o romano ridotto ad uso di vasca per lavare gli erbaggi'. *Ibid.*, p. 374.

57. 'Giacché la misera ciotola era nascosta nel cavo di un grande orcio di tufo o di terracotta, il quale, dissepolto con ogni cura, veniva per lo più collocato nell'angolo di un giardino e poteva diventare, all'occorrenza, un comodo vaso da piantarvi fiori o qualche alberello di arancio o di limo'. *Ibid.*, p. 662.

58. 'E a quel modo che le sue [= del Tevere] acque argillose, ombrate di verde, mi ricordano costantemente la terra etrusca'. *Ibid.*, p. 472.

59. 'E se volete farvi un'idea dell'Etruria […] pensate alla Toscana del Medioevo, agli affreschi dell'Orcagna, alla *geologia* dantesca. Etrusco è Leonar-

do, nella sua *negromantica* famigliarità con la natura. Etrusca è la mente di Machiavelli, *inesplorabile caverna*'. *Ibid.* p. 530.
60. Maurizio Harari, 'Non si va senza duca in questo Inferno. D'Annunzio e il mito etrusco', p. 242.
61. 'Personaggio ormai lontano e favoloso, antico come le rupi del mio paese'. Cardarelli, *Opere*, p. 409.
62. '[Sor Ettore] era di professione scalpellino e, naturalmente, uomo di poche lettere, ma parlava come un dio Toscano di buona razza, si rappresentava i fatti e gli uomini della storia come *se ci avesse vissuto in mezzo*, con uno spirito, cioè, al tutto confidenziale. [...] Imparai dal sor Ettore a conoscere il carattere toscano e quel modo di parlare lento, energico e proprio ch'è di certi *vecchi toscani*'. *Ibid.*, p. 446.
63. 'Il silenzio e la solitudine hanno del sovrumano'. *Ibid.*, p. 337.

The Problem of Distance: Giorgio Bassani, The Etruscans and the Limits of Compassion

Martina Piperno

Moral philosophers have always been particularly intrigued by phenomena of distance – whether spatial, temporal, emotive or cultural, or a combination of any of these, for distance seems to impact the human capacity to feel empathy or compassion. Giorgio Bassani, in his 1962 novel *The Garden of the Finzi-Continis* (henceforth *Garden*),[1] suggests how to expand our capacity for compassion to break down distance (or at least to overcome it in part) and guarantee the survival of memory and humanity; and he does so by using the symbolic heritage of Etruscan culture. The *Garden* can be considered the most successful Italian novel about life in the Italian Jewish community before the Shoah.[2] The main character, the author's *alter ego*, tells us about his visits at the Finzi-Contini family house in the crucial months following the promulgation of the Italian racial laws in September 1938: by the end of the novel the entire family is caught and deported, while the narrator survives. Before starting his memorial endeavour, the narrator tells us, in an eloquent *Prologue*, that he had never felt a real urge to tell the story of the Finzi-Continis until the spring of 1957, when he happened to visit, together with a group of friends, the Etruscan necropolis of La Banditaccia in the municipality of Cerveteri, not far from Rome. This suggests that there is something in the necropolis that inspires a mourning ritual, and an urgent need to tell the stories of the lost and the disappeared before it is too late. Let us unpack the extremely refined and allusive way in which Bassani stages this illumination, and the beginning of his epic narration.

Before entering the Etruscan cemetery, the youngest of the group, Giannina, a nine-year-old girl, asks her dad an apparently simple question:

'- Papa, why are old tombs less sad than new ones?'[3]

Her father attempts an answer:

'Well, [...] the recent dead are closer to us, and so it makes sense that we care more about them. The Etruscans, they have been dead such a long time [...] it's as though they'd never lived, as though they were always dead'.[4]

To which Giannina responds:

> 'But now that you say that [...] it makes me think [...] that the Etruscans really did live, and that I care about them just as much as about the others'.[5]

This sentence seems to impact very much the other visitors: 'The whole visit to the necropolis that followed was infused by the extraordinary tenderness of this remark'[6] and so is, we are led to suppose, the narration of the whole novel starting in the following chapter.

What Giannina does, in this passage dense of implications, is to offer a solution to what Carlo Ginzburg, in *Wooden Eyes* (*Occhiacci di legno*, 1998), drawing on Aristotle, Diderot, Balzac, Hume, Sade, and Benjamin, calls the moral problem of distance. As humans, we are naturally inclined to feel piety and compassion for people who are relatively close. Not too close, or identification would prevail. Not too distant, because our capacity for compassion has some limits. 'Too great a distance gives rise to indifference; too great proximity may awaken compassion, or provoke [...] rivalry'.[7] Aristotle's *Rhetoric* (1386a) provides a first assessment of this feature of the human mind: people 'pity those like themselves in age, in character, in habits, in rank, in birth; for in all these cases something seems more to apply also to the self; [...] people pity things happening to others in so far as they fear for themselves. [...] People do not feel pity, or not in the same way, about things ten thousand years in the past or future'. According to Aristotle, we are not wired to be emotionally connected to those who are far away, in either time – up to 10,000 years – or in space: 'no one rivals [...] those who live at the Pillars of Heracles' (*Rhetoric*, 1388a). This also applies to people who are unlike us, in age, language, perspective or culture. This is why, argues Ginzburg, is so difficult to feel compassion for animals, and for some animals in particular, like insects.'[8]

This principle has profound implications as it makes evident the limits of our moral imagination. As Ginzburg points out, several thinkers reflected on this topic in the eighteenth century: for example, Diderot, in *Entretien d'un père avec ses enfants, ou du danger de se mettre au-dessus des lois* (1773), tells about a murderer who escaped miles away from the crime scene. Guilt is in fact inspired by the fear of punishment rather than by moral scruples: 'distance in place and time perhaps to some extent weakened feeling and awareness of all kinds, even the consciousness of crime'. For this reason, anyone would kill a human being if men and women were smaller ('no larger than a swallow'), argues Diderot in *Lettre sur les aveugles à l'usage de ceux qui voient* (1749). The theme, Ginzburg synthesises, crosses the centuries: responding to a passage of Chateaubriand's

Génie du Christianisme (1802), Balzac, in *Père Goriot* (1834), argues provocatively that killing a Chinese is perceived as less serious than killing a European, because of the spatial, cultural and emotive distance.

This principle, identified by Aristotle and reverberating in modern thought, is still active today, even when technology challenges spatial distance and time zones. The essays collected in *Wooden eyes* were written during the Gulf War, in the early Nineties: at the time people discussed widely the so-called 'intelligent bombs', supposedly capable of minimising disruption by hitting specific targets: 'Airplanes and missiles have shown how right Diderot was.'[9] Nowadays, most wars are fought with drones, meaning that technological warfare has progressed further in the same direction. Besides, the COVID-19 pandemic has made the emotive problem of distance dramatically evident. At the time of Bassani, Europe was still learning about the Nazi concentration camps, where millions were killed not only 'away from the eyes of the many' ('do not we too cease to feel compassion once distance, or the smallness of objects, produces the effect on us that the lack of sight produces on the blind?', wrote Diderot in the *Lettre sur les aveugles*), but also 'at a distance' with gas, like the Finzi-Contini family in the novel. People were slowly coming to terms with the Shoah, object of a collective removal, if not denial, fuelled by misinformation. As known, Primo Levi's *If this is a man* was initially rejected by Einaudi, apparently in the person of Natalia Ginzburg, and was released by a small publisher in 1947, remaining mostly unknown. The second edition, published by Einaudi in 1958, had contributed to starting a difficult conversation about what happened in Nazi concentration camps, becoming Italy's 'critical conscience'.[10] Italian society, at the time the *Garden* was written, was just starting to overcome the spatial, temporal and informative distance with the tragic scale of the Nazi-Fascist genocide.

How can humans counteract the effects of distance? To clarify this, we may take into account one of Ginzburg's sources, Hume's *Treatise of Human Nature* (1739); Ginzburg refers in particular to its section 'On Contiguity and Distance in Space and Time', which immediately follows a chapter entitled 'On the Influence of Imagination on the Passions'. Imagination is an element of crucial importance, in that it determines our passions: 'nothing, which affects the former, can be entirely indifferent to the latter'; secondly, imagination is influenced by contiguity and distance: 'the contiguous […] approach an impression in force and vivacity'; 'the remote […] appear in a weaker and more imperfect light. This is their effect on the imagination.' Therefore, the human faculty that is capable of counteracting the indifference resulting from distance, according to Hume, is imagination. A child is, according to a long tradition of Western philosophy, the most imaginative being. Perfectly in line with Hume's reasoning, Bassani bestows the young Giannina, a child, with the responsibility of reducing, if not erasing completely, the distance between the visitors to the Etruscan necropolis and the dead Etruscans who once inhabited the place. Accordingly, Giannina's moral sensibility is still sufficiently flexible to 'care' for the disappeared Etruscans, and to influence everyone around her.

The Etruscans symbolically stand for the Jews massacred in the Nazi concentration camps. This is implicit, but also allusively suggested by another question by Giannina: 'Papa, who d'you think were the oldest, the Etruscans or the Jews?', to which the father replies laughing 'Try asking that gentleman', thus informing us that the narrative 'I' is a Jew.[11] The analogy between Etruscans and Jews is interesting and problematic, as Andreas Steiner has already pointed out:[12] both are ancient peoples, whose origins date back millennia. Both were migrants, who left their native lands to escape famine (the Etruscans, according to Herodotus) or persecution (the Jews). When the narrator visits the noble tomb of the 'Matuta' family (in fact 'Matunas'; the tomb is now known as 'Tomba dei rilievi/Tomb of the Reliefs'), it reminds him of the monumental tomb of the Finzi-Continis back in the Jewish cemetery of Ferrara. The narrator notices the 'everyday objects of their lives', mostly hunting and artisanal tools, 'hoes, rakes, axes, scissors, spades, knives, bows, arrows, even hunting dogs and marsh birds',[13] which may suggest a comparison with the everyday objects that victims left behind in the concentration camps (those that are exposed at the Auschwitz-Birkenau Memorial and Museum in Oświęcim, Poland, and are now part of mass culture; although the museum had already opened in 1947, Bassani visited it only after the 1970s).[14] The objects that are laid out in the Etruscan tomb are 'fiercely functional and assertive' and 'affirm the [Matunas] family's will to domesticate a hostile environment',[15] yet their collocation in a tomb, deprived of their original function, suggests a sense of surrender. It may be interesting to notice that D. H. Lawrence, who visited the same tomb in 1928 (he calls it the 'Grotta Bella Tomb') and wrote about it in *Etruscan Places* (1932), observed the same objects but he described them as 'mostly warriors' arms and insignia: 'shields, helmets, corselets, greaves for the legs, swords, spears, shoes, belts, the necklace of the noble: and then the sacred drinking bowl, the sceptre [...]. All these are represented on the walls', which shows the polysemantic nature of the symbolic space of the necropolis.[16]

The comparison between the Jews and the Etruscans is therefore full of implications. While the Etruscans are perceived as 'lost' in time, 'distant' at least a couple of millennia, modern Jews were, before the racial laws, very much alive and integrated into Italian society. Yet after the racial laws Jews felt doomed, resigned like 'the late Etruscans of Cerveteri', and restricted in ghettos and exclusive spaces. Micòl's family garden, with its tennis court, which welcomed those excluded by regular sport clubs in 1938, is one of those restricted and protected spaces, even if it maintains an Edenic illusory appearance. 'New civilisations, cruder and less refined, but also stronger and more warlike, by this stage held the field. But in the end, what did it matter? [...] The future could overturn the world as it pleased.' Furthermore, the monumental 'appearance' of Etruscan funerary art and architecture as opposed to the fragility of the city of the living, which makes all things Etruscan a symbol of death and decadence in non-specialised culture,[17] further highlights the astonishing, disquieting 'disappearance' of the bodies of the deported, who do not have a grave. It is not a coincidence, then, that the mind of the narrator wanders first to the Finzi-Contini monumental tomb, which is almost empty, 'only one of the Finzi-Contini I had known and loved had actually achieved this repose. [...] Alberto [...] who died in 1942 of a lymphogranuloma' –, and then to those of whom 'no one knows whether they have any grave at all'. As Millicent Marcus has synthesised, 'the spectacle of the intact Etruscan family whose second life is seen as continuous with the first [...] presents the greatest possible contrast to the fate of the Finzi-Continis, dispersed, dispossessed, and dismembered'.[18]

In his account of his visit to another Etruscan town, Tarquinia, Lawrence had anticipated Bassani in drawing a comparison between the fascist as heir of the Romans and the Etruscans as their victims:

> Tarquinia [...] was known for centuries, as Corneto – Corgnetum or Cornetium – and forgotten was its Etruscan past. Then [...] the Fascist regime [...] glorying in the Italian origins of Italy, has now struck out the Corneto, so the town is once more, simply, Tarquinia. [...] So the wheel of revolution turns. There stands the Etruscan word – Latinised Etruscan – beside the mediaeval gate, put up by the Fascist power to name and unname. The Fascists, who consider themselves in all things Roman, Roman of the Caesars, heirs of Empire and world power, are beside the mark restoring the rags of dignity to Etruscan places.[19]

Bassani seems to remember this page, but the parallel between ancient and modern peoples is more nuanced here. The identification between modern Jews menaced by the Fascists and ancient, decadent Etruscans endangered by the Roman conquest hides Bassani's criticism of the 'garden mentality', which

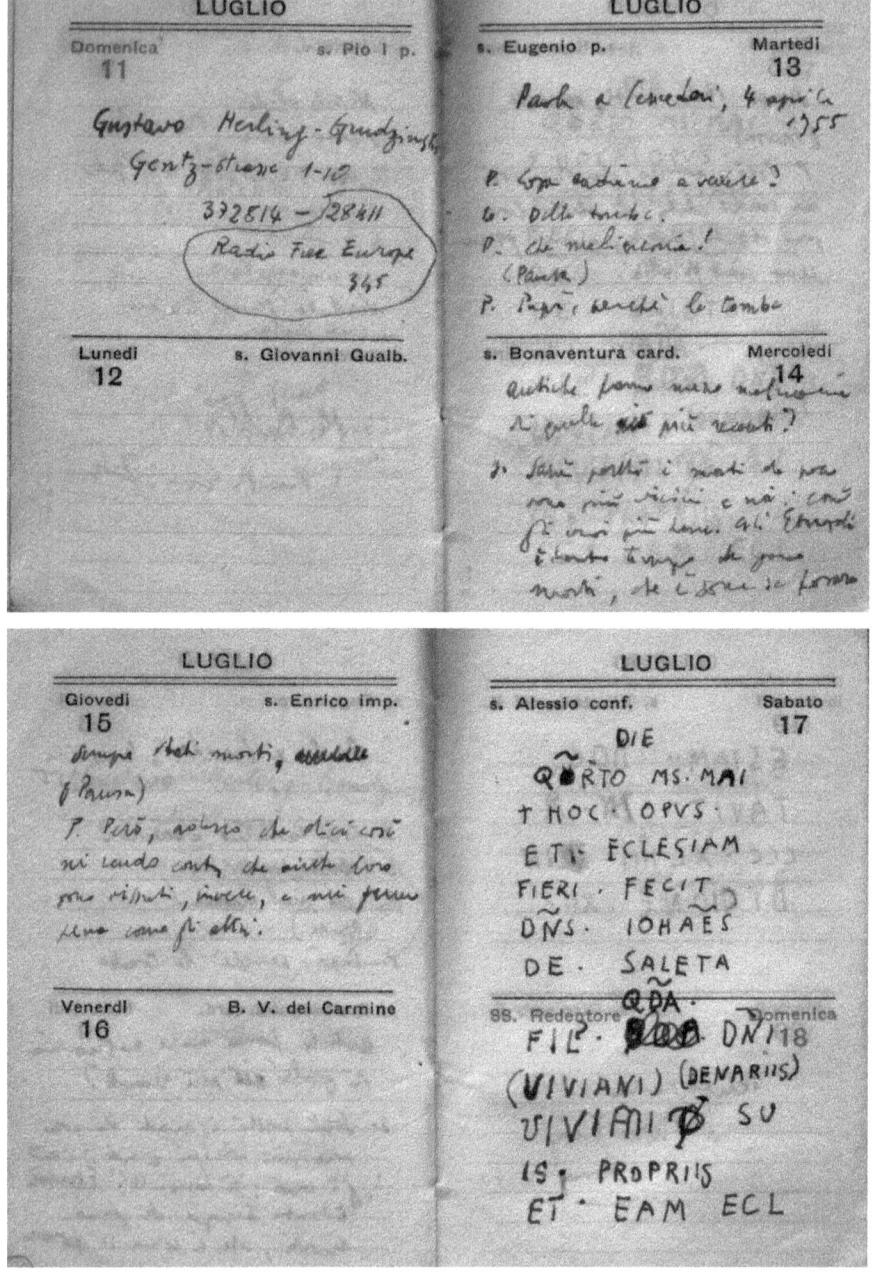

Fig. 8.1 & 8.2 Giorgio Bassani's agenda. Archivio eredi Bassani, Fondo Manoscritti, Serie Taccuini e agende, Agenda 2, cc. 42-43 Permission: Fondazione Bassani.

passively awaits history's verdict'[20] of the Jewish bourgeoisie, who had reacted to racist law-making and persecution with resignation. At the same time, this parallel carries a terrible admonition: deceased Jews risk the complete oblivion and anonymity that now surrounds the Etruscans, as the new victims of the Nazi-Fascist power to name and unname, to use Lawrence's words. It is time to talk about them, to remove the collective block that has prevented the conversation about those who left for the concentration camps and never returned.

We know from various sources that Bassani actually visited the Etruscan necropolis of Cerveteri in the Fifties accompanied by friends and family, and that Giannina's character is in fact a reflection of his eldest daughter, Paola. A marginal note in an agenda used as a notebook shows that, originally, Giannina's questions were Paola's questions, and that the Etruscan tour happened on 4 April 1955, not in 1957 as in the novelistic fiction.[21] In an interview with Vittorio Sereni, Bassani revealed the discrepancies between real life and fiction: 'the episode was slightly corrected [...]. The character of the child [...] which I have delegated to a friend [...] was my daughter Paola at around nine or ten years of age.'[22] In the novel's fiction, therefore, the dialogue happens two years later, and with a child much 'more distant' from the narrator than she was in real life. Bassani does not explain why he felt the need to put some *distance* between himself as an author/narrator and the real elements inspiring him. Sergio Parussa has provided an answer to this question on a practical level, exploring Bassani's creative process;[23] here I might attempt an answer on a philosophical level. It is likely, in fact, that this had to do with Aristotle's principle quoted above: excessive distance compromises empathy, but excessive proximity induces identification and compromises compassion as well as distance. It is likely, therefore, that this putting some distance between real life events and the novel is a response to the need of a balanced 'distance' from the original events guaranteeing objective and credible storytelling as well as an adequate emotive response from the reader. (Fig. 8.1 & Fig. 8.2)

Bassani's *Prologue* is part of and pays homage to the traditional genre of sepulchral literature and poetry; in particular, it echoes a canonised text of Italian literature: Ugo Foscolo's classic poem *Dei sepolcri* [On sepulchers, 1807], written during the Napoleonic sovereignty over Northern Italy. Foscolo's poem was inspired by the Décret Impérial sur les Sépultures (1804), known as Edict of Saint-Cloud, which forbade burial in churches and in towns and prescribed instead the construction of cemeteries *at a distance*, outside city walls; furthermore, it prescribed tombs should all look the same, to avoid discrimination, and epitaphs on the graves of illustrious men to be approved by a commission. In a word, the Edict negated *proximity* and *presence* to the graves of the dead and prescribed hygienic *distance* and *uniformity* to the graves. As Foscolo puts it:

> And yet today a new law
> *hides the tombs from loving eyes*
> and robs the dead even of their names. [...]
> Tombs gave silent witness of glory,
> were altars for those who came after; from the tomb
> rose the *household* gods' answers
> to prayer; an oath sworn *by the bones*
> *of ancestors* struck awe in the heart.
> Through such rites, as the long years turned,
> the cult of the dead passed down the virtues
> of the tribe and family devotion [...]
> and those who *stopped* [Italian: 'sedea', sat]
> to pour libations of milk and tell
> their sorrows to the beloved dead breathed
> a fragrance like the air of the Elysian fields—
> loving delusion: it endears the groves
> that shade the dead at *town's edge*
> to British maidens, drawn by love
> of the mother they have lost.[24]

Foscolo argues that to maintain their key societal function, tombs must be part of everyday life: they must therefore be close and familiar as they were in the ancient times when relatives were incinerated and their remains kept at home (Lares), or more recently in the cemeteries sung by British graveyard poets. The focus is on proximity and familiarity, which ensures the continuation of a dialogue with the dead, a 'communion of devoted hearts' ('corrispondenza d'amorosi sensi'). Similarly, Bassani evokes the *proximity* between Etruscan cemeteries and cities, which ensures a melancholic continuation of the relationship with the departed.

> Just as, still today, in small Italian provincial towns, the cemetery gate is the obligatory terminus for every evening passeggiata [stroll], they came from the inhabited *vicinity* almost always *on foot* – I imagined – gathered in groups of relatives and blood kindred [...], in groups, or else in pairs, lovers,

or even alone, *to wander among the conical tombs* […].Yes, everything was changing – they must have told themselves as they walked along the paved way which crossed the cemetery from one end to the other, the centre of which, over centuries of *wear*, had been *gradually incised* by the iron wheel-rims of their vehicles, *leaving two deep parallel grooves*. […] Once across the cemetery's threshold […] each of them owned *a second home*, and inside it the already prepared bed-like structure on which, soon enough, they would be laid alongside their forefathers, eternity did not perhaps appear to be such an illusion, a fable, a hieratic promise. The future could overturn the world as it pleased.[25]

This paragraph evokes habit ('quasi sempre'), closeness (tombs are at walking distance), domesticity ('una seconda casa') and even consumption ('inciso a poco a poco') determined by frequentation; the evening stroll to the cemetery is described as long-standing tradition of provincial Italy. Bassani romanticises specific elements of Etruscan culture such as the importance of funerary art and the closeness between the city of the dead and the city of the living (which has profound theological implications) to reassess the importance of a continuous dialogue with one's ancestors and the closeness of bodily remains. Furthermore, the tomb ensures at least the transmission of a family name, the Matunas, an exception in the anonymity of the Etruscan people. Finally, the funerary art conserved in the 'Tomba dei rilievi' celebrates and monumentalises life, giving Bassani inspiration for his own commemorative project.

The dialogue between Bassani and Foscolo does not end here. As we have seen, the narrator says that the visit to Cerveteri was the necessary push to remember and tell the long-hidden story of a family who had disappeared. He therefore proposes himself as a witness, but also as a rhapsode: a modern Homer who takes up the responsibility of safeguarding the memory of what risks to be lost in time. In the final stanza of *On Sepulchers*, Foscolo symbolically constructs the social role of poetry in a similar way. Poetry is in fact personified in the classic figure of Homer, described as wandering in the region of Troy and then descending into the ancient tombs of Trojan heroes. There, he would listen to the lament of the tombs themselves, collecting the stories he would later combine to form the *Iliad*. Clearly, this passage is a re-elaboration of the mythological models of the *katabasis* (descent in Hell, as in the case i.e. of Orpheus) and *nekya* (necromancy; dialogue with the dead), examples of which are present also in the Homeric poems (i.e. Odysseus's decent into Hell and dialogue with Tiresias in *Odyssey* Canto XI). Through this process, argues Foscolo, the memory of the deeds of Dardanus' bloodline will be remembered forever:

> Some day you will watch a blind beggar
> wander [Italian: 'errar'] in your venerable shade, groping
> his way into the graves to embrace the urns
> and question them. The hidden vaults will moan
> and the whole tomb will tell of Troy
> razed twice, twice resurrected
> in splendour from its silent streets, only
> to add to the final triumph of Peleus'
> murderous line. The holy bard,
> soothing those anguished souls with his song,
> will make the princes of Greece immortal
> in every land great father Ocean
> holds in his embrace. And you, Hector,
> will have homage of tears, wherever tears
> are shed for the blood that heroes spill
> to hallow the fatherland, and as long as sunlight
> falls on the horrors of our human kind.[26]

It is possible to notice some similarities with Bassani's prologue; the poet-narrator and his friends find themselves in the Etruscan necropolis as a result of their (apparently) casual wandering (an 'errare') on a relaxed April Sunday on the coastline near Rome. Upon entering the necropolis, Bassani's narrator, like Foscolo's 'holy bard' ('sacro vate'), descends into a tomb, the 'Tombs of the Reliefs', as seen above: another *katabasis*, which preludes to the new dialogue with the dead. Down there, he has the opportunity to contemplate the habitual tools of everyday life that the dead have left behind, which brings him back to the objects left in the mansion of the Finzi-Contini, the objects that Micòl loved. Additionally, his mind starts to wander back and forth between ancient times and recent history, allowing traumatic flashes to resurface: 'the conical tombs [were] hulking and solid as the bunkers German soldiers vainly scattered about Europe during the last war'.[27]

By the time the visit is over, during a slow boring journey back to Rome (the rhythm of the movement has indeed changed completely to allow the grieving process) the narrator is portrayed as pondering and mulling over his memories, starting his recollections and giving shape to the novel. Given that Foscolo's poem was definitely a familiar reference for any Italian who received formal education in the twentieth century, which most of his readers could recognise, it can be argued that Bassani engages in an intertextual dialogue with the illustrious, foundational model and in this way transforms the *Prologue* into an extremely refined manifesto of poetics. The classical, erudite references are however concealed in an apparently linear and discreet prose, fluid but full of hidden implications.

Framing the Finzi-Contini story as a recollection, as something that is inherently past and gone, must have been very important for Bassani. In 1970, Vittorio De Sica directed a film based on the novel; the author, who was not involved in the final version of the screenplay, was so let down by the result that he wrote an open letter about it, entitled 'The Garden Betrayed' ('Il giardino tradito'). In this article, he complained vigorously that the filmmakers ignored his idea of inserting into the main narrative obsessive flash forwards showing the deportation of the Jews in 1943 in black and white, 'the colour of documentary chronicles' ('il colore della cronoaca documentaria'). Bassani believed such a feature was necessary to convey the structure of the novel which is built 'on two distinct temporal levels' that of 1957 (trip to Cerveteri) and 1938-39 (the core of the novel). It looks like including the episode of the Etruscan necropolis in the cinematic version was never an option, but according to the author the structure of the movie should have at least echoed the mnemonic and memorial stance of the narrative, as well as the tragic irony that pervades it, by showing beforehand that the story was going to end dramatically. The loss of this temporal dyscrasia, for Bassani, compromises the artistic value of the movie.[28]

Let us return to the Etruscan theme. Bassani builds the suggestive power of his stroll around Cerveteri on the implicit idea that the Etruscans were forgotten because only a limited number of extremely brief sources on the Etruscans is available; that is, because there was no Etruscan Homer. It is worth recalling that the idea that the Etruscans were not only practically wiped away by the Romans, but also actively forgotten by Greek and Latin historians, had been commonplace in scholarly studies on the topic for centuries. According to Mario Guarnacci, author of the treatise *Origini italiche* (1767-72), the Romans are responsible for the loss of historical accounts on the Etruscans: 'the old Fathers, who do sing and sing again nothing other than old Greek and Roman glories, [talk about the Etruscans] only rapidly and synthetically'('vecchi Padri, che quasi null'altro cantano, e ricantano, che le glorie Greche, e le Romane, queste altre cose le dicono troncamente, e di passaggio'). Old Etruscan books were 'killed' and 'proscribed' ('Come mai dunque è seguito un tanto eccidio, ed una tanta proscrizione dei vecchi libri Italici?').[29] Historian Ridolfino Venuti blames the 'notorious ambition of the Greeks of arrogating everything to themselves' ('nota ambizione de' greci di tirar tutto a sé').[30] Similarly Girolamo Tiraboschi argues that ancient historians were 'only preoccupied to glorify their Romans' ('unicamente intenti a innalzare la gloria de' lor Romani').[31] Luigi Lanzi reflects melancholically: 'there were heroes [...] even before Agamemnon, but they did not have a poet, and therefore they are buried in oblivion. Troy itself, Philostratus says, would not even exist, if it was not for Homer' ('vissero de'prodi [...] anche prima di Agamennone, ma perché a loro mancò un poeta, perciò è che sepolti sono in una lunga obblivione. Troia istessa, dice Filostrato, quasi non sarebbe stata, se Omero stato non fosse');[32] a statement that recalls the role of poetry and narration to keep the memory of ancient peoples alive – as reassessed also by Foscolo's *Sepolcri*. Instead, historian and politician Vincenzo Cuoco, in his novel *Platone in Italia* (1804-1806) tries to imaginatively reconstruct pre-Roman history. To do so, he uses a traditional literary device: the novel is based on an incomplete fictional manuscript found by his grandfather. 'If only it was complete, o Reader, we would have a history of Magna Graecia [...] and a history of Italic philosophy' ('se esso ci fosse pervenuto intero, avremmo, o lettore, una storia della Magna Grecia [...] ed una storia della filosofia italica').[33] And finally, also Lawrence had something to say on the topic:

> We know nothing about the Etruscans except what we find in their tombs. There are references to them in Latin writers. But of first-hand knowledge we have nothing except what the tombs offer. [...] Besides, the Etruscans were vicious. We know it, because their enemies and exterminators said so. Just as we knew the unspeakable depths of our enemies in the late war. Who isn't vicious to his enemy? To my detractors I am a very effigy of vice.[34]

In addition to this sense of lost secrets, mystery, and deceit, Cerveteri's necropolis is definitely an eerie, disquieting place. As in the definition by Mark Fischer, the sense of the eerie belongs to 'landscapes partially emptied of the human. What happened to produce these ruins, this disappearance? What kind of entity was involved?'. As we have seen, in fact, the necropolis evokes 'the most fundamental metaphysical questions one could pose, questions to do with existence and non-existence', like those formulated by Giannina – even if nuanced by the sensibility of the child (it is noticeable, though, that while Giannina expresses a sweet, tender feeling – 'voglio bene [agli Etruschi]' – the young Paola Bassani instead had expressed compassion and pain – 'mi fanno pena': see above). '*Why is there something here when there should be nothing? Why is there nothing here when there should be something?*'.[35] Answering these questions leads to enquire into the violence of human civilisations and to 'brush history against the grain',[36] to quote Walter Benjamin. This slow entrance prepares the reader to access the story of the Finzi-Contini with a sense of the depth of the issues and questions that the contemplation of their destiny unfolds.

Bassani constructs his novel as a powerful tool capable of expanding compassion beyond the mere numbers and to tell the story of the victims of the Shoah, returning to them their names and their identities, annihilating not only spatial and temporal *distance*, but also the collective removal of the death of millions of people. The prologue shows that this endeavour takes as much effort as to bring the Etruscans, dead for centuries, back within the limited range of human compassion. By taking up the responsibility of telling the story of the Finzi-Contini, which might have been the story of any well-to-do Jewish-Italian family between 1938 and 1943, by showing us the magnitude and the difficulty of such enterprise through the Etruscan metaphor, Bassani is using what Benjamin, quoted by Ginzburg in his conclusion, calls the 'Messianic power' that every generation is endowed with; that is, a capability for providing redemption, memory, and recognition to those who came before us. For Benjamin, it is a 'weak Messianic power' but still 'a power to which the past has a claim'.[37]

For Ginzburg, Bassani's generation (as well as his own generation) had been endowed instead with a very strong Messianic power, in the light of what happened in the Second World War; yet Ginzburg is sceptical that these generations are up to the task: 'the sphere of what Aristotle called 'common law' seems to have become much broader. But to express compassion for those distant fellow humans would be, I suspect, an act of mere rhetoric. Our capacity to pollute and destroy the present, the past, and the future is incomparably greater than our feeble moral imagination.'[38] Instead, the reader of the *Garden* turns the page with a sense of confidence, eager to start the commemorative enterprise: Bassani seems indeed to believe in the power of literature to build a memorial to the disappeared, an 'appropriate Etruscan burial in its dignity, and its plenitude of life'.[39]

Notes

1. Quotations are from Giorgio Bassani, 'The Garden of the Finzi-Continis', in *The Novel of Ferrara*, translated by Jamie McKendrick (Oxford: Penguin, 2019), pp. 243-457 (*Garden*), and Giorgio Bassani, *Il giardino dei Finzi-Contini*, in *Opere*, Roberto Cotroneo (ed.) (Milan: Mondadori, 1998), pp. 315-577 (*Giardino*).
2. See Robert Gordon, *Holocaust in Italian literature* (Stanford: Stanford University Press, 2010), pp. 22-23, 69. *Ibid*, 'La Shoah nella letteratura italiana', in *La Shoah in Italia*, vol. II: *Vicende, memorie, rappresentazioni*, Marcello Flores and others (eds) (Turin: UTET, 2010), pp. 359-383 (pp. 370-371).
3. *Garden*, p. 245. ('- Papà [...] perché le tombe antiche fanno meno malinconia di quelle più nuove?'). *Giardino*, p. 319.
4. *Garden*, pp. 247-8. ('Si capisce, [...] I morti da poco sono più vicini a noi, e appunto per questo gli vogliamo più bene. Gli etruschi, vedi, è

tanto tempo che sono morti [...] che è come se non siano mai vissuti, come se siano *sempre* stati morti'. *Giardino*, p. 320, emphasis in the text).
5. *Garden*, p. 248. ('Però, adesso che dici così [...] mi fai pensare che anche gli etruschi sono vissuti, invece, e voglio bene a loro come a tutti gli altri., *Giardino*, p. 320).
6. *Garden*, p. 248. ('La successiva visita alla necropoli si svolse proprio nel segno della straordinaria tnerezza di questa frase'. *Giardino*, p. 320).
7. Carlo Ginzburg, *Wooden Eyes. Nine Reflections on Distance*, Eng. trans. by Martin Ryle and Kate Soper (New York: Columbia University Press, 2001), p. 160.
8. *Ibid.*, p. 163.
9. *Ibid.*, p. 167. See Paolo Pecere, Introduction to Carlo Ginzburg. 'Uccidere un mandarino cinese. Le implicazioni morali della distanza', *Minimaetmoralia* online blog, published 03 April 2020 on the wake of the pandemic, URL: https://www.minimaetmoralia.it/wp/altro/uccidere-un-mandarino-cinese-le-implicazioni-morali-della-distanza/. (Accessed April 2021).
10. Marco Belpoliti, 'Primo Levi testimone e coscienza critica', in *La Shoah in Italia*, vol. II: *Vicende, memorie, rappresentazioni* (Milan: Utet, 2010), pp. 384-401. Cfr. also Domenico Scarpa, 'Littératures des chambres à gaz', in *1947. Almanach littéraire*, David Martens, Bart Van Den Bossche, and MDRN (eds) (Brussels: Les Impressions Nouvelles, 2017), pp. 247-256.
11. *Garden*, p. 248. ('Papà, secondo te sono più antichi gli etruschi o gli ebrei?'; 'Prova a chiedere a quel signore'. *Giardino*, p. 320).
12. Andreas Steiner, 'Etruschi ed ebrei nel Novecento: Giorgio Bassani ed Elie Wiesel', in *Gli Etruschi nella cultura e nell'immaginario del mondo moderno*, Atti del XXIV Convegno Internazionale di Studi sulla Storia e l'Archeologia dell'Etruria, Giuseppe M. Della Fina (ed.) (Orvieto: Quasar, 2017), pp. 55-61. See also Martina Piperno, *L'antichità "crudele". Etruschi e Italici nella letteratura italiana del Novecento*, pp. 113-144.
13. *Garden*, p. 249. ('Cari, fidati oggetti della vita di tutti i giorni'; 'zappe, funi, accette, forbici, vanghe, coltelli, archi, frecce, perfino cani da caccia e volatili di palude'. *Giardino*, p. 322).
14. Information disclosed by Paola Bassani. I would like to thank her for her collaboration. Tiny, apparently insignificant objects, destined to oblivion and decay are an important element characterising the house of the Finzi-Contini, a house-museum full of antiques and relics, and particularly Micòl, the novel's female protagonist who is portrayed as obsessed by useless things and collectables and by preventing them from being damaged, lost or discarded. This happens in the case of the *làttimi*, things made of milky glass, that Micòl collects.
15. Millicent Marcus, *Filmmaking by the Book. Italian Cinema and Literary Adaptation* (Baltimore: John Hopkins University Press, 1993), p. 98.
16. According to Portia Prebys, Bassani had read *Etruscan Places* in English: see 'Una domenica d'aprile del 1957 e un'ultima visita: il prologo al *Giardino dei Finzi-Contini*', in *Gli intellettuali/scrittori ebrei e il dovere della testimonianza: in ricordo di Giorgio Bassani*, Anna Dolfi (ed.) (Florence: Florence University Press, 2017), pp. 459-474.
17. 'The Etruscans built everything of wood – houses, temples – all save walls for fortification, great gates, bridges, and drainage works. So that the Etruscan cities vanished as completely as flowers. Only the tombs, the bulbs, were underground'. D. H. Lawrence, *Etruscan Places* (London: Martin Secker, 1932), p. 17.
18. Millicent Marcus, *Filmmaking by the Book*, p. 98.
19. D. H. Lawrence, *Etruscan Places*, pp. 44-45.
20. Millicent Marcus, *Filmmaking by the Book*, p. 98.
21. Archivio eredi Bassani, Fondo Manoscritti, Serie Taccuini e agende, Agenda 2, cc. 42-43 (Img. 1 and 2). Transcription: 'Paola a Cerveteri, 4 aprile 1955. P: Cosa andiamo a vedere? / Io: Delle tombe. / P: Che malinconia! / (Pausa) / P: Papà, perché le tombe antiche fanno meno malinconia di quelle più recenti? / Io: Sarà perché i morti da poco sono più vicini a noi: così gli vuoi più bene. Gli Etruschi è tanto tempo che sono morti, che è come se fossero sempre stati morti. / (Pausa) / P: Però, adesso che dici così mi rendo che anche loro sono vissuti, invece, mi fanno pena come gli altri'. ('Paola in Cerveteri, 4 April, 1955. P: What are we going to see? / Me: Some tombs. / P: How sad! / (Pause) / P: Papa, why are ancient tombs less sad than new ones? / Me; Probably because the recently dead are closer to us: so that you love them more. The Etruscans have been dead such a long time, that it is as if they were always dead. / (Pause) / P: But, now that you say that, I realise that they also lived and this makes me sad for them like all the others.'). Translation by Martina Piperno.
22. 'Leggermente truccato [...]. Il personaggio della bambina [...] che io ho accollato a un mio amico [...] era mia figlia [...] Paola dell'età di nove o dieci anni'. The interview is available online, URL: https://www.fondazionegiorgiobassani.it/vittorio-sereni-intervista-giorgio-bassani-1968/. (Accessed May 2022).
23. Sergio Parussa, '*Non de me fabula narratur*. Nuove note sulla genesi del "Giardino" attraverso le carte d'archivio', in *Verso il "Giardino". Lab-*

oratorio Bassani 3, Beatrice Pecchiari (ed.) (Ravenna: Giorgio Pozzi, 2022), pp. 61-96 (p. 87-89).

24. Ugo Foscolo, *Sepulchers. Translation with Introduction and Notes by Peter Burian*, in *Literary Imagination*, 4.1 (2002), pp. 17-30, ll. 52-55, 99-106, 128-135, my emphases. ('Pur nuova legge impone oggi i sepolcri / *fuor de' guardi pietosi*, e il nome a' morti / contende. / [...] / Testimonianza a' fasti eran le tombe, / ed are a' figli; e uscìan quindi i responsi / de' *domestici* Lari, e fu temuto/*su la polve degli avi* il giuramento: / Religïon che con diversi riti / le virtù patrie e la pietà congiunta/tradussero per lungo ordine d'anni. / [...] / e chi *sedea* / a libar latte o a raccontar sue pene / ai cari estinti, una fragranza intorno / sentia qual d'aura de' beati Elisi. / pietosa insania che fa cari gli orti / de' *suburbani avelli* alle britanne / Vergini, dove le conduce amore / della perduta madre, ove clementi / pregaro i Geni del ritorno al prode / che tronca fe' la trîonfata nave / del maggior pino, e si scavò la bara.' Ugo Foscolo, *Dei sepolcri. Carme*, critical edition by Giovanni Biancardi and Alberto Cadioli (Milan: Hoepli 2012), ll. 51-53, 97-103, 126-136, my emphases).

25. *Garden*, pp. 248-49. ('Esattamente come ancor oggi, nei paesi della provincia italiana, il cancello del camposanto – il termine obbligato di ogni passeggiata serale, venivano *dal vicino abitato* quasi sempre *a piedi* – fantasticavo – raccolti in gruppi di parenti e consanguinei, di semplici amici, [...] oppure in coppia con la persona amata, e anche da soli, per poi inoltrarsi fra le tombe a cono [...]. Tutto, sì, stava cambiando – dovevano dirsi mentre camminavano lungo la via lastricata che attraversava da un capo all'altro il cimitero, al centro della quale le ruote ferrate dei trasporti avevano *inciso a poco a poco, durante i secoli, due profondi solchi paralleli* – Varcata la soglia del cimitero dove ciascuno di loro possedeva *una seconda casa*, e dentro questa il giaciglio già pronto su cui, tra breve, sarebbe stato coricato accanto ai padri, l'eternità non doveva più sembrare un'illusione, una favola, una promessa da sacerdoti. Il futuro avrebbe stravolto il mondo a suo piacere'. *Giardino*, pp. 321-22).

26. Foscolo, *Sepulchers*, ll. 284-300. ('[...] Un dì vedrete mendico un cieco errar sotto le vostre / antichissime ombre, e brancolando / penetrar negli avelli, e abbracciar l'urne, / e interrogarle. Gemeranno gli antri / secreti, e tutta narrerà la tomba / Ilio raso due volte e due risorto / splendidamente su le mute vie / per far più bello l'ultimo trofeo / ai fatati Pelìdi. Il sacro vate, / placando quelle afflitte alme col canto, / i prenci argivi eternerà per quante / abbraccia terre il gran padre Oceàno. / E tu, onore di pianti, Ettore, avrai, / ove fia santo e lagrimato il sangue / per la patria versato, e finchè il Sole / risplenderà su le sciagure umane.'. Ugo Foscolo, *Dei sepolcri*, ll. 279-295.)

27. *Garden*, p. 249. ('le tombe a cono [erano] solide e massicce come i bunkers di cui i soldati tedeschi hanno sparso invano l'Europa durante quest'ultima guerra'. *Giardino*, p. 321).

28. Giorgio Bassani, 'Il giardino tradito', in *Opere*, pp. 1255-65 (p. 1257-58 and 1561), translation by Martina Piperno. See Millicent Marcus, *Filmmaking*, pp. 104-105.

29. Mario Guarnacci, *Origini italiche o siano Memorie istorico-etrusche sopra l'antichissimo regno d'Italia e sopra i di lei primi abitatori nei secoli più remoti*, 3 vols. (Lucca: Venturini, 1767-1772), vol. I, pp. 1, 6, 10, translation by Martina Piperno.

30. Ridolfino Venuti, 'Sull'antica città di Cortona', in *Saggi dell'Accademia Etrusca di Cortona*, 4, 1741, pp. 1-32 (p. 27), translation by Martina Piperno.

31. Girolamo Tiraboschi, *Storia della letteratura italiana*, vol. I: *Che comprende la storia della letteratura degli Etruschi, de' popoli della Magna Grecia, e dell'antica Sicilia, e de' Romani fino alla morte d'Augusto* (Venice: Società tipografica, 1772), p. 3, translation by Martina Piperno.

32. Luigi Lanzi, *Saggio di lingua etrusca e di altre antiche d'Italia per servire alla storia de' popoli, delle lingue e delle belle arti*, 2 vol. (Rome: Pagliarini, 1789), vol. II, p. 174, translation by Martina Piperno.

33. Vincenzo Cuoco, *Opere*, vol. I: *Platone in Italia*, ed. by Antonino De Francesco and Annalisa Andreoni (Bari: Laterza, 2006), p. 11, translation by Martina Piperno.

34. D. H. Lawrence, *Etruscan Places*, pp. 9-10.

35. Mark Fisher, *The Weird and the Eerie* (London: Repeater, 2016), pp. 11-12; italics in the original.

36. Walter Benjamin, *Illuminations* (New York: Shocken Books, 1999), pp. 256-257.

37. *Ibid.*, p. 253.

38. Carlo Ginzburg, *Wooden Eyes*, p. 172.

39. Millicent Marcus, *Filmmaking*, p. 98.

A Compromised Antiquity: The Post-war Italian Rejection of the Etruscan Past

Andrea Avalli

The post-war years still represent an open historical field for researchers of reception and use of the ancient past in Italian culture. Such a theme is clearly relevant to several historiographical approaches: classical reception studies, literary studies, art history and history of ideas. Moreover, one of the hypotheses that could be verified is that the fall of Fascism in 1943-1945 has put an end to the political uses of 'romanità' that the regime had promoted on different cultural levels to foster a national and racial Italian identity.[1] It is still necessary to trace, through the history of literature, modern art and classical studies, how the representations of the ancient past changed in post-fascist Italian culture. This contribution asserts that one of the changes was the post-war rejection of Etruscology, the question of the Etruscan origins and the very interest in the Etruscan past, now considered in non-academic culture as a rhetorical and reactionary topic, useless to the post-fascist renewal of Italian culture and society. My main sources will be Luciano Bianciardi's short stories from the 1950s and two Italian films produced in 1962: *Il sorpasso* (*The Easy Life*) and *La voglia matta* (*The Crazy Urge*). It is not my intention to argue that such a rejection has been the only way in which post-war Italian art and literature have dealt with Etruscan identity or with the ancient world. In fact, it has already been explored, how, especially during the 1960s, the Etruscans have been depicted as victims of a genocide perpetrated by the Romans, memorialised as an equivalent to twentieth century Jews and represented through the memory of the Holocaust.[2] This chapter will rather aim to outline a contemporary but different reception of the Etruscan past, one which – far from reflecting on antiquity through the lens of a tragic memory – refused to accept ancient history as a useless heritage, corrupted and compromised by fascist ideology and propaganda, worthless to post-war Italians. As such, it appears to me to be an enlightening perspective on the need for a new beginning and a radical cultural change that many Italian writers and artists felt after Fascism.

An ideal case study for the post-war rejection of the Etruscans is represented by the Tuscan writer Luciano Bianciardi (1922-1971).[3] Born in Grosseto in 1922, Bianciardi studied philosophy at the University of Pisa during the war years, adhering to liberal-socialist anti-fascist groups.[4] However, in 1943 he had to quit his studies to be enrolled in the Italian army. By the fall of the regime that summer, he found himself stuck in Allied-occupied Apulia, where he spent the last two years of the war serving as an interpreter for the Allied army. After the Liberation of Italy in 1945, he managed to return to Tuscany and adhered to the liberal-socialist Partito d'Azione, one of the main Resistance parties. Thanks to an examination reserved for war veterans and partisans, he was able to resume his studies at the Scuola Normale Superiore in Pisa, where he finally obtained his degree in philosophy.[5] In his post-war diary, Bianciardi kept note of his impatience towards material legacies of the former regime: while visiting Rome in May 1946, he wrote: 'Rome was built in the eighteenth century, by Church people. What was made before and after isn't interesting. Ancient stuff is in museums, dead stuff (even when it remains in streets) while modern stuff should be destroyed'.[6] In particular, the young veteran expressed his repulsion for the new campus of the Sapienza university of Rome built by the regime in the 1930s, with 'square columns, the Minerva statue and Latin inscriptions'[7] – referring to the famous Minerva statue sculpted by Arturo Martini, one of the main Etruscan-inspired fascist artists.[8] Bianciardi therefore appears to be fundamentally dismissive of the fascist uses of antiquity.

After graduating in 1948, Bianciardi found a job in his home town Grosseto as a high school teacher and, from 1951 onwards, as director of the public library Biblioteca Chelliana. During this period, after the demise of the Partito d'Azione, he joined the electoral campaign of the centre-left group Unità Popolare (1953).[9] At the same time, he regularly contributed to left-wing periodicals and newspapers like *La Gazzetta*, the daily paper of Livorno's communist party[10] and *Avanti!*, the historical newspaper of the socialist party, where he published several articles against the former regime and present fascist nostalgia.[11] As a left-wing journalist and writer, Bianciardi started publicly expressing his own critique of the fascist use of antiquity and, more specifically, his rejection of the Etruscans. In fact, anti-bourgeois and anti-Etruscan satire represents one of the main literary features of Bianciardi's writing during the 1950s. In his satirical story 'Il campanile' (1952), Bianciardi narrated the provincial life of a wealthy and cultivated Tuscan lawyer, who flaunts his parochial rhetoric on the 'Pelasgic walls'[12] of his town, while criticising foreign scholars who had belittled pre-Roman history because 'they envy us such an ancient civilisation'.[13] Rather unsurprisingly, the lawyer also evokes the 'very ancient Etruscan origin'[14] of local society, as well as the 'millennial wisdom of the Tyrrhenians, who came by sea from Lydia to teach the Romans the foundation of the law that has rightly made us famous worldwide'.[15] Such a nationalist rhetoric was later ridiculed by the author in the end, when the lawyer reveals himself as a supporter of the Christian Democratic government and he affirms to be ready to turn the Tuscan hills into a 'parking lot'.[16] Bianciardi therefore denounced the continuity between fascist nationalism and its use of antiquity, on the one hand, and many of the views of the post-war Christian Democratic middle class on the other hand. In another short story, he portrayed a similar provincial character, the accountant Belletti, who becomes passionate about Etruscology during his perpetual search of ephemeral interests to follow. To get into this new activity, Belletti

> borrowed a copy of Pallottino, six yearly issues of *Studi Etruschi*, an epigraphical collection, and locked himself at home for two weeks. Then, he wanted to engage himself in archaeological enterprises, directly facing excavation. He also wrote a letter to the newspapers, protesting the 'disgrace' of Etruscological studies being stuck because of the bad will of the powerful, and reclaiming from public institutions a share of money to immediately start an excavation in the Chamars necropolis. Nobody ever knew where Chamars really was; perhaps near Chiusi, perhaps in the Po Valley, but it cannot be excluded that it had never existed.[17]

The accountant is then described as he becomes an amateur archaeologist, searching for Etruscan remains while 'such a glory, that is only ours and that is envied by many foreigners, is buried two metres under'.[18] As his Etruscological passion is at its peak, Belletti collects his notes in a folder that he suggests for publication to a 'young Florentine publisher',[19] but he refuses the proposal: 'Who could ever be interested in the Chamars necropolis? And listen, don't get me wrong, but I'm convinced that all this necropolis stuff is just a story, made up by you archaeologists. The Etruscans… do you want to know what I think? I think they have never existed'.[20] Faced with the general lack of interest towards the Etruscans, the accountant eventually decides to give up his passion.

Such a satirical representation of the provincial middle class therefore contains the mocking of Etruscology, depicted as a localist, nationalist, reactionary activity, useless for society. Another example is provided by the short story 'L'imperiale' and its description of a fascist teacher of Latin and his rhetorical myth of 'romanità'. The teacher is convinced of the inner superiority of Italians – excluding Italian Jews, though – in every field of human culture across history, from antiquity to Fascism. One of the things he discusses is radio, stressing how Guglielmo Marconi makes it a 'work of an Italian genius, product of the talent of a scientist of a very ancient Italic, Bolognese, that is Felsinean, Etruscan, descent'.[21] The teacher's fascist rhetoric is later mocked by Bianciardi, who contrasts it with the ideas of one of his pupils, for whom Rome doesn't evoke 'romanità' but just the city's football team.[22] A further satire of the reactionary myth of the Etruscans (or pre-Roman history) can be found in the story called 'I localisti', in which the author depicted provincial erudites, inspired by a bourgeois myth of urban décor and tourism:

> Because the most important element, in any case, is antiquity: the great fortune of the Etruscans is based on this: on their antiquity (but also, perhaps, on the alleged mystery of their origin and their pre-Roman localisation, which enables a sort of exceptional nationalism). Our localists would melt in the air, as an organic group, if it could be possible to demonstrate – which is desirable – that the Etruscans have never existed.[23]

Bianciardi's dispute against local erudites, or 'localisti', has a concrete dimension in his direction of the Biblioteca Chelliana in Grosseto. In fact, the writer claims that, under his control, the library is no longer attended only by local history experts, but has opened itself to the working class, promoting culture and reading among all citizens, even literally bringing books in the country on a 'bibliobus' – a library-owned bus full of them.[24]

From 1952 on, Bianciardi – also in collaboration with the writer Carlo Cassola, a fellow supporter of Unità Popolare – wrote a series of enquiries into the social conditions of the Maremma miners, published in *Avanti!*, Adriano Olivetti's *Comunità* and the communist periodical *Il contemporaneo*.[25] In the same period, on 4 May 1954, forty-three Ribolla mine workers lost their lives in a gas explosion. The accident was caused by precarious working conditions, exacerbated by the ownership's hostility towards the miners' left-wing union. The publisher Laterza, interested in such a tragedy, offered Bianciardi and Cassola the possibility to turn their enquiries into a book, later published in 1956.[26] The writers' perspective on the Ribolla mine disaster was an accusation of the mine's ownership, in solidarity with the Confederazione Generale Italiana del Lavoro (CGIL) union and local communists. In the book, together with Cassola, Bianciardi briefly traced a social, economic and political history of Maremma, developing some lines of thought which he had already published in his previous enquiries. In 1952, he had criticised localist histories that indulged in a traditionalist take on Tuscan society. Etruscology is included in the range of reactionary historical perspectives, criticised by Bianciardi, as he thought that 'the Etruscans are an interesting theme (except for serious archaeologists, of course) only to those who want to entertain themselves with the vague and amateurish idols of their illustrious origins'.[27] For Bianciardi, to look at Maremma and Grosseto only through the lens of Etruscan identity was tantamount to 'an attitude of convenience, conservative'.[28] Earlier that same year, mocking, as usual, 'the erudite historians and local tradition fanatics'[29] and their Etruscan myth, he had written:

> As for the Etruscans, we must undoubtedly recognise them the great merit of providing the region with a hydraulic regulation which prevented, through ingenious systems, the creation of marshes. But it is not right, only because of this, to mythologise the Etruscans as if they were the direct ancestors of today's Maremmans. Or maybe the localists, without noticing, have a point, because the Etruscans were also basically less an ethnically identifiable people than a very active group of heterogenous formation, who controlled such activities as do the Maremmans now.[30]

In Bianciardi's words, all this was just 'literature':[31] he preferred to talk about modernity, wishing that 'in a fairer world, in a democratic and socialist Italy',[32] Maremma could grow with workers from all over Italy, which – regardless of their origins – would be considered as the new 'Maremmani'.[33] In an article from 1954 on the left-leaning periodical *Cinema nuovo*, Bianciardi came back to the Etruscans, stating that all the local historians 'convinced (and someone still is) that in Maremman veins flows some amount of Etruscan blood' have been supporters of the fascist regime.[34] The identitarian myth of the Etruscans was thus discredited and rejected as inherently reactionary and fascist. It is therefore not a coincidence that, in their social enquiry on the Ribolla mine disaster, Bianciardi and Cassola almost never approached the Etruscans, preferring instead to base their book on a rigorously historical and rational perspective. To trace the social history of mining in Maremma, the two writers began their reconstruction by a geographical and economic description of the region. Claiming the concreteness of their analysis, they criticised previous literary depictions of Tuscany:

> Even if tradition (and literature) made it possible that the average Italian thinks of Maremma as the land of pastures, endless wheat fields, marshes, 'butteri' and boar hunts, today Maremma is above all an area of great mineral wealth. The province of Grosseto produces almost 90 percent of Italian pyrite. Until last year, Ribolla was the biggest Italian black lignite mine. Mount Amiata produces a third of the world's mercury.[35]

The two writers refused to represent Maremma as an eternally rural, backward and – as Bianciardi had pointed out – Etruscan country, rather choosing to trace a historical report of mining and political struggles in the area. Its starting point precisely focussed on the Etruscans. However, the two authors did not indulge in literary praises of them: in fact, they simply wrote that Etruscan mining skills had been 'very rudimentary' and ineffective, and that the Middle Ages had brought better techniques.[36]

After the 1954 Ribolla disaster, Bianciardi's contacts with several members of the cultural commission of the Italian Communist Party (PCI) like Antonello Trombadori and Carlo Salinari, allowed him to move to Milan to work for the communist publisher Giangiacomo Feltrinelli.[37] From the capital of the post-war economic boom, he remembered his earlier provincial life in Tuscany and wrote a book later published by Feltrinelli in 1957. This autobiographical memoir, entitled 'Il lavoro culturale', traced Bianciardi's youth in Grosseto and his activism in local communist cultural policy. The book significantly echoed many aspects of his newspaper articles published since 1952, including the rejection of the Etruscan heritage. The very beginning of the book was dedicated to the Etruscans: Bianciardi started his memoir from a critique of the problem of their origins.

> The problem of the origins has always seduced and strained the mind of sages, wise men and intellectuals: origins of mankind, of the species; origins of evil and inequality. People have calculated the passing of years by the origins of a city or a religion and to say 'original' means to acknowledge a merit. In sum, it seems – who knows for what reason – that people care more about the past, remote past, incapable of hurting any more, than about the future, near future, always, as we know well, threatening and impending.[38]

The author then recalled, in his hometown, the existence of three factions of intellectuals and their relationship with the past and the myth of the origins. The first faction, that of the 'erudites',[39] gathered amateur researchers of local medieval history. Bianciardi mocked them as boring members of the local historical society and passionate attenders of archives, being ironic about their obsession for the preservation of every ancient and abandoned building.[40] He therefore rejected a fetishist, or overprotective, relationship with the material legacies of the past. The author then moved on to criticise the second intellectual faction, the 'archaeologists'.[41] These people were depicted as former anarchists returned to order and readers of George Dennis and Pericle Ducati,[42] or as teachers, lawyers, self-taught researchers, even engineers and dowsers, each one engaged in claiming the importance of the Etruscan civilisation.[43] Bianciardi quoted the main theories on the Etruscan origins, also sarcastically reporting the alleged 'affinity of the Etruscans with the American redskins'[44] and their association with autochthonous 'giants', 'a very ancient and advanced race, unfortunately still mysterious and unknown'.[45] After recalling local erudites and archaeologists, the author started to describe his own intellectual faction, returning to his provocative claim that the Etruscans had never existed:

> Eventually there we were, the young, the rebels without a cause: determined to break up with traditions and start everything anew. Of course, we argued with the others, the medievalist erudites and the archaeologists. What did they both want? What did they mean, the futile and clumsy stuffiness of the first, the antiquarian fury of the latter? Time had come to stop such amateurism, such a futile erudition, this mythology of the ancient origins. Italian culture, we said, was already sufficiently dried up and mortified by these reactionary and provincial forms, by parochialism, by stupid municipalism. The Etruscans? They have never existed. You ask yourselves where they came from, whether from the continent, or from Asia Minor, or from America; you also suggest the hypothesis that they had always been here. Well, you're all right and all wrong, that is you ask yourselves a pointless question. Would it make sense to ask where did the Piedmontese, the Tuscans, the Milanese come from? There have never existed any people who, in perfect agreement, took to the sea (where could they find all those ships, after all?) and went somewhere else.[46]

Bianciardi therefore depicted a generational, cultural and political conflict with local erudites and reactionary archaeologists. The Etruscan question was approached provocatively, rejecting to accept the rhetoric of the origins and the theories on immigration. Because of his refusal to accept of the problem of the origins as 'a pointless question', Bianciardi's ideas could be linked to Massimo Pallottino's 'formation' theory.[47] In this new, post-fascist reception of the Etruscan question, the Tuscan writer compared the ethnic formation of the Etruscans to the contemporary formation of the Milanese 'people' in post-war Milan, the destination for working immigrants from all Italy:

> Where did the Milanese come from? Who knows? Many came from outside: somebody arrived because he couldn't find a job in his home town, someone else came in his youth to go to the army, then got married and never moved. Others have been born and live and work there: maybe they would like to leave, for Capri, Brazil, or Australia, but they can't because they can't

afford the journey, nor hope to survive in another country. What if someone would say to you that the Milanese came from Dalmatia? You would certainly answer that it's a wrong assumption, isn't it? Then why do you trust people who say that the Etruscans came from Asia Minor?

In fact, the Etruscans were like the Milanese; they were those who inhabited this and other areas, a long time ago and they were called, by the others, by their neighbours, by this name. Where did they come from? Who knows? From where they found right to come. But what about the alphabet, the language, this mysterious and indecipherable language? What are you talking about? – we answered. What's the point in deciphering the so-called Etruscan language, when the biggest fragment is about five hundred words long? Or perhaps, we added, if you really want to somehow save your Etruscans, well, then we answer that the Etruscans did exist, but they were not an actual people: they were a minority which ruled over our land and subjugated the poor people, forcing them to work; a minority of ship owners and big businessmen, and priests. Didn't you say that Roman religion took part of its liturgy from the Etruscan one? A minority, besides, of politicians, nay, of Fascists. Wasn't the first fasces founded in Volterra, a city, as you say, very ancient (even if not as ours) and of Etruscan foundation?

All this we, the young war veterans, said, with great anger and indignation by the archaeologists.[48]

The critique of the Etruscan question went as far as an outright denial of any interest whatsoever in the Etruscans, their language or culture. To Bianciardi, it was useless to decipher the 'so-called' Etruscan language, because the remaining fragments were few. In fact, anthropological and linguistic research was considered a form of pointless erudition and the whole Etruscology was regarded as a useless and reactionary interest. The writer came to criticise, from an anti-fascist perspective, the Etruscans as a minority of exploitative bourgeois, priests and fascists who oppressed the autochthonous people ('the poor people' of 'our land').

Bianciardi significantly characterised his critique from a generational point of view; he spoke of 'giovani, la generazione bruciata' (*Gioventù bruciata*, which is the Italian title of Nicholas Ray's iconic *Rebel Without a Cause*, had been released two years earlier) and of 'we, the young war veterans'[49]. Moreover, the generational detachment from the fascist past was as radical as the drive towards the future. Bianciardi's young intellectuals were 'enthusiastic' about the 'victorious march'[50] of their home town towards the country, about the growth of the suburbs, technical modernisation and cultural de-provincialization: 'The true sense of the city, on which those erudite medievalist bats and those archaeologist crows can't focus, there it is: the all-suburb city, open to the winds and foreigners, made of people from all countries.'⁵¹ The myth of the frontier was rather unsurprisingly linked to the American myth, introduced by Bianciardi through the character of Lieutenant Bucker:

> Lieutenant Bucker was a young American teacher, arrived with his army, during the war, who stated indeed that his home town, Kansas City, looked like ours. And we liked this comparison, making a symbol of it: Kansas City, Kansas City is our reality, no jokes! The origins of the city? The foundation year? 1944, no more and no less. Before then, it didn't exist, it was founded by the Americans who, arriving among us, had paved a field to let the airplanes land, opened Coca-Cola shops, food stores, dancings [in English], material deposits, suddenly creating a new trading centre. From everywhere, then, crowds of people had come to this brand-new mecca [...].⁵²

In the young generation's imagery, Americans replaced the Etruscans as founders of the city, while its origin was pushed from the Iron Age to the 1944 Liberation. From an identitarian point of view, the myth of the Etruscan descent was superseded by the myth of the developing city, a melting pot for different people. The very name of the city of Grosseto was never mentioned by Bianciardi, who renamed it 'Kansas City', officially implying the need for a post-fascist re-establishment of the city.⁵³

Bianciardi's Tuscan province was therefore no more the base of a traditionalist and racist identity tracing its origins back to the Etruscans, but instead, the frontier of modernisation and re-foundation of Italian culture and identity. Nonetheless, the province remained a fundamental identitarian space: in Bianciardi's book, we find critical hints towards Rome, which is called a 'parasitic city',⁵⁴ and Milan, blamed for depriving intellectuals of their traditional status of 'clan' and 'corporation'⁵⁵ and transforming them into ordinary workers of cultural industry.⁵⁶ Bianciardi's anti-Etruscan perspective allowed for the coexistence of the provincial myth and the rejection of an antiquity-oriented racial identity, the respect for rural workers and the anti-nationalist myth of American modernity. 'In our city', Bianciardi wrote, 'one could start all over anew, and Italy, as for culture (but also for the rest), just needed to start all over again'.⁵⁷ The increasing disillusion of Bianciardi regarding communist cultural policy and Milanese social modernity, expressed in books such as *Il lavoro culturale* (1957), *L'integrazione* (1960) and especially *La vita agra* (1962), finally led him to elaborate a radical critique of industrial modernity, both in its capitalist and in its socialist version, and to imagine a primitivist utopia.⁵⁸ Apart from these further developments, Bianciardi's articles of the 1950s and the beginning of *Il lavoro culturale* recorded how the post-war desire for a post-fascist re-foundation of Italian society and culture led young people to consider Etruscology as a reactionary form of erudition, useless to the present reconstruction. In particular, the provocative claim of the Etruscans' inexistence remained a staple of Bianciardi's literary imagery for the rest of his short life.[59] However, Bianciardi did not seem to rule out the possibility of different readings of the Etruscan identity in the post-war years, for in 1968 he wrote a short story in which he connected the history of Etruria with that of Zionism, contemporary Israel, and the Israeli-Palestinian conflict, referring to the Etruscans as victims of a genocide.[60]

Apart from Bianciardi's, other forms of rejection of the Etruscans can be found in two 1962 films taking their cue from the new post-war and consumerist society. Dino Risi's *Il sorpasso* famously stages the road trip, from Rome to Tuscany, of a young law student (Roberto, played by Jean-Louis Trintignant) and a working-class man (Bruno, played by Vittorio Gassman), exuberant in his Roman accent, the symbol of the average man of the economic boom. The latter flaunts his unprejudiced approach towards life and women, extending it to his relationship with the past (both ancient and fascist). There are several examples for this attitude. Regarding relationships with women, Bruno explains to his young fellow that in modern society it is not necessary to engage, and that it is normal to have many partners. He recalls how, as a child, he wanted to boldly affirm his heterosexual identity by trying to touch his schoolteacher Rosa Maltini, (adding 'not Maltoni', therefore making an irreverent reference to Benito Mussolini's mother). Bruno's ex-wife (played by Catherine Spaak) tells Roberto that she first met him in 1945, when he used to wear an American marine uniform just because he liked the outfit. Bruno's national identity therefore appears as very relaxed compared to fascist standards. This also applies to his attitude towards race. At some point Bruno tells the student a 'Jewish proverb'[61] on women, which generates an embarrassing debate on racial issues:

> Roberto: Tell me, was your grandmother a Jew?
> Bruno: Why, are you a racist?
> Roberto: No, of course not…and you?
> Bruno: Me? [he laughs] You don't know me…I've once been with a woman who was a Jew and a negress![62]

The denial of racism peacefully coexists with the continuity of fascist, racist and sexist stereotypes. In another scene, Bruno, in his car, follows two German women he wants to pick up. He only listens to Roberto's protests and stops when they eventually find out that the women were heading to a German war cemetery. Even if Roberto is younger than Bruno and envies his vitality, in *Il sorpasso* he plays the role of the keeper of traditional ethics and respect for the past. The student comes from a bourgeois family and his cousin is a Fascist nostalgic. Therefore, the generational and cultural conflict depicted by Bianciardi, in this case, is reproduced in the movie: the mature Bruno represents future Italy, while the young Roberto stands for traditional Italy. Roberto is aware of his own family contradictions, but he remains tied to traditional society and culture, while Bruno emancipates himself from them with ease. In a well-known scene, on the road outside Rome leading to Tuscany, the young student addresses Bruno, who is driving his car:

> Roberto: You know, here there are some beautiful Etruscan tombs…
> Bruno: Oh, yeah? Well the Etruscan tombs can go … themselves! [he laughs and drives faster][63]

Facing the opportunity to take a turn and head to the archaeological Etruscan site, the driver refuses and comically flaunts his lack of interest in the Etruscans. What had been narrated by Giorgio Bassani in *Il giardino dei Finzi-Contini*, published that same year (1962), repeats itself with opposite effects: in Bassani's novel, a group of intellectual friends, on their way back to Rome, take the turn to the Cerveteri necropolis, immersing themselves in archaeology and private memories of the Holocaust. The only one who is discontent is the youngest member of the group, Giannina, who initially finds the visit sad and boring.[64] In Risi's *Il sorpasso*, instead, the car is headed outside Rome in search of fun and the driver is completely uninterested in the possibility of stopping and reflecting on history and on the memory of a tragic past. Bruno's rejection of the Etruscans is consistent with his attitude towards life, Fascism and the war, and it assumes a childish and liberating attitude compared to the severity inspired by archaeology and the necropolis. From this point of view, Bruno speeding up after his anti-Etruscan joke can easily be read as a metaphor for his drive towards the future, away from the past. The very car Bruno is so proud of is a symbol of industrial technology and consumerism which attests to his own adherence to modernity. Roberto, who had proposed a detour past the Etruscan tombs and suffered the driver's rejection and joke, is thus mocked for his attachment to traditional and humanistic culture. From this point of view, it is unsurprising that he gets ridiculed by the average man, the consumerist, post-Fascist Bruno. Hesitating between resistance and exaltation, Roberto gets transported towards Italy's future by a fellow countryman, an enthusiast of modernity. The end of the film is explicitly pessimistic on such a relationship: the car accident caused by Bruno's eagerness, and the sudden death of Roberto, imply a negative judgement on the social costs of the economic boom, as well as on the survival chances of traditional culture after the impact with modernity. The only survivor is the average post-Fascist man who mocks the Etruscans, void of historical memory and lacking in cultural interests beyond consumerism.

That same year, the Etruscans were briefly, if significantly, evoked in Luciano Salce's film *La voglia matta*. This movie stages another generational and cultural conflict between a conservative, Catholic engineer in his forties (played by Ugo Tognazzi), who falls in love with a fifteen-year-old girl (played by Catherine Spaak) on holiday with her group of rich, unconventional and arrogant friends. Like Roberto's attraction for Bruno's attitude in *Il sorpasso*, in *La voglia matta*, the engineer's forbidden love for a teenager can be read as a symbol for the attraction of old and conservative Italy to modernity. The difference between the two generations is radical and particularly involves the memory of Fascism and the war. During the war, the engineer had fought in Africa, where he had killed an English soldier, and such a dramatic event still torments his conscience. Such an unresolved relationship between the memory of violence and the Fascist war re-emerges when, just like in *Il giardino dei Finzi-Contini* and *Il sorpasso*, the film sets one of its scenes in a cemetery. The engineer enters there by night just to show the group of teenagers that he's not afraid, but he is victim of a macabre prank played by them, revealing himself terrified of meeting the ghost of the English soldier killed in Africa. Unlike him, the teenagers born after the war do not fear such a memory and do not show any sacred respect for a cemetery; instead, they flaunt their lack of interest in politics, hoping that a new war breaks out just to avoid their school exams. They also listen to a vinyl recording of Nazi chants without knowing German, just to feel the 'intonation',[65] the girl loved by the engineer says 'Mussolini who? The father of the piano player?'[66] and a boy dreams of becoming a revolutionary while listening to Cuban music. Their relationship with politics and the memory of fascism is already filtered through unconventionality, cynicism and lack of interest. They represent a future devoid of historical memory, while the 40-year-old engineer belongs to the old Italy.

The Etruscans are again evoked in such a conflict. Some teenage girls comment on the engineer's look, in youth language 'He is not that bad looking', and one of them says, with dissatisfaction, that 'He's an Etruscan'.[67] In this case, the Etruscan identity is used by new generations negatively, as hyperbole and as a synonym of the old-fashioned, outdated, ugly and boring. The unconventional and rich youngsters, who do not show any respect for the past and the memory of the dictatorship and the war, look impatiently upon the old generation. Mature men are discredited as 'Etruscan' because of their roots in an archaic and obsolete culture. Just as in Bianciardi's writings and in *Il sorpasso*, and partially in Giannina's attitude in *Il giardino dei Finzi-Contini*, the generational and cultural conflict between old, traditional Italy and new, post-fascist Italy is also made by the rejection of the Etruscans as an obsolete, boring and useless theme.

As a provisional conclusion, waiting for further and broader studies of the post-fascist reception of the Etruscans, it can be suggested that the fall of fascism sparked new and unexpected relations with the distant past in Italian culture. The interpretation of some literary and cinematographic sources, such as those I discussed in this contribution, justifies the assertion that one of these relationships, not the only one, of course, is the post-fascist repulsion of ancient history. Such an antipathy regarding antiquity can be read as a post-war intolerance for the former regime's nationalist and racist ideology and propaganda, a key aspect of which had been the political use of ancient history. The new rejection of antiquity first targets 'romanità' as the most ideologically compromised historical period; consistent with American sword-and-sandal films, Italian post-war cinematographic representations of ancient Rome stage the Roman Empire as a murderous, anti-Christian and genocidal dictatorship.[68] As for the Etruscans, the condemnation of Rome as a totalitarian and genocidal regime in post-war cultural imagery enables their subsequent reception as victims. However, as Luciano Bianciardi's writings from the 1950s and films by Dino Risi and Luciano Salce show, sometimes the post-fascist refusal to accept antiquity can also involve the Etruscans. In such sources, Etruscology is often mocked as a symbol of cultural irrelevance, a futile localist erudition, if not of a reactionary and fascist cultural interest. In *La voglia matta*, the very ethnonym 'Etruscan' is used as a synonym for something archaic and useless. The curiosity for the Etruscan past seems to be generally refused as a laughable, pointless – or worse, reactionary – activity, which is of no interest for the future of Italy. As I have tried to outline, such a rejection is consistent with the drive towards modernity of post-war Italian society and readable through the contemporary impatience for fascist culture and its uses of antiquity.

Notes

1. Andrea Giardina and Andrè Vauchez, *Il mito di Roma. Da Carlo Magno a Mussolini* [2000] (Rome Bari: Laterza, 2016), pp. 212-302; Joshua Arthurs, *Excavating Modernity. The Roman past in Fascist Italy* (Ithaca London: Cornell University Press, 2012); Paola Salvatori, *Mussolini e la storia. Dal socialismo al fascismo (1900-1922)* (Rome: Viella, 2016).
2. See Martina Piperno's chapter in this book, see also Martina Piperno, *L'antichità "crudele". Etruschi e Italici nella letteratura italiana del Novecento* (Rome: Carocci, 2020), pp. 113-144.
3. I thank Francesco Cassata for giving me the idea to study Luciano Bianciardi for this topic.
4. On Italian liberal-socialist anti-fascism, see Marco Bresciani, *Quale antifascismo? Storia di Giustizia e Libertà* (Rome: Carocci, 2017).
5. Cf. Luciano Bianciardi, *Il cattivo profeta. Romanzi, racconti, saggi e diari* (Milan: Il saggiatore, 2018), p. 1478; Pino Corrias, *Vita agra di un anarchico. Luciano Bianciardi a Milano* [1993] (Milan: Feltrinelli, 2009).
6. 'Roma è stata costruita nel '700, e da gente di Chiesa. Quello che è stato fatto prima e dopo non interessa. La roba antica è nei musei, roba morta (anche quando è sulle piazze) quella moderna bisognerebbe distruggerla'. *Impressioni di Roma e del Congresso*, in Luciano Bianciardi, *Il cattivo profeta. Romanzi, racconti, saggi e diari*, p. 1470. All translations are by Andrea Avalli.
7. 'le colonne quadrate, la statua di Minerva e le iscrizioni in latino'. *Ibid.* p. 1470.
8. Giulia Fusconi, 'Il periodo etrusco di Arturo Martini', *Xenia Antiqua*, 6 (1997), pp. 195-220; Giulia Fusconi, 'Io sono il vero etrusco', in *Arturo Martini*, Claudia Gian Ferrari, Elena Pontiggia and Livia Velani (eds) (Milan: Skira, 2006), pp. 81-86; Maria Vittoria Marini Clarelli, 'Arturo Martini a Roma dalla Secessione alla Quadriennale', in *Arturo Martini*; Flavio Fergonzi, '"L'uomo più assimilatore che si conosca". Un rapido percorso su Martini e l'uso delle fonti scultoree', in *Arturo Martini*; Federica Grossi, 'Gli Etruschi di Arturo Martini: rielaborazioni d'avanguardia', in *Fascino etrusco nel primo Novecento, conversando di arti e di storia delle arti*, Giovanna Bagnasco Gianni (ed.), *Aristonothos. Scritti per il Mediterraneo antico*, vol. 11 (Milan: Ledizioni, 2016), pp. 111-142. Nico Stringa, 'Arturo Martini e gli Etruschi', in *Gli etruschi nella cultura e nell'immaginario del mondo moderno*, Giuseppe Maria Della Fina (ed.) (Rome: Quasar, 2017), pp. 359-370; Martina Corgnati, *L'ombra lunga degli etruschi: echi e suggestioni nell'arte del Novecento* (Monza: Johan & Levi, 2018).
9. 'Da molte parti le voci antiche', in *La Gazzetta*, 22 October 1952, now in Luciano Bianciardi, *L'antimeridiano. Tutte le opere*, vol. II: *Scritti giornalistici* (Milan: ExCogita, 2008), pp. 128-131; 'Nascita di uomini democratici', in *Belfagor*, 31 July 1952, now in *L'antimeridiano. Tutte le opere*, pp. 293-294; 'Previsioni', in *La Gazzetta*, 25 May 1953, now in *L'antimeridiano. Tutte le opere*, pp. 188-191. Cf. Pino Corrias, *Vita agra di un anarchico. Luciano Bianciardi a Milano*.
10. Massimo Coppola and Alberto Piccinini, 'La mosca sul muro', in Luciano Bianciardi, *L'antimeridiano. Tutte le opere*, p. XIX.
11. Cf. Luciano Bianciardi, *L'antimeridiano. Tutte le opere*, pp. 11-15; 20-22; 30-32; 37-39; 54-56; 73-75; 85-87; 88-90; 91-93; 94-96; 110-112; 116-118; 138-140; 144-146; 173-175; 185-187.
12. 'Mura pelasgiche'. 'Il campanile', in *La Gazzetta*, 20 May 1952, now in *L'antimeridiano. Tutte le opere*, p. 47.
13. 'ci invidiano una civiltà così antica'. *Ibid.*, p. 48.
14. 'antichissima origine etrusca'. *Ibid.*, p. 48.
15. 'millenaria saggezza dei tirreni, venuti dal mare della Lidia, per insegnare ai padri romani i fondamenti del diritto che ci ha resi giustamente famosi nel mondo'. *Ibid.*, p. 48.
16. 'parcheggio di automobili'. *Ibid.*, p. 49.
17. 'si fece prestare una copia del Pallottino, sei annate di *Studi etruschi*, una raccolta di epigrafi, e si chiuse in casa per due settimane. Poi volle dedicarsi anche lui ad imprese di fondo, affrontare direttamente gli scavi. Scrisse anche una lettera ai giornali, protestando contro «lo sconcio» degli studi di etruscologia che restavano fermi per la cattiva volontà dei potenti, e reclamando da ogni ente pubblico una quota in denaro per iniziare subito gli scavi di ricerca della necropoli dell'antica Chamars. Dove sia Chamars nessuno l'ha mai saputo: forse nei pressi di Chiusi, forse nella pianura padana, ma non è da escludersi che non sia mai esistita. 'Il ragioniere', in *La Gazzetta*, 8 June 1952, now in *L'antimeridiano. Tutte le opere*, p. 62.
18. 'questa gloria, che è soltanto nostra e che tanti stranieri ci invidiano, resta sepolta sotto un paio di metri di terra'. *Ibid.*, p. 62.
19. 'un giovane editore fiorentino'. *Ibid.*, p. 62.
20. 'Cosa vuole che interessi la necropoli di Chamars? E poi senta, non si arrabbi, ma io son convinto che questa delle necropoli sia tutta una storia, l'avete inventata voi archeologi. Gli etrus-

chi...lo vuol sapere? Secondo me non sono mai esistiti'. *Ibid.*, pp. 62-63.
21. 'frutto dell'ingegno di uno scienziato di stirpe italica antichissima, bolognese, cioè felsinea, etrusca'. 'L'imperiale', in *La Gazzetta*, 8 July 1952, now in *L'antimeridiano. Tutte le opere*, p. 78.
22. *Ibid.*, pp. 76-78.
23. 'Perché l'elemento più importante, in ogni caso, è l'antichità: su questo si fonda la grande fortuna degli etruschi: sulla loro antichità (ma anche, forse, sul preteso mistero della loro origine e sulla loro localizzazione preromana, che permette una specie di nazionalismo d'eccezione). I nostri localisti sparirebbero, come gruppo organico, se fosse possibile dimostrare, ciò che è augurabile, che gli etruschi non sono mai esistiti'. 'I localisti', in *La Gazzetta*, 13 September 1952, now in *L'antimeridiano. Tutte le opere*, p. 105.
24. 'La cultura su quattro ruote', in *La Gazzetta*, 26 July 1953, now in *L'antimeridiano. Tutte le opere*, pp. 210-213.
25. 'Da molte parti le voci antiche', in *L'antimeridiano. Tutte le opere*, pp. 128-131; Luciano Bianciardi and Carlo Cassola, 'Gli inizi del fascismo in Maremma', in *Comunità*, 23 February 1954, now in *L'antimeridiano. Tutte le opere*, pp. 625-642; 'La lambretta dei minatori', in *Il Contemporaneo*, 27 March 1954, now in *L'antimeridiano. Tutte le opere*, pp. 659-666; 'Ira e lacrime a Ribolla', in *Il Contemporaneo*, 15th May 1954, now in *L'antimeridiano. Tutte le opere*, pp. 676-680; Pino Corrias, *Vita agra di un anarchico. Luciano Bianciardi a Milano*, p. 70.
26. Massimo Coppola, Alberto Piccinini, 'La mosca sul muro', in Luciano Bianciardi, *L'antimeridiano. Tutte le opere*, p. XII. Cf. 'I minatori della maremma', in *Cultura moderna*, April 1956, now in *L'antimeridiano. Tutte le opere*, pp. 827-831.
27. 'Gli etruschi sono un tema allettante (oltre che per gli archeologi seri, s'intende) solo per chi vuol trastullarsi coi fumosi e dilettanteschi idoli della origine illustre'. 'La periferia di Grosseto avanza verso la campagna', in *Avanti!*, 25 November 1952, now in *L'antimeridiano. Tutte le opere*, p. 305.
28. 'un atteggiamento di comodo, conservatore'. *Ibid.*, p. 306.
29. 'Gli storici eruditi ed i fanatici delle tradizioni locali'. 'C'è posto in Maremma per migliaia di lavoratori', in *Avanti!*, 4 December 1952, now in *L'antimeridiano. Tutte le opere*, p. 310.
30. 'Quanto agli etruschi, dobbiamo senz'altro riconoscere loro il grosso merito di aver saputo dare alla zona una regola idraulica che impediva, con ingegnosi impianti, la formazione del padule. Ma non par giusto, soltanto per quello, mitizzare gli etruschi come se fossero i diretti progenitori dei maremmani d'oggi. O forse i localisti, senz'avvedersene, hanno ragione, nel senso che anche gli etruschi, in fondo, più che un popolo etnicamente identificabile, furono un gruppo attivissimo, e di formazione eterogenea, che tenne allora queste cose, come le tengono oggi i maremmani'. *Ibid.*, p. 310.
31. 'letteratura'. *Ibid.*, p. 310.
32. 'In un mondo più giusto, in un'Italia democratica e socialista'. *Ibid.*, p. 311.
33. 'C'è posto in Maremma per migliaia di lavoratori', in *Avanti!*, 4 December 1952, now in *L'antimeridiano. Tutte le opere*, pp. 310-311.
34. 'convinti (e qualcuno lo è ancora) che nelle vene maremmane scorresse qualche misura di sangue etrusco'. 'Per Ribolla soltanto la INCOM', in *Cinema nuovo*, 10 December 1954, now in *L'antimeridiano. Tutte le opere*, pp. 733-734.
35. 'Anche se la tradizione (e la letteratura) ha fatto sì che l'italiano medio pensi alla Maremma come alla terra dei pascoli, degli sterminati campi di grado, del palude, dei butteri, delle cacciate al cinghiale, oggi la Maremma è soprattutto una zona di grande ricchezza mineraria. La provincia di Grosseto produce quasi il 90 per cento della pirite italiana. Ribolla era, fino allo scorso anno, la maggiore miniera di lignite picea d'Italia. L'Amiata produce un terzo del mercurio mondiale'. Luciano Bianciardi and Carlo Cassola, 'I minatori della Maremma', in Luciano Bianciardi, *Il cattivo profeta. Romanzi, racconti, saggi e diari* [1956], pp. 29-30. Cf. 'Boschi e miniere nella terra dei butteri', in Luciano Bianciardi, *L'antimeridiano. Tutte le opere*, p. 600.
36. '[M]olto rudimentali'. Luciano Bianciardi and Carlo Cassola, 'I minatori della Maremma', in Luciano Bianciardi, *Il cattivo profeta. Romanzi, racconti, saggi e diari*, p. 30.
37. His job for the Feltrinelli publishing house and life in Milan were later recalled by Bianciardi in his novels *L'integrazione* (1960), now in Luciano Bianciardi, *Il cattivo profeta. Romanzi, racconti, saggi e diari*, pp. 365-436, and *La vita agra* (1962), now in *Il cattivo profeta*, pp. 437-563. Cf. Pino Corrias, *Vita agra di un anarchico. Luciano Bianciardi a Milano*, p. 84; Carlo Feltrinelli, *Senior Service* [1999] (Milan: Feltrinelli, 2014).
38. 'Il problema delle origini ha sempre sedotto e affaticato la mente di saggi, sapienti e intellettuali: origini dell'uomo, della specie, della società; origini del male e della disuguaglianza. Dalle origini di una città o di una religione si son calcolati gli anni, e dire "originale" significa riconoscere un merito. Insomma pare – e chissà poi per quale ragione – che alla gente importi più del

passato, del remoto passato, incapace ormai di far male ad alcuno, che dell'avvenire, prossimo avvenire, sempre, come ben sappiamo, minaccioso e incombente'. 'Il lavoro culturale', in Luciano Bianciardi, *Il cattivo profeta. Romanzi, racconti, saggi e diari* [1957], p. 167.
39. '[E]ruditi'. *Ibid.* p. 167.
40. *Ibid.*, pp. 167-168.
41. '[A]rcheologi'. *Ibid.*, p. 168.
42. *Ibid.*, p. 168
43. *Ibid.*, p. 169.
44. '[A]ffinità degli etruschi con i pellerossa d'America'. *Ibid.*, p. 170.
45. '[G]iganti, cioè di una razza civilissima e assai progredita anche se, purtroppo, ancora misteriosa e sconosciuta'. *Ibid.*, p. 170.
46. 'Infine c'eravamo noi, i giovani, la generazione bruciata: decisi a rompere con le tradizioni ed a rifare tutto daccapo. Naturalmente eravamo in polemica con tutti gli altri, coi medievalisti eruditi e con gli archeologi. Cosa volevano, gli uni e gli altri? Cosa significavano le sterili e goffe pidocchierie dei primi, cosa significavano i furori antiquarii dei secondi? Era l'ora di finirla con questo dilettantismo, con questa sterile erudizione, con questa mitologia delle origini antichissime. La cultura italiana, dicevamo noi, era già abbastanza aduggiata e mortificata da queste forme reazionarie e provinciali, dal campanile, dallo sciocco municipalismo. Gli etruschi? Ma gli etruschi non sono mai esistiti. Voi vi chiedete da dove sono venuti, se dal continente, o dall'Asia Minore, o dall'America: avanzate anche l'ipotesi che siano sempre stati qui. Ebbene, avete tutti ragione e tutti torto, cioè vi ponete un problema che non ha senso. Avrebbe senso chiedersi da dove sono venuti i piemontesi, o i toscani, o i milanesi? Non esistono popoli che, tutti d'accordo, un bel giorno prendono il mare (dove trovano tante navi, oltre tutto?) e se ne vanno altrove'. *Ibid.*, p. 171.
47. Cf. Vincenzo Bellelli, 'Alla ricerca delle origini etrusche', in *Le origini degli Etruschi: storia archeologia antropologia*, Vincenzo Bellelli (ed.) (Rome: L'Erma, 2012), pp. 17-48.
48. 'Da dove vengono i milanesi? E chi lo sa? Molti da fuori: qualcuno è venuto su perché a casa sua non trovava lavoro, qualche altro venne, da giovane, a farci il militare, e poi ha preso moglie e non si è mosso più. Altri ci sono nati e ci stanno e ci lavorano: magari vorrebbero andarsene, a Capri, o in Brasile o in Australia, ma non possono perché non hanno soldi per il viaggio, né speranza di poter campare, lontani dalla loro città. Se vi dicessero che i milanesi vengono dalla Dalmazia, cosa fareste voi? Direste certamente che è un'ipotesi sballata, no? E allora perché credere a chi sostiene che gli etruschi vennero dall'Asia minore? Gli etruschi erano appunto come i milanesi; erano quelli che abitavano in questa zona, e da altre parti, molto tempo fa e venivano chiamati, dagli altri, dai loro vicini, con questo nome. Da dove son venuti? Chi lo sa? Da dove gli era parso giusto venire. Ma l'alfabeto, la lingua, questa lingua misteriosa e indecifrabile? Macché indecifrabile, rispondevamo noi. A che serve cercar di decifrare la cosiddetta lingua etrusca, se il frammento più lungo è di cinquecento parole in tutto?
O forse, aggiungevamo, se proprio vi preme di salvare in un qualsiasi modo i vostri etruschi, ebbene, allora vi diciamo che gli etruschi esistevano, ma non erano un popolo: erano una minoranza che governava la nostra terra, e teneva soggetta la povera gente, e la faceva sgobbare; una minoranza di armatori navali e di grossi commercianti, e di preti. Non avete forse detto che la religione romana prese da quella etrusca una parte della sua liturgia? Una minoranza, oltre tutto, di politicanti, anzi, di fascisti. Il primo fascio littorio non è stato forse trovato a Volterra, città, come voi dite, antichissima (sebbene non quanto la nostra) e di fondazione etrusca? Tutto questo dicevamo noi giovani usciti dalla guerra, con grave ira e sdegno degli archeologi'. 'Il lavoro culturale', in Luciano Bianciardi, *Il cattivo profeta. Romanzi, racconti, saggi e diari*, pp. 171-172.
49. '[N]oi giovani usciti dalla guerra'. *Ibid.* p. 172.
50. '[E]ntusiasti [...] della marcia vittoriosa'. *Ibid.*, p. 172.
51. 'Il senso vero della città, proprio quello che sfuggiva a queste talpe di medievalisti eruditi, ed a quelle cornacchie di archeologi, eccolo qui: la città tutta periferia, aperta, aperta ai venti ed ai forestieri, fatta di gente di tutti i paesi'. *Ibid.*, p. 172.
52. 'Il tenente Bucker era un giovane professore americano, venuto su con il suo esercito, durante la guerra, ed affermava appunto che la sua città, Kansas City, somigliava alla nostra. Ed a noi questo paragone era piaciuto, ne avevamo fatto un simbolo: Kansas City, Kansas City è la nostra realtà, altro che storie! Le origini della città? L'anno di fondazione? Ma era il 1944, né più né meno. Prima di allora non esisteva, era stata fondata dagli americani, che, giungendo fra noi, avevano spianato un campo per farvi atterrare gli aerei, aperto rivendite di coca-cola, spacci di generi alimentari, dancings, depositi di materiale, creando all'improvviso un centro di traffici nuovo. Da ogni dove, allora, erano accorse folle di gente a quella nuovissima mecca'. *Ibid.*, p. 172.

53. The idea of Grosseto as Kansas City and the provincial myth had already emerged in previous writings: cf. 'Vitelloni anche loro', in *La Gazzetta*, 27th October 1953, now in *Il cattivo profeta. Romanzi, racconti, saggi e diari*, p. 244; 'Cresce a vista d'occhio l'improvvisa e frettolosa periferia', in *Il Nuovo Corriere. La Gazzetta*, 4th July 1954, now in *Il cattivo profeta. Romanzi, racconti, saggi e diari*, pp. 279-281. In 1954, the reference to Kansas City became popular in Italy also because of the movie *Un americano a Roma*, starring Alberto Sordi in the role of an enthusiast of American culture – I thank the editors of the volume for this suggestion.
54. '[C]ittà parassitaria'. 'Il lavoro culturale', in Luciano Bianciardi, *Il cattivo profeta. Romanzi, racconti, saggi e diari*, p. 175.
55. '[C]lan', 'corporazione'. *Ibid.*, p. 175.
56. 'Il lavoro culturale', in Luciano Bianciardi, *Il cattivo profeta. Romanzi, racconti, saggi e diari*, pp. 174-175.
57. 'Nella nostra città si poteva ricominciare tutto daccapo, e in Italia, quanto a cultura (ma anche per il resto) c'era proprio gran bisogno di ricominciare tutto daccapo'. *Ibid.*, pp. 174-175.
58. Cfr. *La vita agra*, in *Ibid.*, p. 478 and pp. 539-541.
59. Cfr. 'Il favoloso Cagliari', in *Epoca*, 26 April 1970, now in Luciano Bianciardi, *L'antimeridiano. Tutte le opere*, pp. 1799-1800.
60. 'Exodus' [1968], in Luciano Bianciardi, *Il cattivo profeta. Romanzi, racconti, saggi e diari*, pp. 1321-1326. A first reconstruction of Bianciardi's literary uses of the Etruscans is Mariagrazia Celuzza, 'Luciano Bianciardi, gli Etruschi, il Medioevo e Grosseto: una questione di identità?', in *Antico e non antico. Scritti multidisciplinari offerti a Giuseppe Pucci*, Valentino Nizzo and Antonio Pizzo (eds) (Milan Udine: Mimesis, 2018), pp. 105-114. For a positive judgement on Israel as a secular and socialist political model, see 'La Bibbia manuale di civiltà', in *Le ore*, 11 April 1963, now in Luciano Bianciardi, *Il cattivo profeta. Romanzi, racconti, saggi e diari*, pp. 896-897. Bianciardi visited Israel the following year, in 1969: cf. 'E se la rivoluzione fosse già scoppiata?', in *Kent*, May 1969, now in *Il cattivo profeta. Romanzi, racconti, saggi e diari*, pp. 1544-1552; 'Canestri in terrasanta', in *Kent*, September 1969, now in *Il cattivo profeta. Romanzi, racconti, saggi e diari*, pp. 1553-1560.
61. 'Proverbio ebreo'. *Il sorpasso*.
62. 'Roberto: 'Dì, era ebrea tua nonna?'. Bruno: 'Perché, sei razzista?'. Roberto: 'Ma no…e tu?'. Bruno: 'Io? Figurati, non mi conosci…una volta sono stato con una che era ebrea e pure negra!'. *Il sorpasso*.
63. Roberto: 'Sai, qua vicino ci sono delle belle tombe etrusche…'. Bruno: 'Ah, sì? Beh, io le tombe etrusche me le attacco al c…'. *Il sorpasso*.
64. See Martina Piperno's chapter in this book, and Ead. *L'antichità "crudele". Etruschi e Italici nella letteratura italiana del Novecento*, pp. 113-128.
65. 'L'intonazione'. *La voglia matta*.
66. 'Mussolini chi? Il padre del pianista?'. *La voglia matta*. The quote alluded to one of Mussolini's sons, Romano (1927-2006), who in the post-war years became known as a jazz piano player.
67. 'Non è mica proprio un cesso'. 'È un etrusco'. I have found this use of the Etruscans in *Il sorpasso 1962-2012. I filobus sono pieni di gente onesta*, ed. by Oreste De Fornari (Alessandria: Falsopiano, 2012), p. 42.
68. Martin M. Winkler, 'The Roman Empire in American Cinema after 1945', *The Classical Journal*, vol. 2, no. 93 (1997), pp. 167-196; Andrea Avalli, 'I film peplum e la fine del mito fascista della romanità', *Thersites*, 10 (2019), pp. 50-65.

About the Authors

Gennaro Ambrosino (University of Warwick) is a PhD student in Italian Studies. His project focusses on the intersections between archaeology and the 'unconscious' in Italian culture from the late 18th through the mid-19th centuries. He completed a Bachelor's degree in Modern Literature at the University of Naples 'Federico II', a Master's degree in Modern Philology at the University of Rome 'La Sapienza' and a Master's degree in Western Literature at KU Leuven. He worked on the Mesmeric imaginary in Italian literature of the late 18th and early 19th centuries with a particular focus on the figure of Francesco Orioli: contributions were published in the *Enthymema* and *Incontri* journals.

Andrea Avalli (Scuola Superiore di Studi Storici, San Marino) holds a PhD in contemporary history from the University of Genova and the Université de Picardie Jules Verne. His thesis focusses on the debate on the Etruscan ethnic origins under Italian Fascism. His main research interests are the history of Fascist Italy, nationalism, racism, Marxism, history of historiography and history of science.

Marie-Laurence Haack (Université de Picardie Jules Verne) is an associate professor of Ancient history at the department of History and Geography. She is member of the *Institut Universitaire de France* and her research interests include Etruscology, Italic Archaeology, Reception Studies, Ideology and Historiography. She recently published *La construction de l'étruscologie au début du XXe siècle* (2015), *Les Étrusques au temps du fascism* (2016) et *Étruscologie dans l'Europe d'après-guerre* (2017).

Martin Miller (Italienisches Kulturinstitut Stuttgart) was born 1962 in Tübingen and studied Classical Archaeology, Ancient History and Art History at the universities of Tübingen and Perugia. His PhD dissertation (1992) was on fortifications in Italy from the 8th to 3rd centuries BC, after which he was awarded a travel grant from the German Archaeological Institute. From 1994 to 1999, he worked at the *Antikensammlung* at the *Staatliche Museen zu Berlin*, especially in the museum archives. Martin Miller has excavated in Orvieto, Fregellae (Ceprano), Castellina del Marangone (Civitavecchia) and Cancho Roano (Zalamea de la Serena, Spain), in addition to doing fieldwork (field survey) in Kyaneai (Lycia). Since 2002 he is a member of the Italian Institute of Culture in Stuttgart. Miller has been studying the history of archaeology for many years, especially the history of Etruscology. His most important works include a biography of the classical archaeologist Otto Wilhelm von Vacano, and studies on German archaeologists and linguists, on the *Istituto di Studi Etruschi* before the Second World War, on Alfred Rosenberg, the Etruscans and Rome.

Francesca Orestano (Università degli Studi di Milano) is Professor of English Literature at the department of Languages and Literatures and has authored books on the American Renaissance (*Dal Neoclassico al Classico*); on Rev. William Gilpin and the picturesque (*Paesaggio e finzione*); and on visual studies (*La parola e lo sguardo*). She has edited books on children's literature, on Charles Dickens, on Jakob Burckhardt's response to the Italian Renaissance, on John Ruskin's art criticism and chemistry, and on the grid of modernity in *Cahiers Victoriens et Edouardiens*. Her essay on Little Dorrit is in *The Oxford Handbook of Charles Dickens*. Recent work includes publications on Virginia Woolf, Giuseppe Tomasi di Lampedusa, Giovanni Arpino, George Eliot, on Limehouse and the Chinese community in the 19th century, gardens from the 18th century to present. In 2020, she edited the issue of *Questione Romantica* devoted to 'Romanticism and Cultural Memory'. She also worked on material culture and English travel literature in Etruria, which she explored in her article 'Gli Etruschi nella memoria culturale britannica, tra Otto e Novecento: ovvero il sublime fascino di un braccialetto' (2016).

Lisa C. Pieraccini (University of California, Berkeley) is Associate Adjunct Professor at the department of History of Art and works on the art and archaeology of the first millennium BC in Italy, with special emphasis on the Etruscans and early Romans. She lived in Italy for many years where she taught and conducted research in Rome and southern Etruria. Her interests include Etruscan craft connectivity, international trade, funerary art and ritual, and issues of identity. Dr. Pieraccini has published a variety of articles and chapters on aspects of Etruscan tomb painting, the Etruscan contextualization of Greek myth, the use, decor, and agency of cylinder stamped ware as well as the reception of Etruscan art from the 17th to 20th century. Dr. Pieraccini is an elected member of the Istituto di Studi Etruschi ed Italici in Florence. She has co-organized a number of international conferences in the US and Italy. She is author of *Around the Hearth: Cylinder Stamped Braziers* (2003, L'Erma di Bretschneider), editor of

Pithoi Stampigliati: Una Classe Originale di Ceramica Etrusca (2010, L'Erma di Bretschneider), co-editor of the series *Cities of the Etruscans* (with Nancy de Grummond) published by Texas University Press and consulting editor of the journal *Etruscan and Italic Studies*. Before joining the History of Art Department, Dr. Pieraccini taught for the Classics Department and Italian Studies at UC Berkeley, Stanford University as well as Temple University in Rome.

Martina Piperno (Università di Roma La Sapienza, honorary fellow MDRN/KU Leuven) is Assistant Professor of Italian Studies. She was awarded her PhD from the University of Warwick in 2016 and she held postdoc positions at University College Cork, in Ireland (2017-2019), and KU Leuven (2019-2021), and was Assistant Professor in Italian at the University of Durham, UK (2021-2023). Her first book, *Rebuilding Post-Revolutionary Italy. Leopardi and Vico's "New Science"* (Oxford 2018) has won the Scaglione Prize for Italian Studies issued by the Modern Language Association of America. She has recently published the monograph *L'antichità crudele. Etruschi e Italici nella letteratura italiana del Novecento* (Rome 2020).

Bart Van Den Bossche (MDRN/KU Leuven) is Professor of Italian Literature at the University of Leuven (KU Leuven) and founding member of the research lab MDRN based at KU Leuven. His main research areas are modern and contemporary Italian literature, in particular, myth and literature, avant-garde, modernism, realism and poetry. He is currently involved in a large-scale research project on "Literary Knowledge in the Modernist Period". He published a book on Cesare Pavese (*"Nulla è veramente accaduto". Strategie discorsive del mito nell'opera di Cesare Pavese*, Lovanio-Firenze, Leuven University Press-Franco Cesati editore, 2001), and a book on myth in twentieth-century literature *Trasformazioni ed elaborazioni: il mito nella letteratura italiana del Novecento* (Leuven-Firenze, Leuven University Press-Franco Cesati editore, 2007). Among the most recent volumes he co-edited figure *Futurism. A microhistory*, eds Sascha Bru, Luca Somigli and Bart Van Den Bossche, Oxford, Legenda ("Italian Perspectives" 36), 2017; *1947. Almanach littéraire*, David Martens, Bart Van Den Bossche & MDRN (eds), Brussels, Les Impressions Nouvelles, 2017, and *Iconografie pirandelliane. Immagini e cultura visiva nell'opera di Luigi Pirandello*, Bart Van Den Bossche & Bart Dreesen (eds), Oxford/Bern/Brussels, Peter Lang, 2019.

Chiara Zampieri (MDRN/KU Leuven) is Junior Researcher at KU Leuven (Belgium). She holds a PhD in Comparative Literature awarded by the KU Leuven. Her thesis, titled *Voix d'Étrurie: la représentation de l'antiquité étrusque* *dans la littérature européenne (1840-1940)*, was part of the larger interdisciplinary research programme *Literary Knowledge (1890-1950): Modernisms and the Sciences in Europe*. Within this larger programme, her research project 'Modern Etruscans' focussed on the reception of the Etruscans and their culture in the French, Italian and English literature of the modernist period. She actively collaborates with the Museo Nazionale Etrusco di Villa Giulia, in Rome. She is part of the research networks Patrimonialitté (which investigates the relationships between literature and heritage) and RIMELL (Recherches Interdisciplinaires sur la Muséographie et l'Exposition de la Littérature et du Livre).

Index

A

Addington Symonds, John 31
Ainsley, Samuel 26
Alighieri, Dante 56, 128, 136-141
Alvaro, Corrado 9, 12, 13, 18, 20, 64-66, 68, 70-72, 74, 75
Anti, Carlo 49
Apollinaire, Guillaume 56
Argento, Dario 88
Aristotle 148, 149, 153, 159
Augustus, Caesar 101

B

Balzac, Honoré de 148, 149
Bassani, Giorgio 12, 14, 21, 147, 149, 150, 151, 153-157, 159, 173
Bassani, Paola 153, 158
Beals, Carleton 50, 52, 55, 57
Benjamin, Walter 148, 159
Bianchi Bandinelli, Ranuccio 10
Bianciardi, Luciano 12, 163-173, 175
Boccaccio, Giovanni 56
Böcklin, Arnold 100
Bonaparte, Luciano 129
Bontempelli, Massimo 56
Botticelli, Sandro 31
Brachmann, Wilhelm 104
Breton, André 56
Brett, Dorothy 115
Brewster, Earl 65, 115
Brodribb, William Jackson 117
Broglie, de, Victor 99
Brunelleschi, Filippo 29, 30
Burchiello 56

C

Campana, Dino 56
Campana, Giovanni Pietro 129
Campanari 15, 24, 26
Campigli, Massimo 12, 33, 34, 36, 45
Cardarelli, Vincenzo 9, 12-14, 18, 20, 64, 68-70, 74, 75, 127-141
Cassola, Carlo 166, 167
Cato, de Censor 101

Caylus, Comte de 23
Cecchi, Emilio 56
Cézanne, Paul 32
Chateaubriand, de, François-René 148, 149
Church, Alfred John 117
Ciampi, Sebastiano 99
Cimabue 29
Comte, Jules 48
Cord, Alex 88
Cox, Brian 89
Crawford, Alexander William 83
Crispino, Armando 88
Cronin, Patricia 21, 85-87
Cumont, Franz 48, 49, 57
Cuoco, Vincenzo 129, 158

D

D'Annunzio, Gabriele 9, 31, 37, 47, 100, 137
Däubler, Theodor 100
De Chirico, Giorgio 33, 38
Della Seta, Alessandro 11, 35, 36
Dennis, George 17, 26, 27, 168
De Pisis, Filippo 33
De Sica, Vittorio 157
Diderot, Denis 148, 149
Digby Wyatt, Matthew 25
Ducati, Pericle 11, 18, 116, 120, 168
Duras, Marguerite 9

F

Feltrinelli, Giangiacomo 168
Fischer, Mark 158
Foscolo, Ugo 21, 153-156, 158
France, Anatole 9
Francesca, della, Piero 57
Freud, Sigmund 136
Fry, Roger 28, 32

G

Galleppini, Aurelio 91, 92
Gassman, Vittorio 172
Gerhard, Eduard 99
Gertler, Mark 118

Giacometti, Alberto 12, 36, 37, 45
Gibbon, Edward 118, 119
Giglioli, Giulio Quirino 9, 11, 18, 44, 46-49, 57
Gilpin, William 28
Ginzburg, Carlo 148, 149, 159
Ginzburg, Natalia 149
Giotto 29, 30, 37, 57
Goethe, Johann Caspar 97
Goethe, Johann Wolfgang 97-99
Gori, Anton Francesco 97
Grant, Arthur James 117
Gratz Collins, Vere Henry 117
Gray, Cecil 118
Grünwedel, Albert 97, 102-104, 106
Guarnacci, Mario 157

H

Hamilton Grey, Elisabeth Caroline 26
Hancarville, de, Pierre-Francois 23
Hawthorne, Nathaniel 31
Hegner, Jakob 100
Heracles 30, 148
Herbig, Gustav 102
Herder, Johann Gottfried 98, 99
Heyse, Theodor 100
Hildebrand, von, Adolf 100
Hillebrand, Karl 100
Homer 155, 157, 158
Hube, von, Rodolph 117
Hume, David 148-150
Huxley, Aldous 9, 51, 52, 54, 55, 57

I

Ilzhöfer, Otto 103
Inghirami, Francesco 99

J

Jaffe, Else 120
James, Henry 31
Jones, Owen 25

K

Kass, Deborah 85
Kestner, August 99, 108
Klagges, Dietrich 104, 105
Kluge, Theodor 104
Kuhn, Ernst 103, 104
Kurz, Edgar 100
Kurz, Isolde 100

L

Lacan, Jacques 132
Lanzi, Luigi 158
Larousse, Pierre 43
Lasca 56
Lawrence, D. H. 9, 12-14, 18, 20, 32, 33, 38, 64-68, 70, 73-75, 90, 115-123, 150, 151, 153, 158
Lawrence, Frieda 117
Lee, Vernon 31
Leopardi, Giacomo 128, 131, 132, 141
Levi, Primo 149
Lévi-Strauss, Claude 67
Livius, Titus 99

M

Machiavelli 140
Malaparte, Curzio 9, 20, 54-57, 100, 130
Manzoni, Alessandro 128
Marconi, Guglielmo 166
Marini, Marino 34, 35, 36, 45
Martha, Jules 10, 11, 45
Martini, Arturo 12, 34, 36, 45, 164
Masaccio 57
Micali, Giuseppe 129
Michelangelo 30, 37, 140
Minto, Antonio 116
Mommsen, Theodor 10, 11, 45, 119, 120
Moore, Henry 37, 38
Müller, Karl Otfried 99
Mussolini, Benito 38, 172, 174

N

Nerval, de, Gérard 56
Nietzsche, Friedrich 52
Nilhén, Staffan 36

O

Orcagna 140

P

Palazzeschi, Aldo 56
Pallottino, Massimo 16, 132, 165, 169
Papini, Giovanni 130
Parasuco, Salvatore 94
Pater, Walter 31
Peterich, Eckart 100, 106
Peterich, Paul 100
Phidias 30
Piranesi, Giovan Battista 24
Pisano, Giovanni 37
Plutarch 117
Poe, Edgar Allan 135
Proust, Marcel 31

R
Raphael, Sanzio 32
Ray, Nicholas 170
Reinach, Salomon 9, 57
Risi, Dino 172, 175
Rodin, Auguste 49
Rosenberg, Alfred 19, 101-106
Ruskin, John 13, 17, 23, 27-33, 35, 36, 38

S
Sacchetti, Franco 56
Sade 148
Salce Luciano 174, 175
Salinari, Carlo 168
Savinio, Alberto 13, 18, 20, 33, 38, 39, 56, 64-66, 68, 74, 75, 132
Schlegel, August Wilhelm 99
Schubart, Wilhelm 102
Schubert, Johannes 103
Sereni, Vittorio 153
Serrano, Andres 92-94
Seume, Johann Gottfried 98, 99
Sir Leonard 93, 94, 96
Sironi, Mario 45
Spaak, Catherine 172, 174
Stackelberg, von, Otto Magnus 99
Staël-Holstein, Baroness von, Anne-Louise-Germaine 99
St. Francis 30, 98
Storer, Edward 45, 46, 49, 50, 52, 55, 57
Suetonius, Gaius 117
Sulla, Lucius Cornelius 101

T
Tacitus, Publius Cornelius 117
Tiraboschi, Girolamo 158
Tognazzi, Ugo 174
Trintignant, Jean-Louis 172
Trombadori, Antonello 168
Trumpp, Ernst 103
Tubières, de, Anne-Claude-Philippe 23

V
Venuti, Ridolfino 157
Vico, Giambattista 138
Viele, Egbert Ludovicus 81-85
Vinci, da, Leonardo 140
Virgil 137
Viterbo, da, Annio 97
Vulca 52

W
Wallace, Brian Edgar 88
Wedgwood, Josiah 23
Weege, Fritz 120
Weinberg, von, Guido Kaschnitz 101
Wharton, Edith 31
Winckelmann, Johann Joachim 10, 11, 45
Woolf, Virginia 26, 32

Z
Zannoni, Giovanni Battista 99

Printed in the USA
CPSIA information can be obtained
at www.ICGtesting.com
LVHW010440101223
766105LV00004B/201